THE SUCCESSFUL BUSINESS LIBRARY

W9-BXZ-347

FOURTH EDITION

FRANCHISE BIBLE

How To Buy A Franchise
OR
Franchise Your Own Business

BY ERWIN J. KEUP

The Oasis Press®/PSI Research
Central Point, Oregon

Published by The Oasis Press®
© 1990, 1991, 1994, 1995, 1996, and 2000 by Erwin J. Keup

This publication is designed to provide accurate and authoritative information in
regard to the subject matter covered. It is sold with the understanding that the
publisher is not engaged in rendering legal, accounting, or other professional
service. If legal advice or other expert assistance is required, the services of a
competent professional person should be sought.
> — *from a declaration of principles jointly adopted by a committee of*
> *the American Bar Association and a committee of publishers*

Editors: Vickie Reierson, Linda Pinkham, and Erin H. Wait
Book Designer, 1st Edition: Constance C. Dickinson
Compositors: Jan Olsson, Debbie Johnson, and Erin H. Wait
Managing Editor: Constance C. Dickinson
Cover Designer: Steven Burns

Please direct any comments, questions, or suggestions regarding this book to:

> Editorial Department
> The Oasis Press®/PSI Research
> P.O. Box 3727
> Central Point, OR 97502
> (541) 479-9464

The Oasis Press® is a Registered Trademark of Publishing Services, Inc.,
an Oregon corporation doing business as PSI Research.

Keup, Erwin J.
     Franchise bible : how to buy a franchise or franchise your own business / by Erwin J.
Keup. — 4th ed.
     p.   cm. — (The Oasis Press' successful business library)
     Includes index.
     ISBN 1-55571-526-5 (pbk.)
     1. Franchises (Retail trade)—United States—Forms. 2. Franchises (Retail trade)—Law
and legislation—United States. I. Title. II. Series.

HF5429.235.U5 K478 2000
658.8'708—dc21   00-029794

Printed in the United States of America
Fourth edition 10 9 8 7 6 5 4 3 2 1

Table of Contents

Part III   Appendices

Checklists and Worksheets in this Book

Index

What's New in this Edition – A Note from the Author

The fourth edition of *Franchise Bible* has been dramatically revised to reflect the changes since the introduction of the new Uniform Franchise Offering Circular (UFOC) adopted by the Federal Trade Commission and the registration states that went into effect January 1, 1995. This edition illustrates that service oriented businesses, such as coffee bars and auto service businesses, are definitely in the new millennium picture. The sample offering circular in Appendix A features a franchise offering that involves the servicing of the public's craze for coffee beverages and the servicing of the public's vehicles, both on the same premises at the same time with both operations being self-sufficient yet complimentary to each other.

In the 1970s and 1980s, franchising was predominately seen in the areas of restaurants, retail stores in nonfood products, and hotels and motels. The recessionary period in the late 1980s and early 1990s, however, caused franchisors and franchisees alike to turn to businesses involving the maintenance, reconstruction, restoration, preservation, and servicing of major consumer products — big-ticket items like automobiles, homes, furnishings, and major appliances.

In addition, the 1990s saw a marked rise in the number of relatively low-cost franchises catering to the educational, business, and social needs of Americans — franchises that require a higher degree of expertise in the franchisee.

My personal experiences with registering franchisors over the past few years have confirmed these new trends in franchising. The new franchisors of the 2000s are and will continue to be well-read entrepreneurs in successful service maintenance businesses who have not only survived the recessionary period, but who are making a profit and wish to expand their businesses through available franchise methods. They will be choosing franchisees that have the potential management skills and motivation necessary to successfully carry out their expansion process.

The 1990s have also seen a revolt by some franchisees of major franchisors concerning what they feel are "unfair and unconscionable" terms in their franchise agreements, many of which were signed in the 1980s. This has culminated not only in franchisees forming their own associations, but also in the International Franchise Association (IFA), formerly an association primarily of franchisors, now counting 25,000 franchisees as new members.

Iowa was the first state to enact legislation protecting franchisees, which became effective on July 1, 1992. As many as 19 states are pondering franchise-related bills ranging from technical changes in existing laws to comprehensive measures patterned after the Iowa statute.

In addition, shortly after Iowa's bill became law, two federal bills were introduced. One such bill attempted to curb franchise abuse by creating federal standards for the franchisor-franchisee relationship and strengthening federal guidelines concerning disclosures. This first bill included such revisions as the prohibition of franchisee termination without cause, allowance of franchisees to purchase equipment from their own sources, and granting franchisees the right to sue in their own state. The second bill was to expand the disclosures required of the franchisor, including information on franchise failures, turnovers, litigation, contractual obligations, and potential competition between franchisors and franchisees.

Sample Uniform Franchise Offering Circular

On April 25, 1993, the North American Securities Administrators Association (NASAA) adopted extensive revisions to the Uniform Franchise Offering Circular (UFOC) Guidelines. These revisions became binding upon franchisors on January 1, 1995, having been adopted by each of the 14 registration states and approved by the Federal Trade Commission. (See Appendix E for a listing of the 14 registration states.)

The sample offering circular in Appendix A will give you a much clearer picture of how the new UFOC rules will affect you. In addition, the new UFOC guidelines as adopted by the State of California are reproduced in Appendix F. These guidelines include specific instructions on how to prepare a UFOC, and samples and illustrations for each of the items of the Uniform Franchise Offering Circular.

In the field of franchising, both parties, the franchisor and the franchisee, have one major thing in common — the franchise agreement, which is, in essence, their mutual "Bill of Rights." Whether you are a potential franchisee, independent-business buyer, franchisor, or business seller, I encourage you to read this book in its entirety. What you will learn will only help you succeed in your franchising endeavor.

ERWIN J. KEUP

About the Author

Erwin J. Keup is a practicing attorney with offices in Newport Beach, California. For the past 42 years, Mr. Keup has specialized in franchise law, franchise consulting, and general corporate and business law, including trademarks and service marks. He has provided legal and business counseling in a variety of fields.

Mr. Keup graduated from Marquette University in 1953 with a B.S. degree in business administration and from Marquette Law School in 1958 with a J.D. degree. He also served as a member of the Marquette University Law Review while in law school. Before establishing his private law practice in Newport Beach, California in 1975, Mr. Keup held corporate law department positions with Miller Brewing Company in Milwaukee, Wisconsin, and Glidden Paint Company in Cleveland, Ohio. He was also vice president and general counsel of Snelling and Snelling, Inc., the world's largest personnel agency franchisor.

Mr. Keup is a member of the American, California, and Orange County bar associations. He is a member of the Ohio Bar and a former member of the Wisconsin Bar Association. Mr. Keup is also a member of the American Bar Association's Forum on Franchising and a former member of the California Bar Association's Franchise Legislation Committee. He is listed in *Who's Who in American Law* of 1987–88.

Mr. Keup is an arbitrator/mediator with the American Arbitration Association, FAM (Franchise Arbitration and Mediation, Inc.), and British Columbia International Commercial Arbitration Centre, specializing in franchisor/franchisee disputes. He has conducted seminars on franchising and has taught the business and legal aspects of franchising at private business schools. Mr. Keup is the author of The Oasis Press' *Mail Order Legal Guide*, as well as numerous business articles on franchising. He is married and the father of eight children.

Acknowledgments

This work is the result of 42 years of practicing law, much of it in the franchise- and distributorship-agreement fields, and dealing with the many business aspects of franchising, including several years as an executive and general counsel to a major franchisor.

I would like to thank the designer, editors, and compositors of The Oasis Press for their fine work on each edition of *Franchise Bible*.

My sincere gratitude also goes to my franchise clients, many of whom have become close friends, for allowing me to share in their vast business experience. I am also indebted to Glenn Arnesen, not only for allowing the reproduction of his Lube N Latte® offering circular for illustration purposes in Appendix A, but also for allowing me to incorporate some of my ideas in the Lube N Latte system.

Introduction

Whether you are interested in franchising your business or buying a franchise operation, *Franchise Bible* will be a valuable resource for you in your research and investigation of franchising.

To begin, franchising, in business language, is a method of marketing through which successful business owners (potential franchisors) expand the retail distribution of their goods or services by contracting with independent, third parties. These third parties (potential franchisees) agree to operate the retail sales or service outlets featuring the franchisor's original trademarked goods or services and implementing marketing methods at their capital costs. In exchange for this opportunity to share in the net proceeds from the sale of trademarked goods or services, the franchisees pay an initial fee and ongoing royalties to the franchisor. Franchising is not a method of generating income solely through the sale of franchises. The franchise itself is not what made a franchisor wealthy; it was the particular product or service. Any potential franchisor or franchisee should bear this fact in mind.

There are two main parts to the text of *Franchise Bible*. Part I is concerned with the individuals who are interested in going into business by buying a franchise or existing small business. Part II of the text addresses business owners who have started a business, made it successful, and now wish to expand by franchising the business. Whether you are a successful business owner desiring to expand your market through franchising, or an individual desiring to go into business for yourself, read both parts of this book thoroughly.

Hopefully, by reading this book, the business owner intending to franchise his or her business will gain some insight into what a franchisee looks for when evaluating a franchise agreement and initial offering circular. Likewise, the person seeking to buy a franchise can find valuable information in this book regarding the desired methods of operation a good franchisor should utilize. If a prospective franchisee has some idea of what constitutes a well-run franchise system, he or she can make an informed choice. By the same token, many successful franchisors started out as franchisees themselves, developing franchises and subsequently selling them, using their knowledge in franchising new business entities in a role-reversal situation.

To help you in your quest for more information on franchising in general, *Franchise Bible* features several sample franchise documents and additional franchising resources. Part III contains six appendices, each with its own unique content of information. Be sure to review these appendices while reading the text in the first two parts.

The prospect of owning a franchise or franchising your business is a very exciting and challenging one. Let *Franchise Bible* take some of the worry out by informing you more about the laws, documents, and responsibilities of being a franchisor or franchisee.

Part I

Buying a Franchise or Small Business

Chapter 1

Buying a Franchise

Introduction

Are you currently working for someone but longing to be your own boss by owning your own business? Are you a retired person looking for a way to get back into a new line of work, or a recent college graduate wanting to get into your own business? Whatever your situation, if you are looking for new business ownership opportunities, then the first part of *Franchise Bible* — chapters 1–4 — is definitely for you. This section of the book is specifically intended for the person who wants to buy either a franchise or an existing business that is not a franchise. It is not intended to help you start a business from scratch.

When looking for new business opportunities, buying a franchise or existing business may be the way for you to go. But how do you select your own business? As a new business purchaser, you must first select a particular field of business you like and then decide whether or not that endeavor is suitable to your past experience and talents. Once this is accomplished, you can pursue a more established course of action.

When starting your own business, you have three different options. First, you can start your business from scratch, using your own name, knowledge, and background. Secondly, you can buy an existing business wherein you will own the business outright and operate it without any controls from a third party. Or lastly, you could purchase a form of license to sell a product or service utilizing the name, good will, marketing techniques, and operating procedures from a franchisor.

This initial chapter is mostly concerned with purchasing a franchise, while Chapter 2 discusses the details regarding an offering circular and franchise agreement. If you are also interested in learning about purchasing an existing business that is not a franchise, Chapter 3 discusses some of the activity involved there. Chapter 4 deals with purchasing a franchise from a local franchisee and helping you evaluate potential franchisors and sellers.

Once you have given adequate consideration to the advantages and disadvantages of buying outright or franchising and have carefully weighed your conclusions along these lines with your conclusions about other forms of business, you can then decide how best to invest your savings and fulfill your dream of being your own boss. According to statistics provided each year by the U.S. Department of Commerce, the chances of success in a franchise operation are generally recognized as much greater than those of operating a business from scratch or even purchasing an existing business. You must also realize, however, that the purchase of a franchise does not necessarily bring less autonomy than is found operating under the other two alternatives.

In addition, any prospective business owner should remember that the risk of failure exists in purchasing any business, be it a franchise or a local business venture. One important item to keep in mind in any business purchase is the ground rules set forth in the purchase agreement. These ground rules are often a determining factor in the success or failure of any purchased entity. It is not so much that the purchase agreement must contain legal loopholes or escape clauses that allow a buyer to regain his or her compensation if the business should fail — which is often not the case when a franchise is purchased — but the terms must be workable for both parties. To be workable and successful, the terms should include that the initial and ongoing fees and obligations provide a reasonable profit to the franchisor or seller and are also affordable to the buyer.

To begin this discussion on purchasing a franchise, you first need to understand the two different definitions of franchising. Franchising can be defined from two different perspectives — the business owner's perspective and the legal statutory perspective.

Business Owner's Definition of Franchising

The business owner's definition is the most important definition to both the franchisor and franchisee because if the franchise entity does not succeed, any legal statutory requirements are a moot point. The business owner's definition of franchising is as follows:

Franchising is a method of market expansion utilized by a successful business entity wanting to expand its distribution of services or products through retail entities owned by independent operators using the trademarks or service marks, marketing techniques, and controls of the expanding business entity in return for the payment of fees and royalties from the retail outlet.

Essentially, the franchisee is a substitute for the franchisor's company-owned office in the retail distribution of the franchisor's services or products. The success or failure of one party to this unique relationship generally determines the success or failure of the other party. If the franchisor and franchisee keep this business relationship definition in mind, the self-centered attitudes that appear to arise under the legal definition can be avoided.

The Legal Definition of Franchising

The legal definition of a franchise differs among the several states that have passed franchise registration statutes and the Federal Trade Commission (FTC). California was the first state to pass a franchising law, and its definition is similar to the definition of franchise used by the other states that have franchise registration statutes. The California definition, taken from California Business and Professions Code, Section 2001, defines "franchise" as follows:

Franchise means a contract or agreement, express or implied, whether oral or written, between two or more persons by which:

- *A franchisee is granted the right to engage in the business of offering, selling, or distributing goods or services under a marketing plan or system prescribed in substantial part by a franchisor;*
- *The operation of the franchisee's business pursuant to that plan or system as substantially associated with the franchisor's trademark, service mark, trade name, logotype, advertising, or other commercial symbol designating the franchisor or its affiliates; and*
- *The franchisee is required to pay, directly or indirectly, a franchise fee.*

The cited business definition mentioned previously does meet the elements of the legal definition; however, the attitudes of the franchisor and franchisee in looking upon the franchise as the "marketing arm" or the "independent company-owned office substitute" of the franchisor set the franchising concept in the proper business perspective.

Thus, as a potential franchisee, you should not purchase a franchise from any franchisor that you would not consider for a top employment position, and any franchisor should not sell a franchise to any person he or she would not consider a top choice for a lifetime manager of a company-owned office. By the same token, a franchisor should give you the same care and support as he or she would give to his or her top managers of the company-owned outlets.

Why Buy a Franchise?

With so many options available and all the potential pitfalls possible in buying a business or franchise, you may be wondering why you should invest your time and money into a franchise opportunity. To help you get an idea of some of the advantages you would enjoy as a new franchisee, review the list below. As a franchisee, you will enjoy:

- Group advertising power;
- Owning your own business and making day-to-day decisions yourself, guided by the franchisor's experience;

- The ability to sell products and services to markets that cannot be serviced by company-owned outlets because of higher operational costs and lower motivation of employees in company-owned outlets;
- The benefit of identification of service marks, trademarks, proprietary information, patents, and designs;
- Systematic training from experts;
- A lower risk of failure and/or loss of investments than if you were to start your own business from scratch;
- Being a part of a uniform operation throughout the country, which means all franchises will share the same interior and exterior physical appearance, same product, and same service and product quality;
- Assistance in financial and accounting matters from the franchisor, as well as ongoing support; and
- The enhancement of your management abilities and being the recipient of an opportunity you could not have had in most employment situations.

In addition, you may wonder how to go about ensuring you make the best decision possible. Investing in your own business takes guts and the willingness to make important decisions. As a result, you will need to carefully research the statistics regarding new business start ups versus the purchase of an existing business from a nonfranchisor. Once you have done this, compare these statistics with research on franchised endeavors. What you find may be useful in helping you make a sound business decision and helping you understand why franchising may be more beneficial for you. Here are some helpful facts of franchising.

- The U.S. Department of Commerce, in its edition of *Franchising in the Economy,* has cited very interesting statistics that conclude franchising has increased phenomenally in recent years and is a significant part of the U.S. marketing system. Franchising offers tremendous opportunities to individuals and companies seeking wider distribution of their products and services. The U.S. Department of Commerce also points out that retail sales from franchise establishments comprise about one-third of all U.S. retail sales.
- John Naisbitt, in the Naisbitt Group's *The Future of Franchising,* has predicted that more than one-half of all retail sales will be made through franchise sales by the year 2010.
- Government research indicates that the success rate for franchise-owned endeavors is significantly better than the rate for nonfranchise-owned small businesses. These same findings also show that 80 percent of all new small businesses fail, many within the first year. By contrast less than 2 percent of new franchises are discontinued over a three-year period.

In short, the good news is that franchising is a growing part of the national economy and presents a much better chance for success to the new franchisee. The bad news is that not every franchise is a sure-fire way to multiply your savings and provide you with an enjoyable occupation for your remaining days on this planet.

Buyer Beware

More and more buyers are seeking franchises from relatively unknown franchisors with little-known brand names and service marks. At the same time, an increasing number of people, particularly those who have not been in business before, are also interested in purchasing existing small businesses from independent business owners operating in a geographically limited neighborhood area. This scenario usually takes the form of older sellers who purportedly wish to dispose of their business as they reach retirement age. Since spending your savings on a business is one of the most important decisions of your life, if not the most important decision, always heed the key words, "buyer beware."

In the late 1950s and 1960s, all kinds of charlatans jumped on the bandwagon and franchised nearly everything imaginable, on a global scale. A buyer didn't always know what he or she was getting into. Typical of our society, help eventually came from legislative enactments which swung the pendulum the other way, at least as far as paperwork is concerned. As a result, franchising today is a much more exacting and time-consuming process because of required procedures and restrictions. But all this activity has resulted in more protection for you, the franchise buyer.

Franchising and the Law

Part of the flurry of new regulations and legislation that were implemented to help protect franchisees included an FTC rule, applicable before January 1, 1995, that required a written disclosure statement, referred to as an FTC offering circular. The FTC offering circular contained certain specified areas of information to be presented to prospective franchisees at certain points in time. This FTC rule regarding offering circulars applied to those states that had not passed franchise acts. Fourteen states passed their own franchise acts which require registration, while the FTC, which governs all the states, does not require registration.

Under the new franchise laws effective January 1, 1995, the FTC and all 50 states use the same Uniform Franchise Offering Circular, although the states retain the right to impose stricter provisions if they so desire, including registration. In all instances, the federal and state statutes do not provide a means of deciding whether or not a franchise is of any value or even whether or not the information submitted by the franchisor is true or not. The statutes merely force the franchisor to make certain representations and reveal certain information which, if untrue, would subject the franchisor to civil and criminal lawsuits.

The bottom line is no legislation will ever eliminate crime, nor will legislation eliminate the naiveté of some potential business owners who invariably are obsessed with seeing only the good parts of a transaction and none of the bad. As a prospective franchisee, you must be aware of the con artists that are hard at work trying to present the best possible image of their particular opportunity, and who call their business endeavors "partnerships" or "licenses."

This does not mean, however, that all partnerships or license agreements are franchises, or fraudulent schemes. Because licensing and franchising have become almost synonymous, the modern-day con artists seem to look to arrangements called "partnerships" as convenient labels for the purpose of circumventing the disclosure requirements of federal and state law. These types of partnerships usually offer the use of the same business name and style, but the seller is a partner whose interest is eventually purchased by the business-seeking entrepreneur. The major drawback to this type of arrangement is that the selling partner does not have the capital and does not wish to reveal information about him or herself. This would not be the case if the seller was a franchisor. In addition, before the purchase of a partnership by the new business-seeking entrepreneur, the business is usually subject to the control of the selling "partner."

In conclusion, beware of an offered entity that supposedly gives you a going business under a trade name and has you start out as a partner and end up eventually as a sole owner, along with other individuals who also purchased a partnership interest in other areas and became owners, using the same name as yours.

Are You Franchise Material?

Now that you have a better understanding of what a franchise is and some of its history and background, you need to consider if you are cut out to be a franchise owner and operator. To do this, you need to take a hard look at yourself and evaluate how you would handle the responsibilities and operations of a franchise. Obviously, you want to do this before you make what could be the biggest investment of your life.

Most people have the false notion that in franchising, a lot of money can be made with a minimum amount of effort. This is a serious misconception. The franchisee who works the hardest, profits the most from a franchise business. Initially at least, you must be able to make sacrifices. You must lay a strong foundation even for the most successful franchise operation. Be prepared to put in long hours of hard work, and above all, to be disappointed by your employees to a certain extent. The extent of this disappointment is directly related to how good you are at selecting and supervising people. The next consideration is how well you are organized, and last, but not least, is the state of your health.

One thing is certain: If the franchisor is merely interested in your money and does not evaluate you under certain standard criteria geared to determine your potential to succeed, there is something wrong with your franchisor. However, before you even see a franchisor, evaluate yourself.

Ask yourself such questions as:

- Will your franchise be taking a considerable amount of your time away from your family? If so, how do you feel about that?

- Is your family enthused about the franchise? Will you enjoy working with them if they will be employees?
- Do you enjoy working with others?
- Do you have the background or character traits necessary to succeed in self-ownership?
- Do you have the necessary capital resources, and can you make the financial sacrifices?
- Are you emotionally prepared for working long, hard hours?

Don't be afraid to check with friends and acquaintances as to their opinions on your abilities along these lines. Don't rely on just one opinion; get a consensus of opinions. To help determine your suitability to buying and running a franchise operation or small business, use the Checklist for Evaluating Your Suitability as a Franchisee or Small Business Buyer, which is located at the end of this chapter.

Conclusion

Once you have determined that buying a franchise is what you want, and you are prepared for the franchising challenge, you need to become more familiar with the franchise transaction and protect yourself by investigating each opportunity very carefully and thoroughly. Chapter 2 is designed to help you in this endeavor by describing what is involved in both an offering circular and franchise agreement.

Checklist for Evaluating Your Suitability as a Franchisee or Small Business Buyer

Carefully consider these questions before buying your own franchise or small business.

Financial

Yes No

☐ ☐ Have you and your spouse and knowledgeable family members discussed the idea of going into business for yourselves?

☐ ☐ Are you in complete agreement?

☐ ☐ Do you have the financial resources required to buy a franchise or small business? If not, where are you going to get the capital?

_____

_____

☐ ☐ Are you and your spouse ready to make the necessary sacrifices in the way of money and time in order to operate a franchise or small business?

☐ ☐ Will the possible loss of company benefits, including retirement plans, be outweighed by the potential monetary and self-pride rewards that would come from owning your own business?

☐ ☐ Have you made a thorough written balance sheet of your assets and liabilities, as well as liquid cash resources?

☐ ☐ Will your savings provide you with a cushion for at least one year after you have paid for the franchise or small business, allowing a one-year period of time to break even?

☐ ☐ Do you have additional sources of financing including friends or relatives who might be able to loan you money in the event that your initial financing proves inadequate?

☐ ☐ Do you realize that most new businesses, including franchises, generally do not break even for at least one year after opening?

☐ ☐ Will one of you remain employed at your current occupation while the franchise or small business is in its initial, pre-profit stage?

Personal

Yes No

☐ ☐ Are you and your spouse physically able to handle the emotional and physical strain involved in operating a franchise or small business, caused by long hours and tedious administrative chores?

☐ ☐ Will your family members, particularly small children, suffer from your absence for several years while you build up your business?

☐ ☐ Are you prepared to give up some independence of action in exchange for the advantages the franchise offers you?

☐ ☐ Have you really examined the type of franchise or business you desire and truthfully concluded that you would enjoy running it for several years or until retirement?

☐ ☐ Have you and your spouse had recent physicals?

☐ ☐ Is the present state of your health and that of your spouse good?

☐ ☐ Do you and your spouse enjoy working with others?

Checklist for Evaluating Your Suitability as a Franchisee or Small Business Buyer (continued)

Yes No

☐ ☐ Do you have the ability and experience to work smoothly and profitably with your franchisor, your employees, and your customers?

☐ ☐ Have you asked your friends and relatives for their candid opinions as to your emotional, mental, and physical suitability to running your own business?

☐ ☐ Do you have a capable, willing heir to take over the business if you become disabled?

☐ ☐ If the franchise or new business is not near your present home, do you realize that it would not be beneficial to sell your home and buy one closer until the new venture is successful?

Business

Yes No

☐ ☐ Do you and your spouse have past experience in business that will qualify you for the particular type of franchise or business you desire?

☐ ☐ Is it possible for either you or your spouse to become employed in the type of business you seek to buy before any purchase?

☐ ☐ Have you conducted independent research on the industry you are contemplating entering?

☐ ☐ If you have made your choice of franchises, have you researched the background and experience of your prospective franchisor?

☐ ☐ Have you determined whether the product or service you propose to sell has a market in your prospective territory at the prices you will have to charge?

What will the market for your product or service be like five years from now?

_____

_____

_____

What competition exists in your prospective territory already? _____

From franchise businesses? _____

_____

From nonfranchise businesses? _____

_____

Other Considerations

Yes No

☐ ☐ Do you know an experienced, business-oriented franchise attorney who can evaluate the franchise contract you are considering?

☐ ☐ Do you know an experienced, business-minded accountant?

☐ ☐ Have you prepared a business plan for the franchise or business of your choice?

Notes

Chapter 2

Learning about Franchise Documents

Introduction

When you become interested enough in a franchise opportunity to start gathering information and beginning discussions with a prospective franchisor, you will need to be more familiar with two important documents — the offering circular and the franchise agreement or contract. By learning more about both of these documents and the details they require, you will be better prepared to investigate potential franchise opportunities. This chapter discusses both of these documents in detail and offers tips and strategies on what is involved with each.

The Uniform Franchise Offering Circular

As mentioned in Chapter 1, the Federal Trade Commission (FTC) implemented a rule that required franchisors to present would-be franchisees with a disclosure statement, also known as an offering circular, that contains certain information regarding a franchise.

This rule has been substantially modified effective January 1, 1995, so that franchisors in all 50 states must provide prospective franchisees with a newly revised Uniform Franchise Offering Circular (UFOC). For a sample of what a UFOC looks like, refer to the sample in Appendix A and to the new UFOC guidelines reproduced in Appendix F. If you are familiar with the old offering circular, the guidelines will give you a clearer picture of the extensive changes now in effect.

Specifically, the franchisor must provide you with a Uniform Franchise Offering Circular:

- At the first face-to-face personal meeting between you and the franchisor, or at the time for making disclosures regarding the terms and conditions of the sale of the franchise;

- Ten days before you make any payment to the franchisor; or
- Ten days before you sign any contract committing you to buy the franchise, whichever occurs first.

In addition, the FTC requires all franchisors to furnish you with completed copies of the documents to be executed at least five days before you sign on the dotted line. Examine the Uniform Franchise Offering Circular very carefully, even if you have gleaned information on your own regarding a particular franchisor and his or her franchise offering.

Before examining an offering circular more carefully, if possible, try to personally do a field investigation of all the franchises offered in the field of your choice, and compare franchisors doing business in the same area. To do a field investigation:

- Begin by checking with existing franchisees about their experiences with their franchisor and whether the franchisor has carried out the representations made in the circular and franchise agreement.

- Try to discern the attitude of the existing franchisees regarding the major people in the franchisor's hierarchy of personnel.

- Contact existing franchisees and determine whether or not the franchisor keeps his or her promises.

- Find out whether franchisees feel that their franchise opening costs were more than what the franchisor originally estimated they would be.

- Determine if the franchisor provided the franchisees with adequate training or whether they were left on their own.

Remember, competitors of the franchisor will generally be more than happy to give you all the "dirt" about other franchisors. The same is true of existing franchisees. If they have a gripe against their franchisor, they will be the first to tell you in no uncertain terms. To help you gather the information you need when talking to franchisees, use the Checklist for Interviewing Existing Franchisees on page 35.

Once you have completed your field investigation, you will be better informed when examining the offering circular or prospectus. The procedures discussed in the following paragraphs will help you better examine the actual document. Remember, if you don't get an offering circular from a franchisor, there is something wrong; for example, your franchisor may have violated an act enforceable by the FTC or a state agency, or both.

The Offering Circular's Cover Page

The Uniform Franchise Offering Circular has a cover page that briefly identifies the business that is being franchised and the amounts of the initial franchise fees.

On January 1, 1995, all 14 registration states and the remaining 36 states governed by the FTC began using the same Uniform Franchise Offering Circular, including a uniform cover page. However, individual state registration regulators may require that the franchisor reveal, in capital letters, additional information regarding risk factors on the cover page. Check with your state regulators to see if your state has any additional requirements.

The cover of the new Uniform Franchise Offering Circular must specify any risk factors in bold print. These risk factors must include, if applicable:

- A warning that the franchise agreement permits the franchisor to arbitrate or sue only in a particular state and whether arbitration or litigation in a state other than the franchisee's home state may force the franchisee to accept a less favorable settlement for disputes;
- The fact that arbitration out of state may cost more;
- Whether the franchise agreement designates the law of a particular state other than the franchisee's home state to govern the agreement; and
- That the out-of-state law might not provide the same protection and benefits as the franchisee's local law, and that the franchisee should compare these laws.

Offering circular cover pages may also include the warning that there may be other risks concerning the franchise. However, if the risks are known, they should be specified on the cover page in bold print.

The new Uniform Franchise Offering Circular as adopted by the FTC is also used in those states that do not have franchise registration laws. Some of these states with no franchise registration laws have what are called business opportunity laws, which also might apply to franchise offerings. Franchise laws cover those businesses where:

- The buyer pays money for the business;
- The buyer uses the trademark of the franchisor so the business appears to be a part of an organization; and
- The buyer is subject to marketing directives or controls, or both, set forth by the seller/franchisor.

Business opportunity laws cover those businesses that have similar aspects of those covered by franchise laws, with the key exception being that business opportunities do not use a trademark as part of the deal between the buyer and the seller. To cover both types of businesses, some states have both franchise laws and business opportunity laws, and you need to check to see if your state is one of them.

Making sure you and your franchisor comply with the new franchise or business opportunity laws should be done by an experienced franchise attorney. Because of the complexity, don't attempt to go it alone. For specific information on state franchise and business opportunity laws, turn to Appendix E, State Franchise Information Guidelines.

The second page of the new Uniform Franchise Offering Circular is a standard form table of contents. The table of contents normally covers 1 1/2 pages and contains 23 paragraph headings, as well as a section setting forth the exhibits. The exhibits include the franchise agreement, any other agreements signed by the franchisee, the franchisor's financials, and in many cases a directory of state administrators and agencies. (See the table of contents in the sample offering circular in Appendix A.)

One of the most innovative requirements under the revised UFOC guidelines is that the actual disclosure portion of the UFOC be in "plain English." The new regulations require that the franchisor address itself by its corporate name or by "we," and that the franchisee be addressed as "you."

If an offering circular is not delivered on time, or if it contains a false, incomplete, inaccurate, or misleading statement, a violation of federal or state law may have occurred, and you should report this violation to the Federal Trade Commission in Washington, D.C. If your state has a registration law, you should contact the state authority that regulates franchising in your state. You can also report state registration violations to the FTC.

Additionally, you will be advised that franchise registration in a state that has a franchise registration agency does not mean that the state recommends it or has verified the information in the offering circular. You will also be advised that if you learn that anything in the offering circular is untrue, you should contact the Federal Trade Commission or your state authority, if there is one in your state. Last but not least, the cover sheet should also indicate the effective date of the offering circular.

The Franchisor, Its Predecessors and Affiliates

An offering circular will give you the franchisor's background and that of its predecessors and affiliates. A predecessor is defined in the new law as a person from whom the franchisor acquired directly or indirectly the major portion of the franchisor's assets. An affiliate is defined in the new law as a person controlled by, controlling, or under common control with the franchisor.

Examine the section on the franchisor, its predecessors and affiliates closely. Read about the background of the business and the business experiences of its principal officers. If possible, run a credit check on the company and its previous officers. In addition, any information you can obtain regarding the record of the previous businesses — including other franchise businesses — in which the principals were associated is of paramount importance in determining whether or not they have a proven track record. This information can also help you make some type of forecast about the possibility of your own success. To assure that you obtain all the background information you need, use the Checklist of Information to Secure from a Franchisor on page 37 as a starting point.

Business Experience and Identity of Key Franchisor Personnel

This section of a circular will give you some personal information on the officers and directors of the franchise company. Again, if you can check out their backgrounds, both their business experience and the views of their former acquaintances or competitors, you will enhance your chances of succeeding with your new endeavor. In addition, you should make every attempt to get to know these people as much as you can. Ask to see the head person before you put your money down. Remember, this person will be a vital cog in your story of success since his or her endeavors will directly affect the success of your endeavors.

Check out any affiliates listed in the second section of the circular to make sure that all vital items or services are not supplied by relatives or friends of the franchisor. If some services arc supplied by family and friends, this may drastically change the profitability of your franchise because of inflated, noncompetitive prices.

Litigation Involving the Franchisor

Pay particular attention to this section of the circular, and stay away from any prospective franchisor that is under some current effective injunction or restrictive order, particularly one that could result in a drastic change in the franchise operation itself or possibly a cessation of the franchise in the future. In addition, determine whether or not the franchisor — or any of the franchisor's key employees — has been convicted of crimes or has a record of unfavorable determinations handed down by courts or government agencies.

If any such investigations, convictions, or proceedings are mentioned in the offering circular or prospectus, view these as warning signs and rethink whether or not you want to purchase the franchise. If, all other things being equal, you still wish to purchase it, at least check out the proceedings as documented in the courts or government agencies and determine what has taken place in regard to this litigation.

Always remember the franchisor's side is only one side of the story. Beware if this section reveals any lawsuits against the franchisor by former or existing franchisees. If it does, call or write the court clerks where the cases are being litigated to find out the name of the attorneys representing the plaintiffs; then contact the attorneys and their clients.

If the litigation is local, secure the information by a personal visit to the courthouse and talk to the attorney of record. Contact the plaintiffs and ask them why they are dissatisfied with the franchisor and why they are suing or have sued.

Prior Franchisor Bankruptcies

Many great people have incurred numerous failures in their lives before reaching a pinnacle of success. Abraham Lincoln is just one of many such examples. However, as a rule, people who have failed in the past will fail in the future. Carefully check over the section of the offering circular that refers to prior bankruptcies. It is not uncommon to find that certain franchise founders have started several previous franchises in different business areas, while compiling a track record of failing in each and every one of them. Each endeavor may be subject to a bankruptcy, but the founder may walk away with a million dollars that is not subject to the proceedings involving his or her corporate entity.

Initial Franchise Fee

Your offering circular should contain valuable information on the range of minimum to maximum fees that are charged upfront by the franchisor. The basis for these ranges is stated under this section of the circular. Examine the basis for initial franchise fees very carefully. Use the information as a basis for your personal projections of how much money you will have to spend.

Generally, you will be required to pay a certain amount of money down in order to purchase the franchise. This is commonly referred to as "the initial franchise fee" or "front money." In addition, you may be required to pay other types of money upfront for certain services. It is very important that you determine from this section of the circular precisely what you will receive in the way of services, inventory, and other benefits in return for your front money.

Once again, the franchisor's most valued personnel should be contacted and bombarded with questions regarding the benefits you will receive for this front money. If there are existing franchisees, contact as many of them as you can to find out if they were satisfied with the benefits they received upon paying this front money.

This is one area where inexperienced franchisors can create franchises that are destined to fail or that will be unmarketable because they choose high figures out of the sky. A franchisor should realistically consider what it would cost to open the franchise and the wealth of the typical type of franchisee that will purchase this franchise.

Franchisors need to consider these factors rather than what other franchisors in the same industry charge. If the franchisor breaks even on the sale of each franchise, he or she can still succeed with reasonable royalties and profits from goods and services sold to the "captive franchisee."

Before you purchase the franchise, ask the franchisor how the initial franchise fee is determined, and see what he or she says. If the franchisor can project that the initial franchise fee charges are only for the amounts he or she feels are necessary for the franchisor to break even (and these are reasonable charges), then you can be more secure that the franchisor is someone who knows how to make a successful franchise offering.

A high initial franchise fee does not necessarily mean the franchise is a better investment or even a good one. Take the franchise expansion story of Book Rack Franchising Corporation of Fort Lauderdale, Florida, which was originally founded by Virginia Darnell in 1963. According to *The Franchise Redbook, 1999 Edition* by Roger C. Rule, Book Rack has 283 outlets throughout the United States that sell used and new paperback books. The initial franchise fee is only $6,000 with a straight $75-per-month royalty fee. This is quite reasonable. The moral of the story is not to judge a franchise by its initial fees!

In your research, expect to find a wide range of initial fees and royalty payments; however, there should be a uniformity of initial franchise fees within a particular industry. Be sure you are able to determine this average fee for your particular business.

Other Fees

This section of the circular will advise you in tabular form as to whether or not there are any other fees that you will have to pay in addition to your front money, including ongoing royalties, service fees, training fees, renewal fees, advertising fees, and other similar, one-time or ongoing charges that are payable to the franchisor or its affiliates. Check to see if these fees are refundable if you decide to back out after signing the franchise agreement. Again, it is vital that you determine these amounts and project how they will affect your operations. A good accountant is a very valuable asset when purchasing a franchise.

Also remember that if you are required to pay a royalty on gross sales, this percentage will be substantially greater when you figure the same royalty on your net revenues. Ten percent of gross sales could represent a cash payment of 50 percent or more of your net profit after expenses, depending on your overhead expense.

Initial Investment

This section of the circular presents, in tabular form, the franchisor's monetary estimate of what it will cost you to begin operations, including the initial franchise fee, equipment, inventory, rent, working capital, and other miscellaneous costs. The franchisor must adjust this estimate for each particular state where the offering circular is directed. The information outlined in this section is extremely useful when trying to estimate how much of your money will go into the initial phase of the business, and how fast.

Again, if at all possible, contact existing franchisees and see if these cost projections appear fairly accurate according to their experiences with the franchisor. If there are no existing franchisees available, review these listed costs with local contractors and vendors. Also remember that if these figures are materially misrepresented, a violation of the law might have occurred, which you may wish to complain of at a future date.

This also would be an appropriate time for you to determine whether or not you can start your own business financially. Check out the bottom line — that is, will you have enough cash to support yourself and still meet your business obligations during the launching stages of the franchise, which could span a period of a year or more?

Restrictions on Sources of Products and Services

If the circular provides that franchisees must purchase or lease from designated sources, let this be a warning sign for you to investigate the franchise further. If you are tied into purchasing a particular product or leasing your business premises from the franchisor or his or her affiliates, you may be incurring expensive costs as a result of such tie-ins. Find out if these leases or purchase contracts are competitive with nonaffiliated entrepreneurs in the matter of not only costs but in benefits received.

For instance, if you give a ball point pen away, you could make a fine living on selling the refills to the recipient if he or she is required or obligated to buy the refills from you and no one else. Therefore, if at all possible, check with existing franchisees to see whether or not they are happy with any purchase restrictions and whether or not they are receiving their money's worth. Franchisors who spend an extensive amount of time selling or leasing products, equipment, and buildings will generally spread themselves so thin that the chance of the franchise succeeding is slim. In most cases, it is a full-time operation for a franchisor to license, train, promote, and operate a franchise business without being involved in allied businesses selling equipment, inventory, and facilities to the franchisees.

However, if franchisors can lower their royalty fee by getting a portion of the profit they need from selling ingredients or services to their franchisees at a reasonable cost, then both parties benefit. You are apt to be happier paying for tangible products you use in the business than for intangible values, such as a royalty payment.

Franchisee's Obligations

This section of the offering circular includes a table listing your obligations as a franchisee, with references to the sections of your franchise agreement that contain the obligations. The purpose of the table in the new UFOC is to list your principal obligations under the franchise agreement and other agreements. The table should help you find more detailed information about your obligations in these agreements and in other items of the offering circular.

Read over the provisions of the agreements referred to in this section very carefully since they constitute your contractual obligations of the franchise agreement that, if you breach, will probably be grounds for your termination. Make sure that you are capable of complying with the obligations listed here.

When contemplating buying a franchise, if the franchisor has exiting franchisees, contact these franchisees and get their opinions about the obligations listed in this section. Ask them if they have encountered any difficulties complying with the obligations.

Also, be sure to study the quality of the franchisor's product or service and compare it with competitors'. If you find that the franchisor's product or service suffers in comparison, forget about purchasing the franchise.

Financing

With variable interest rates, it may be necessary for you to secure financing through the franchisor or else face the prospect of being unable to purchase the franchise at all. If it is a requirement to finance through the franchisor, a trip to local lending institutions is in order to determine whether or not you will be securing a loan on comparable existing conditions. Show a copy of the financial arrangements portion of the circular to your local banker, and ask for the banker's opinion of such terms and conditions. Again, a credit check on the franchisor would be ideal. If possible, existing franchisees should be contacted to see if information can be solicited from them as to their experiences with financing from the franchisor. Common sense is a requirement for all potential franchisees when investing hard-earned money in a franchise.

Franchisor's Obligations

You are not only initially paying for the right to use a trademark or service mark, you are probably also paying both a cash advance and a percentage of your future profits for other benefits to be provided to you by the franchisor. Determine whether or not you are getting your money's worth. When reviewing this part of the circular, ask yourself:

- Does the franchisor state he or she will furnish a standard plan of specifications vital to the operation of the business, or could you come up with specifications of your own if you started your own business?
- Does the franchisor provide you with starting inventory and training? If he or she does provide training, how, when, and where does the training occur?
- Is a training manual provided? How detailed is the manual?
- What ongoing support does the franchisor provide to you once the franchise is operating?

Make a list of the support items you believe the franchisor needs to provide for you to succeed in the business being sold by the franchisor. The would-be franchisor should reverse this thinking and list the items of support that are necessary in order to ensure you have every possibility of succeeding. Once the list is completed, it should be included as obligations in the franchise agreement. Determine from research in the business reference sections of the public library just what help in the way of training and experience you would need in order to successfully pursue this concern on your own. Answer the following questions:

- Does the franchisor offer these types of services?
- Does the franchisor offer them on a continuing basis?
- Is the franchisor obligated to offer these benefits in the offering circular and the franchise agreement?
- Does the franchisor merely offer them even though he or she is not obligated to do so? (Remember, obligations can be enforced in court while nonobligatory statements cannot.)
- Do the services offered fulfill the franchisee's needs?

Once again, contacting existing franchisees or potential franchisees of a competitor/franchisor can give you a good idea of what to look for in the way of training and advice from a franchisor. Always remember, every franchisee went through the same thing that you are going through. A telephone call to a franchisee of the franchise operation you are interested in, or to a competitor's franchisee, might give you an opportunity to meet the owner and discuss matters. Perhaps an offer of lunch would help ensure his or her cooperation.

Territory

Exclusive areas are extremely important to the franchisee and you need to carefully review this section of the circular. Exclusive area generally means that you will not have any competition, at least as far as location of another franchise is concerned, in a specified area. However, the matter of exclusive areas can cause problems for the franchisor. For instance, it could be a possible antitrust violation for the franchisor to restrict any other franchisee from selling in a specified area from outside that area, as well as a costly litigation nightmare if such a provision had to be enforced by the franchisor.

In addition, the franchise system itself is concerned because it realizes each franchisee must pursue his or her business efforts to the maximum. Therefore, if one franchisee fails to develop his or her particular area, it behooves the system to place another franchisee in competition in that area; this ensures that the particular franchise potential is fully achieved.

The fear that a franchisee will not develop his or her territory is the fear of most franchisors, and the one reason why many franchisors will not grant exclusive areas, prohibiting putting other franchisees in that area. As an alternative to this, some franchise agreements provide that the initial franchisee must meet current minimums or lose the franchise or share the territory with another franchisee. Make sure that territories have specific formulas in determining the size of the territory in order to have an adequate customer base to provide a reasonable profit to a franchisee in each territory. Be sure to research the impact on your sales with such a condition.

It is very unlikely that a franchisor will deliberately try to destroy an area by selling two franchises in a territory that would provide a suitable profit for only one. In many cases, you will find that you do not have an exclusive area. If this is true, find out whether or not the franchisor will offer you a right of first refusal so you can purchase any additional franchises that may be offered in the future adjacent to your specified territory or location. This way, you can expand in a given area without fear that someone else is operating in your area, reaping a part of your profits. One benefit for you, as a prospective franchisee, is a condition set forth by the franchisor that he or she will not open a company-owned office or another franchise in your territory under the same, similar, or different trademark. Some franchisors, however, may retain the right to sell a franchised trademark product or similar product in your territory through supermarkets or other retail outlets. This might hurt your sales.

Careful consideration should be given to termination or loss-of-area exclusivity clauses imposed by the franchisor for failing to meet minimum sales volume. These minimum sales volume quotas could, of course, mean the withdrawal of your franchise if they are not met. If such minimum restrictions are provided for in the franchise you are considering, they should be examined carefully to see if they are realistic. If possible, consult with existing franchisees to see what their experience has been at meeting such minimums. In addition, if your state has a franchise investment act that requires the filing of offering circulars as a public record, contact the state and review the early filings with the idea of determining who the initial franchisees were. Perhaps one of these initial franchisees is no longer in business.

If you can locate a former franchisee of the particular franchise operation you are interested in, you might be able to secure a substantial amount of information from an excellent source. Listen to this person's impressions of the franchisor. If there are many former franchisees, consider this a red flag as to the merits of purchasing a franchise from this particular franchisor. This particular section of the circular can help you tell whether or not the franchisor favors company-owned offices as opposed to franchised offices. In many cases, the franchisor-owned offices may be a result of the reclamation of franchises that failed. A high record of failure by previous franchisees is another red flag in your search.

Trademarks

One of the prime benefits you are paying for when you purchase a franchise is a well-known trade name, trademark, service mark, service name, or logotype. Preferably, you wish to be a licensee of a trademark or service mark that is registered in the *Principal Register* of the U.S. Patent Office. A registered trademark or service mark of this nature gives the franchisor certain legal presumptions as to ownership and the right to use these marks throughout the United States, which can be very valuable to your franchise. Check with the U.S. Patent and Trademark Office in Washington, D.C. and find out if a certificate of registration has actually been granted to the franchisor. A trademark registered in the *Supplemental Register* does not have these presumptive legal rights, and a statement to this effect must be in Item 13 of the Uniform Franchise Offering Circular.

Another consideration is the length of time that the franchisor has held such certificate of registration. An indication that the mark has been applied for but is still pending does not mean that the franchisor has or will attain the registered right to a particular name. Furthermore, the initials "T.M." after the trademarks merely indicate that the franchisor uses a particular name as a trademark, not that he or she has a U.S. registration certificate.

The key to utilizing a trademark or service mark is to federally register it so you can use the trademark or service mark and advertise it with the symbol ® indicating it is a U.S. registered mark. Registration of a trademark is only one element to consider. Other questions to address include:

- Are the trademarks and trade names well known in the market area in which you intend to operate?
- Are they well known throughout the United States?
- Is the trademark or service mark so identified with the franchisor that it will attract customers to the franchise operations?
- Do you have full use of every trademark or service mark registered to the franchisor?

Consideration should also be given to whether or not there is an obligation by the franchisor to protect the trademark and pursue those who violate it. It behooves not only the franchisor but his or her entire franchise system to extensively police the use of the trademark or service mark and immediately stop infringers through litigation, no matter how expensive the litigation may be.

Patents, Copyrights, and Proprietary Information

The section on patents and copyrights is important to you only if patents are material to the franchise itself. If they are, obtain copies of the patents from the U.S. Patent Office and have them reviewed by your patent attorney for depth of coverage and length of time remaining on the patent. Examine if there are any possible limitations of the right of the franchisor to use the patent or any dissolution of the patent through licenses to others, particularly potential competitors. Carefully examine any claims of proprietary right and confidential information designated by the franchisor.

Obligation to Participate in the Actual Operation of the Franchise Business

In the opinion of many franchise professionals, the successful franchisee is the one who manages his or her own business, or at least spends a considerable amount of time supervising the management of the business. The smart franchisor, in many cases, will insist that the franchisee be active in the operation of the business, or at least retain qualified managers who will be. In general, these managers must be approved by the franchisor. Franchisees should be obligated to train managers, preferably at their own expense. But usually, franchisors will obligate themselves to train a manager at the franchisee's expense. Again, be sure you can determine the frequency of the training sessions.

Restrictions on What the Franchisee May Sell

If you wish to conduct a more extensive business while operating the franchise, this section of the offering circular will be important for you to review. It is also important if you are limited to the sale of services or products which, if sold alone, would not give you the required return on your capital. Again, ask either existing franchisees of the franchisor or existing franchisees of a competitor/franchisor about their experiences. There have been instances in the franchise industry when franchisees were limited to one service only. In one case, for example, a franchisee who was limited to only offering a tune-up service for automobiles believed that it would be more profitable if allied services, such as oil changing, were also permitted. The question to ask yourself is whether or not such restrictions on your product sales will permit you to make a reasonable profit.

Renewal, Termination, Transfer, and Dispute Resolution

This particular section of the circular, which is in tabular form, is of major importance to your future success since it dictates the length of time for which you will receive a return on your investment. For many, the best franchises are those that will exist in the name of the franchisees, and their heirs, or their purchasers for as long as the franchisees, their heirs, successors, or purchasers perform the contracted duties in a manner called for by the agreement. In other words, the ideal franchise agreement allows the franchisee, and anyone who purchases the franchise, to automatically renew the franchise agreement as long as the agreement has not been breached. A franchise agreement requiring you to spend ten years of your time, money, and effort only to lose the franchise at the end of ten years is not a good one.

Watch out for clauses that require you to make substantial amounts of repairs and decorations as a contingency to a renewal. Such clauses should be reasonable and have some formula so expenses do not have to be incurred all in one year. The clauses should set some type of standard so any changes in decor and refurbishing are related to staying competitive within the industry.

An ideal franchise is one you can pass on to your heirs or sell to others subject to the approval of the franchisor and possibly at a reasonable transfer fee. If a particular franchisor does not allow such transfers or renewals, and you still wish to purchase the franchise, consider what provisions, if any, you can make for the franchisor to purchase the franchise back and the amount of consideration for such a deal.

If your state has franchise laws regulating franchise renewals and terminations, consult your attorney to see if the circular's renewal and termination clauses comply with them. See Appendix E for more on state franchise laws.

Your ability to change legal forms of business organization — for example, from a sole proprietorship to a partnership, or from a sole proprietorship or partnership to a corporation — should definitely be a part of a good franchise package at no extra fee or at least a minimum fee. Scrutinize very carefully the reasons a franchisor gives for causes of termination when examining this portion of the offering circular or prospectus.

This section also reveals whether or not the franchise business can be offered for sale to others. If the franchisor has the right of first refusal, that right should not reside within the franchisor's discretion when the business is being sold to a blood relative. The more rights you receive regarding the continuation of the franchise, as well as its transfer and sale, the better the franchise package you are getting, both from a practical and legal standpoint.

If the franchise agreement limits your choice of forum to an arbitration forum rather than a court of law, or your choice of the law to be applied is an out-of-state jurisdiction, consult an attorney regarding the affect of this on your rights. The cover page of the circular should also alert you to these restrictions as possible risks.

Arrangements with Public Figures

If the franchisor states that a public figure is being paid to endorse the franchise, find out whether or not you can use the public figure either in personal appearances or in advertising without prior written approval of the franchisor, the frequency of such use, and the cost of such use, if any.

Earnings Claims

In most cases, the franchisor will not provide actual, average, projected, or forecasted financial sales profits or earnings because of federal and state laws requiring written substantiation of such projections. In addition, there are so many variables involved that it is very difficult to forecast projected earnings in a particular area, especially with a franchise operation that is relatively new. However, if the franchisor does provide such information, it should be shown to your accountant for evaluation. This information should also be evaluated against that which may be supplied by competitive franchisors.

Once again, contacting existing franchisees of the franchisor could well provide you with a considerable amount of information as to the veracity of these projections. Even a franchisee of a competitor could give you some insight into the reliability of such projections. If it is not possible for you to contact a franchisee of either the franchisor or a competitor, a suitable alternative would be to contact someone who is not a franchisee but operates a similar business in the same geographical area. This applies to your efforts to ferret out any of the information described above. There is nothing like relying on experience when deciding whether or not to buy a business.

List of Outlets – Information Regarding Franchises of Franchisor

This section of the circular provides you with the names, telephone numbers, and locations of existing franchisees. In addition to accessing this information, you can also determine whether or not a substantial number of failures have occurred within the franchised operation you are investigating. You can also project just how large the system probably will be in a few years according to the estimates of the franchisor.

Generally, the greater the number of franchisees, the greater the franchisor's chances for success regarding future sales of franchises; however, don't take this at face value. Check with the franchisees themselves. It is also a general rule that the greater the number of franchisees, the more money you will pay for the franchise. This is particularly true in situations where the franchisor does not have many company-owned offices. Theoretically, a higher number of franchisees indicates a more extensive distribution of the product and a better public image for the franchise.

Financial Statements

The offering circular will contain an exhibit with audited financial statements. Take the financial statements to your accountant if you do not have the training to properly evaluate them. Remember, the financial condition of the franchisor not only will affect his or her ability to run a financially successful operation in the future, but it will also determine whether or not he or she will go under, leaving you holding the bag. Most good franchisors have their own successful "pilot plant" company-owned offices, which are the basis of their franchise systems.

Most franchisors use a separate corporate entity for selling their franchises. However, if your particular franchisor doesn't, you then have an opportunity to find out whether or not any income was actually made on these company-owned ventures for a period of up to three years. If the franchisor can't make a go of the business, how do you expect to make a go of it?

Financial statements are the financial track record of the franchisor. Examine, analyze, and digest this material. Feel free to ask questions of the main representatives of the franchisor concerning these financial statements. In fact, it is a good idea to take your accountant along with you to such meetings. Retain the services of an experienced accountant and an experienced attorney, familiar with the day-to-day business operations of a franchise, and who specialize in franchise arrangements.

A Comparison of a Circular and Franchise Agreements

Attached to the circular, you will find a copy of the current franchise agreement or contracts, and possibly other ancillary agreements issued by your franchisor. Carefully examine these agreements and compare them with the statements that are made in the circular. Make sure that the statements coincide and there is nothing missing or even additional in the agreement or contract that is not in the circular as previously discussed. See Appendix B for a sample franchise agreement. The rest of this chapter discusses those areas of the agreement you should be aware of, in addition to those that have been discussed in this section.

The Franchise Agreement

In the trade, the franchise agreement or contract is sometimes referred to as "money in the bank" because a good agreement that protects the best interests of the franchisee and franchisor will be a major factor in ensuring future revenues from the franchise business for both parties. Every franchise agreement provides certain basic provisions and conditions.

They may be numbered differently, placed in different locations, or even have different subtitles, but they are basically the same in nature. This section discusses some additional provisions to look for in the agreement and some suggestions of how to handle them.

Generally, franchisors will not agree to negotiate any terms of their agreement, particularly those terms that are material to them. Before the passage of state franchise registration laws, this was not the case. Today, any substantial changes in the agreement require a change in the circular, and many franchisors may be reluctant to make material changes, particularly if they must first obtain approval from a state franchise regulator. However, there is no harm in asking. The rules differ from state to state. For instance:

- California allows a restricted type of negotiation. The franchisor must provide a notice of negotiated sales with the California Commissioner of Corporations within 15 business days after the sale and must amend his or her registered UFOC in order to disclose the terms of the particular item negotiated before another sale is made. The latter disclosure must be made if the negotiated sale occurred within 12 months of the offering being made.

- Illinois allows a one-time-only negotiation without a formal amendment.

- Indiana requires a temporary amendment for negotiating franchises only.

- North and South Dakota seem to favor negotiated franchise agreements and appear not to require an after-amendment referring to the negotiations. This should be checked out periodically with the state authorities.

- Virginia requires the franchisor to negotiate.

- Minnesota requires an amendment prior to selling the franchise.

- New York doesn't permit negotiation prior to filing.

Use of Trademarks

As previously indicated, one of the prime benefits you receive when you purchase a franchise is the use of a well known and registered trademark or service mark. Examine the portion of the agreement that is entitled "License" or "Trademark," and make sure you are getting your money's worth. Consider the following:

- Is the trademark well known?

- Has it been in operation for a substantial amount of time?

- Does the franchisor have an unrestricted right to use and license such trademark or service mark?

- Are there other trademarks, service marks, or logos you are entitled to use?

- Will the franchisor enforce the trademark registration to the exclusion of infringers?

Location of the Franchise

Another factor influencing the success of almost any business is location — franchising is no exception. You will need to ask yourself these questions when reviewing this section of a franchise agreement:

- Do you have an exclusive right to operate a facility within a franchised area? If not, do you have the right of first refusal to open other locations within the area?

- Is the franchisor required to advise you on site selection? If not, are you qualified to select your own site?

- Will the franchisor assist you by providing information and statistics concerning a suitable location? Included at the end of this chapter, on page 41, is a Franchise Site Evaluation Form to assist you in your site selection.

- How close is the nearest other franchisee (of the franchisor) or franchisor-owned outlet to the site proposed for you?

- How close are your competitors?

- If you are unable to renew your lease at its expiration, will the franchisor make every reasonable effort to relocate you in another premise in the same location?

- Will the cost of such relocation be borne by the franchisor or by you?

Term of the Franchise

Regarding the term of your potential franchise, consider these questions:

- Do you have the franchise as long as you live?

- Is your franchise subject to an option to purchase by the franchisor before it expires? If it is, are you paid an amount equal to market value or a certain multiple of earnings, or must you take a lower book value?

- If the franchise is for a stated term, do you have a right to renew? If you have a right to renew, is there a renewal fee? What is the renewal fee? Is it reasonable?

Front Money and Royalties

The answers to the following questions are very pertinent to your decision regarding whether or not an investment should be made in the franchise offered for sale. Some of these concerns are touched upon in other sections of this book as well.

- Is there any front money (initial fee) that must be paid? If so, can you afford the front money?

- What do you receive in the way of services, inventory, and other fringes for the front money?

- When is the front money payable? Will the franchisor finance the front money? Have you calculated your debt service obligations on the total amount borrowed in your projected pro forma financial statements?

- Do you have to pay a royalty? Is the royalty based on net income or gross sales? If based on gross sales, what is the effective percentage on your net income before taxes? After taxes? How often do you have to pay the royalty?

- What records must you submit to the franchisor regarding your earnings?

- Is the payment of the front money and the royalty consistent with the amount of working capital that you have available?

- What type of investment would you have to provide if you started your own business in competition with the existing franchisees of the franchisor?

Leases

Reviewing the portion of the franchise agreement that pertains to leases is another important area to ask specific questions. Here are some sample questions you may want to ask yourself.

- Are you required to lease the location from the franchisor? If so, is the lease reasonable in its term and the monthly amount you must pay to the franchisor?

- Have you checked with comparative landlords to determine if the rent is reasonable?

- Is this a "net lease," meaning, do you have to pay, in addition to the rental fee, utilities costs, parking lot improvement costs, and wage increases based on the standard-of-living clause, as well as increases in property taxes? If so, have you checked out the actual or probable amount of these additional costs?

- Must you lease fixtures, signs, or equipment from the franchisor? If so, are the prices reasonable?

- Have you explored the comparative costs of the fixtures, signs, and equipment offered by suppliers other than the franchisor?

- Are you required to buy a certain amount of inventory?

- Is the cost of the inventory comparable to that of an inventory purchased from a third party?

- Are you required to follow certain customs and standards? Are these customs and standards consistent with the good management of the business and the quality of the products?

Obligations and Duties of the Franchisor

Ask yourself the following questions regarding the franchisor's responsibilities to you:

- Will you receive adequate training from the franchisor? If so, when, where, and how long?

- Do you have to pay for such training? Is such training offered at a convenient location not requiring extensive travel expenses?

- Are you entitled to continuous training throughout the term of your franchise?

- Will you be provided with an operations manual? (See Chapter 10.)

- Will the franchisor give you some idea of the extent of the coverage of the manual before you sign the contract?

- Will the franchisor provide you with advertising at his or her expense? If not, must you secure advanced approval of any advertising copy from the franchisor?

- Are you required to pay an additional fee for advertising? If so, is the franchisor bound to place such an advertising fee in a special account in your name and utilize it for local advertising?

- What are the franchisor's obligations to you after you are in operation? Are they worth the royalty you will be paying?

Obligations and Duties of the Franchisee

Be sure and ask about your responsibilities as a franchisee as well.

- Are your obligations and duties under the contract reasonable?

- Are other franchisees obligated to perform the same procedures?

- Are the obligations necessary to help ensure the uniformity and quality of the service or product?

- Are you required to participate in the franchisor's training?

- Are other franchisees required to participate in initial and ongoing training by the franchisor?

- Are you obligated to actively participate in the franchise? If not, are you obligated to have a manager approved by the franchisor?

- Is there any provision regarding the days that your franchise must be kept open?

- Are there provisions that help ensure that all franchised entities will be clean and kept in an attractive manner?

- Are you subjected to revisions in the contract at various times or when you transfer the contract by sale to others?

- Are you required to keep adequate records and books?

- What records must you submit to the franchisor and how often?

- What are the penalties for not submitting such records?

Transfer of Agreement and Termination

Regarding the transfer of the franchise agreement, or termination of the franchise, consider the following:

- Can you transfer the license to your heirs to a corporation formed by you for that purpose? If so, must you pay a fee? Is such a fee reasonable?

- If you die and you are operating as a sole proprietorship or a partnership, will your personal representative be able to carry on the business?

- Are you required to give a right of first refusal to the franchisor? If the franchisor has a right of first refusal, is the formula for payment of your interest adequate? Will it include a price for goodwill?

- If the franchisor has a right of first refusal, is the purchase price payable in a lump sum rather than spread out in installments?

- When can the franchisor terminate the franchise? Can this be done only with good cause? If so, are the causes listed therein reasonable?

- If the franchisor can terminate for breach of contract, has he or she specified which terms of the agreement are considered material terms, the breach of which will automatically constitute termination?

- What are your rights upon termination? What are the penalties? Can you terminate this venture without cause prior to its term without any liability? Can you compete after termination?

- Are there applicable laws regulating the termination of franchises or distributorships in your state?

Arbitration of Court Jurisdiction

Review the agreement to see if there is a provision relating to the arbitration of disputes. Generally, arbitration is much less costly and certainly quicker than court. It is also ideal if the arbitration can be held in the state where you are located. The downside to arbitration is that it normally does not allow for discovery procedure and is binding and final.

You would benefit greatly from the insertion of a paragraph stating that the laws of the state in which the franchise is operated do prevail. Usually, the franchisor will attempt to have controlling law in the state where he or she is located, thus causing you a great deal of hardship and expense in trying a case outside the state of the franchise area.

Attorney Fees

In addition, review the agreement to see if there is a clause providing that in the event of litigation of a dispute under the franchise agreement, the winning party shall be entitled to an award for his or her attorney fees. This clause often encourages both parties to litigate, each feeling he or she will be victorious and reimbursed for his or her fees by the loser. However, each party is obligated to pay his or her respective attorney fees as litigation progresses. At the conclusion of the trial, the judge can award whatever he or she deems as reasonable attorney fees, no matter what the actual attorney bill is, and the losing party may well be bankrupt at the time of the final award. For cost-saving tips on attorney fees, refer to Chapter 11.

Helpful Publications and Tips to Prospect for a Franchise

To help you get more information on franchises in general, you may want to obtain some of the following publications:

- *The Franchise Redbook: Easy-to-Use Facts and Figures, 1999 Edition* — This publication is the most up-to-date and definitive information source on existing franchises in the United States and Canada that have continuing plans for expansion. This publication also offers detailed information concerning the basic facts and figures about these franchises on an individual basis. The information has been organized to make it easy to compare any one of 1,200 franchises in 142 categories against its competitors without having to flip pages back and forth. You can use the information to do market analysis, prepare marketing plans, complete a business plan, or prepare contact lists. The book is written by Roger C. Rule. To obtain a copy of the book, contact:

The Oasis Press

(541) 479-9464

FAX (541) 476-1479

- *Entrepreneur Magazine* — This monthly magazine usually publishes franchise information in its January and July issues. To subscribe to this helpful magazine, contact:

Entrepreneur Magazine

Subscriber Service
2392 Morse Avenue
Irvine, CA 92713
(800) 421-2300
e-mail: entmag@entrepreneurmag.com

- *The Franchise Handbook* — This is a handy publication that will provide useful information on available franchise opportunities. For more information on this handbook, contact:

Enterprise Magazine, Inc.

1020 North Broadway, Suite 111
Milwaukee, WI 53202
(414) 272-9977
FAX (414) 272-9973
www.franchise1.com

- *Franchise Opportunities Handbook* — This publication is compiled by the U.S. Department of Commerce and available through the Superintendent of Documents. It contains a listing of existing franchising opportunities within the United States. For your copy, write to:

Superintendent of Documents

U.S. Government Printing Office
Washington, DC 20402

You will find that most franchise offerings are advertised in either the business opportunity section of *The Wall Street Journal* on Thursdays, or the Sunday classified section of your local newspaper. When you answer such ads, the franchisor will probably respond by sending you a brochure and franchisee business application and net worth form. Refer to the end of Chapter 11 for a sample of this form. Once the franchisor determines that you have the financial wherewithal, the offering circular will be sent and franchise salespersons will come knocking.

Another way of discovering franchise opportunities is to attend franchise trade shows. Some of the best franchise trade shows are those sponsored by the International Franchise Association (IFA). IFA trade shows take place in major U.S. cities every year.

Conclusion

With the help of some of these above resources, and your own investigating and researching, you will have a good start on prospecting for and purchasing a franchise. To help you in your investigation and research, review the Checklist of Information to Secure from a Franchisor located at the end of this chapter. Make several copies of this checklist so if you are evaluating more than one franchise, you can use the form for each franchise offering.

Checklist for Interviewing Existing Franchisees

Use this questionnaire when trying to investigate different franchise opportunities by interviewing existing franchisees.

Yes No

☐ ☐ Are you satisfied with the franchisor?

☐ ☐ Is your franchise profitable?

☐ ☐ Have you made the profit you expected to make?

☐ ☐ Are your actual costs those stated in the offering circular?

☐ ☐ Is the product or service you sell of good quality?

☐ ☐ Is delivery of goods from the franchisor adequate?

How long did it take you to break even? _____

☐ ☐ Was the training provided to you by the franchisor adequate?

What is your assessment of the training provided? _____

_____

_____

_____

_____

_____

☐ ☐ Is your franchisor fair and easy to work with?

☐ ☐ Does your franchisor listen to your concerns?

☐ ☐ Have you had any disputes with your franchisor? If so, please specify.

_____

_____

_____

_____

_____

☐ ☐ If you have had disputes, were you able to settle them?

How was settlement accomplished? _____

_____

_____

_____

_____

_____

Checklist for Interviewing Existing Franchisees (continued)

Yes No

☐ ☐ Do you know of any trouble the franchisor has had with other franchisees? If so, what was the nature of the problem?

_____

_____

_____

☐ ☐ Do you know of any trouble the franchisor has had with the government?

_____

☐ ☐ Do you know of any trouble the franchisor has had with local authorities?

_____

☐ ☐ Do you know of any trouble the franchisor has had with competitors?

_____

☐ ☐ Are you satisfied with the marketing and promotional assistance the franchisor has provided?

☐ ☐ Have the operations manuals provided by the franchisor helped you?

What do you think of the manuals? _____

_____

☐ ☐ Are the manuals changed frequently? If so, why?

_____

_____

Other comments you would like to make.

_____

_____

_____

_____

_____

_____

_____

_____

_____

_____

_____

_____

Checklist of Information to Secure from a Franchisor

Use this checklist when doing your own investigation and information gathering.

Yes   No

☐   ☐   Is the franchisor a one-person company? or

☐   ☐   Is the franchisor a corporation with an experienced management that is well trained?

☐   ☐   Is the franchisor offering you an exclusive territory for the length of the franchise? or

☐   ☐   Can the franchisor sell a second or third franchise in your market area?

☐   ☐   Do you have the right of first refusal to adjacent areas?

☐   ☐   Will the franchisor sublet space to you? or

☐   ☐   Will he or she assist you in finding a location for your franchise operation?

☐   ☐   Does the franchisor provide financing? If so, what are the terms?

_____

_____

_____

_____

_____

_____

☐   ☐   Does the franchisor require any fees — other than those described in the offering circular — from the franchisee? If so, what are they?

_____

_____

_____

_____

_____

☐   ☐   Has the franchisor given you information regarding actual, average, or forecasted sales?

☐   ☐   Has the franchisor given you information regarding actual, average, or forecasted profits?

☐   ☐   Has the franchisor given you information regarding actual, average, or forecasted earnings?

What information have you received?

_____

_____

_____

_____

☐   ☐   Will the franchisor provide you with the success rates of existing franchisees?

☐   ☐   Will the franchisor provide you with their names and locations?

Checklist of Information to Secure from a Franchisor (continued)

Yes No

☐ ☐ Are there any restrictions on what items you may sell? If so, what are they?

_____

_____

_____

_____

☐ ☐ Does your prospective franchisor allow variances in the contracts of some of his or her other franchisees? What is the nature of the variances?

_____

_____

_____

_____

☐ ☐ In the event you sell your franchise back to your franchisor under the right of first refusal, will you be compensated for the goodwill you have built into the business?

☐ ☐ Does the franchisor have any federally registered trademarks, service marks, trade names, logotypes, and/or symbols?

☐ ☐ Are you, as a franchisee, entitled to use them without reservation? or

☐ ☐ Are there restrictions, exceptions, or conditions? If so, what are they?

_____

_____

_____

_____

☐ ☐ Does the franchisor have existing patents and copyrights on equipment you will use or items you will sell?

☐ ☐ Does the franchisor have endorsement agreements with any public figures for advertising purposes? If so, what are the terms?

_____

_____

_____

☐ ☐ Has the franchisor investigated you carefully enough to assure him or herself that you can successfully operate the franchise at a profit both to him or her and to you?

☐ ☐ Has the franchisor complied with FTC and state disclosure laws?

☐ ☐ Does the franchisor have a reputation for honesty and fair dealing among the local firms holding his or her franchise?

Checklist of Information to Secure from a Franchisor (continued)

Other Questions

How many years has the firm offering you a franchise been in operation? _____

Describe the franchise area offered you.

_____

_____

_____

What is the total investment the franchisor requires from the franchisee?

_____

_____

_____

How does the franchisor use the initial franchise fees?

_____

_____

_____

What is the extent of the training the franchisor will provide for you?

_____

_____

_____

What are your obligations for purchasing or leasing goods or services from the franchisor or other designated sources?

_____

_____

_____

What are your obligations in relation to purchasing or leasing goods or services in accordance with the franchisor's specifications?

_____

_____

_____

What are the terms of your agreement regarding termination, modification, and renewal conditions of the franchise agreement?

_____

_____

_____

_____

Checklist of Information to Secure from a Franchisor (continued)

Under what circumstances can you terminate the franchise agreement?

_____

_____

_____

If you decide to cancel the franchise agreement, what will it cost you?

_____

_____

_____

What is the background experience and achievement records of key personnel (their "track records")?

_____

_____

_____

How successful is the franchise operation? (Use *Dun & Bradstreet* reports or magazine articles, to supplement information the franchisor gives you.)

_____

_____

_____

_____

What is the franchisor's experience in relation to past litigation or prior bankruptcies?

_____

_____

_____

_____

What is the quality of the financial statements the franchisor provides you?

_____

_____

_____

_____

Exactly what can the franchisor do for you that you cannot do for yourself?

_____

_____

_____

_____

Franchise Site Evaluation Form

When trying to evaluate suitable site locations for your potential franchise, use this form as a guideline.

Name of person making report: _____

Address: _____

_____

Phone: _____

Date of report: _____   Address of site: _____

_____

Information on Site, Customers, and Street Traffic

Type of site (strip center, mall, free-standing, drive-through, or other):

_____

Nearest intersections: _____

_____

Distance of nearest intersections from site: _____ , _____ , _____

Nearest stop sign and name of street: _____ ft. _____

Number of lanes on front and side streets:

_____ on _____

_____ on _____

_____ on _____

_____ on _____

Description and number of parking spaces (front, side, and back, as applicable):

_____ spaces _____

_____ spaces _____

_____ spaces _____

_____ spaces _____

Condition of adjacent streets: _____

_____

_____

_____

_____

Observations of traffic on streets at peak hours including time of day observed: _____

_____

_____

_____

Franchise Site Evaluation Form (continued)

Description of adjoining business, including type of building, and products or services offered:

Left Building   Right Building

_____   _____

_____   _____

Frontage measurements: _____

Depth of site: _____

Total square footage: _____

Customer traffic count of adjacent buildings or businesses:

	Left Building	Right Building
6:00–8:00 A.M.	_____	_____
8:00–10:00 A.M.	_____	_____
10:00–noon	_____	_____
noon–1:00 P.M.	_____	_____
1:00–2:00 P.M.	_____	_____
2:00–4:00 P.M.	_____	_____
4:00–6:00 P.M.	_____	_____
6:00–7:00 P.M.	_____	_____
7:00–8:00 P.M.	_____	_____
8:00–midnight	_____	_____
midn't–6:00 A.M.	_____	_____

Major competition within one and one-half miles of site:

Name	Address	Type of Business
_____	_____	_____
_____	_____	_____
_____	_____	_____
_____	_____	_____
_____	_____	_____

Observations made from surveillance of adjacent businesses and discussions with businesspeople regarding general business conditions, customer traffic, parking availability, center advertising, promotions, reasonableness of rent, possible rent increases, possible construction, and other:

Disadvantages   Advantages

_____   _____

_____   _____

_____   _____

_____   _____

_____   _____

Franchise Site Evaluation Form (continued)

Visibility of site from street: North _____ feet   West _____ feet

South _____ feet   East _____ feet

Ingress and egress observations:

_____

_____

_____

_____

General access: Excellent _____   Good _____   Poor _____

Purchase of Real Estate

Purchase price: $ _____

Terms of purchase: _____

_____

Base Rental

Monthly: $ _____

Date and amount of increase: _____ $ _____

Percentage rental: Yes _____ No _____   If yes, describe: _____

_____

_____

Common area costs: Yes _____ No _____   If yes, brief description: _____

_____

_____

Description of utility costs that must be paid and estimated amounts: _____

_____

_____

Description of other costs: _____

_____

_____

Term of lease: _____

Renewal term and increased rental or other increased costs associated therewith: _____

_____

_____

_____

Lease can be cancelled _____ years _____ months from date of possession or on: _____, 19 ___.

Franchise Site Evaluation Form (continued)

Price Comparisons with Competitors within One Mile

Prime competitor: _____

Secondary competitors: _____

_____

_____

List each of your major products or services and insert competitor's price:

_____ $ _____

_____ $ _____

_____ $ _____

_____ $ _____

_____ $ _____

_____ $ _____

Population — Demographics (Minimum Two-Mile Radius)

Population: _____ Year: _____ Increase in last 12 months: _____ %

Per-capita income: $ _____ Median family income: $ _____

Type of housing: _____

Average home, condo, or apartment value: $ _____

General comments: _____

_____

_____

Zoning and Restrictions

Present zoning class: _____

Permissible uses: _____

_____

Required setbacks: Front: _____   Rear: _____

                      Right side: _____   Left side: _____

Number and size of
parking places: Front: _____   Back: _____

                      Left side: _____   Right side: _____

Fire zone: _____   Nearest fire hydrant: _____

Address and distance of closest fire station: _____ feet or miles

_____

_____

Franchise Site Evaluation Form (continued)

Sign Restrictions

Freestanding: _____

_____

Exterior: _____

_____

Interior: _____

_____

Utility Information

	Company Name	Phone Number
Electric	_____	( ) _____
Natural gas	_____	( ) _____
Water	_____	( ) _____
Telephone	_____	( ) _____
Health dept.	_____	( ) _____
Zoning	_____	( ) _____
Other	_____	( ) _____

Problems discovered when contacting utilities: _____

_____

_____

_____

Nearest Industrial Developments

Name and Address	Type of Business	Estimated # of Employees	Distance
_____	_____	_____	_____
_____			
_____	_____	_____	_____
_____			
_____	_____	_____	_____
_____			
_____	_____	_____	_____
_____			
_____	_____	_____	_____
_____			
_____	_____	_____	_____
_____			

Franchise Site Evaluation Form (continued)

Possible Area Business Draws

List all convention facilities, colleges, high schools, grade schools, parks, or churches in the area.

_____

_____

_____

_____

_____

_____

Shopping Areas

Location	Size	Distance from Site	Comparable Rents

Exhibits

1) Strip map showing site in relation to competitors within a one-mile radius.

2) Videotape of location from all directions.

3) Demographic profiles from one- and two-mile radius.

4) Traffic count sheet.

5) Plot plan of site.

6) Other business and development information from brokers, landlords, and others.

7) Names and addresses of real estate brokers used.

Your Evaluation of Suitability of Site

_____

_____

_____

_____

_____

_____

_____

_____

_____

_____

Chapter 3

Buying a Local Business

Introduction

If you are considering purchasing an existing local business rather than a franchise, you will find the factors you need to consider when purchasing a franchise are similar to those for purchasing a local business; however, you will also find some dissimilarities. For instance, the local business owner is not going to supply you with an offering circular or prospectus detailing his or her background and that of the business you are buying. Consequently, you will have to secure this information yourself. To do this, you can have a qualified attorney prepare an agreement which would, in essence, make the seller warrant and represent certain necessary facets of the business which, if untrue, would allow you to bring an action for fraud or rescission, or both. Thus, many of the provisions discussed in Chapter 2 can be incorporated into these warranties and representations.

This chapter focuses on some of the factors you need to consider when purchasing a local business. Review each discussion carefully to get a better idea of what types of actions and responsibilities you will have as a prospective business purchaser.

Purchase Agreements

Many people are under the impression that escrow instructions are the only contracts they need when purchasing a business. This is not true. The escrow agreement is merely an instructional type of agreement wherein both parties advise the escrow agent of what he or she must do to complete the closing, such as what payments are in order and what documents must be received and exchanged. This is not a true sales agreement.

A true sales agreement should require the seller to put in writing and warrant every essential part of the business that will make it a success or failure. This includes warranting that the financials are true and correct; that there are no hidden income tax claims or litigation; that the business has made a certain amount of money and will continue to make a certain amount of money (if that information can be obtained from the seller); and that there are no pending lawsuits. There will be many other details you will want to know about as well, but unless you put them in writing and have them warranted by the seller, they will get lost in the shuffle.

Exhibits of purchase agreements should include:

- Financial statements;
- The type of note that you will sign;
- A list of creditors and accounts receivable;
- A list of claims and pending litigation; and
- A complete list of the outstanding contracts, inventory, fixtures, and equipment you are purchasing, together with their value and the basis of evaluation. (Valuable contracts should be examined to determine if you can assume them.)

The passage of the Clinton Deficit Reduction Act has created certain opposing tax advantages between the seller and the buyer of a business on how the purchase price of a business is allocated to various assets being acquired. This tax legislation, which was passed in August 1993, simplified the allocation process by creating a broad new category of amortizable assets, called Section 197 Intangibles. Consequently, intangible assets purchased after August 1993 may now be amortized over a 15-year period by the purchaser. Intangibles include covenants not to compete, know-how, customer lists, goodwill, and going concern value. For the first time ever, goodwill and going concern value can be amortized by the buyer as Section 197 Intangibles over a 15-year period. See your accountant before signing a purchase agreement that attempts to allocate the purchase price.

Review Financial Statements

The name of the game in any business is the bottom line, or in other words, profit. Again, it cannot be emphasized too clearly that an experienced certified public accountant familiar with business acquisitions should examine not only the existing financial statements of the seller, but any projections or forecasts he or she has made. It would be a good idea to attempt to get the seller to set forth in writing his or her sales and earnings projections.

The local business owner should provide you with updated financial statements and warrant and represent that they are true, accurate, and the basis for your purchase. Don't be afraid to run a credit check on your seller or ask his or her creditors and competitors what they know.

Audited financial statements, including a balance sheet and a profit and loss statement, are extremely desirable. Unaudited statements are much less desirable, but in many cases, the seller will contend that the cost of an audit is too expensive.

If this is the case, you may want to offer sharing the audit's expense. If the financials are unaudited, the purchase agreement should contain a clause in which the seller warrants that such financials are true and correct. Any such warranty should indicate that it will survive the closing of the purchase and sale. Having this warranty could certainly save you from disaster and prevent you from buying "a pig in a poke." Sometimes, the best investment is the investment that is not made.

Beware the seller who refuses to give you a financial statement, whether audited or not.

Bulk Sales Laws

When a business sells all, or substantially all, of its assets or enters into a major transaction that is not part of its ordinary business activities, the bulk sales law applies. While many states have repealed this law, some states still have a bulk sales law, and you need to find out if yours is one of them.

The bulk sales law is of particular importance to you, because as a purchaser of an existing business, you are required to perform certain duties under this law to ensure that the rights of the seller's creditors are protected.

To comply with this law, both you and the seller have certain responsibilities. The recommended approach is to consult your attorney and escrow agent, if one is involved. In fact, retaining an attorney to research bulk sales law requirements, as well as to help write a purchase agreement, is imperative to protecting yourself from potential pitfalls and liabilities. Preferably, try to find an attorney who specializes in business law.

The Purchase Price

Always remember, the purchase of a business is like an investment in any other type of endeavor — you are seeking a fair and reasonable return on your investment. In today's fluctuating, interest-rate market, investments in relatively safe endeavors many times can return an annual rate of five percent. In other words, in a safe investment, within 20 years, you can obtain a return equal to your original investment. The same is true when you are buying a business. If possible, find out how the seller arrived at the sales price and compare it to the sales price of comparable businesses.

Currently in California, business brokers recommend a sales price equal to one year's gross sales, plus the value of the assets on the books. Have your accountant carefully check over the financial statements, including the all-important cash-flow analysis, and have him or her advise you as to when he or she thinks you can secure back your investment. The better the investment, the faster you will recover your initial investment.

You must ask yourself whether or not you can afford the down payment and, in many cases, the installment payments that you will be required to make in future years. Will your payments hinder the support of your family? Will your new business provide enough money to make the current payments and at the same time support your family?

A cash-flow analysis will at least give you some hint as to what prospects you face along these lines. Check your seller's cash-flow analysis and his or her financial statements and determine how much he or she had left over after expenses. In all probability, you will find that the seller did not have the expenses you have since he or she did not have to pay someone else for the purchase of the business.

Look not only at the costs of operating the business but also at the contracts that accompany such costs. For example, leases should be carefully examined to see if they have escalation costs that are not payable now, but will be in the future. In addition, leases should be studied to make sure that you will have the premises for a sufficient number of years to recoup your investment.

Location of the Business

Seriously consider the location of the business you are thinking of buying. Some of the questions you may want to raise include:

- Will this location be available for a substantial number of years?
- Is there any possibility of a major competitor coming to the immediate area? If so, what effect will this have on the business that is for sale?
- Can the business be relocated without loss of profit? Is the present lease assignable?

The latter question can be answered by your making a personal visit to the landlord with the understanding that you wish to have the same terms and conditions as those of the seller. Most leases provide that an assignment cannot be made without the consent of the landlord. In many cases, the landlord is given the right to raise the rent if there is a sale.

Not only is the examination of the lease's contents, assignability, and duration important, but a check with the individual landlord to determine whether or not he or she will abide by such assignment and its existing terms and conditions is imperative. See the section in Chapter 2 entitled, "Leases." This section raises additional questions that should be asked by franchise or independent-business buyers.

Market Analysis

Like all businesses, the life or death of a local business depends on its market. Major companies that are generally successful in opening a new location normally conduct a market feasibility study beforehand. There is no reason why you should not make your own market feasibility study.

There is a wealth of information available from the U.S. Department of Commerce regarding the buying patterns of Americans in relation to particular businesses, including service- and product-oriented businesses. A trip to your local library can provide you with corresponding statistical information. Business publications, such as *The Wall Street Journal*, will give you an idea of the quickly changing attitudes of the American consumer public.

As a prospective business purchaser, you can also acquire information about the customers of a particular entity, either by phone or by requesting that the seller make questionnaires available to his or her customers for a period of 30 to 60 days before you purchase the business. You could establish a contingency that the closing be delayed for a certain period of time until you can conduct your own survey.

If the seller will not go for this, your best bet is to tell him or her that you would like a trial period on the job and that during this trial period, you will contact customers and obtain their viewpoints on the establishment and why they patronize it. If you are buying a small business, you should have permission to contact its customers. To prevent any type of panic, this can be done without your indicating that you would be the new owner. With the help of the seller, you can introduce yourself as someone merely seeking to find out for the owner how the business can be improved.

If you are buying a business whose particular trade name is the key to the purchase, make sure your purchase agreement contains a provision stating that:

- You can use the name; and
- The seller represents and warrants subject to a fraud action that such name is his or hers and is not subject to litigation by some other third party claiming to have rights to the name.

Competition

A thorough check of the market area should be made for existing, as well as potential, competitors. Most real estate agents will advise you of buildings that might be available to competitors in your line of business. Personally canvass the area for existing or potential competing businesses that may lessen your future profits.

In addition, ask the seller if he or she will give a covenant-not-to-compete statement in writing that ensures he or she will not compete with you in a specific geographical area and for a period of time that is reasonable and enforceable under your state laws. Here again, an experienced attorney is a necessity.

Checking the Seller's Background

It is a good idea for every potential purchaser to study the local county court records to determine whether or not any litigation has been brought against the seller.

This can be done by going to the local courthouse and providing clerks with the last names of the sellers and/or the name under which the business entity has operated. Once any case numbers are secured, the actual file should be reviewed to determine what the litigation involved. Follow-up conversations with the plaintiffs and their attorneys are also in order. The seller should then be confronted to see what his or her side of the story is regarding these litigated matters. If real property is part of the deal, a title policy should be secured as part of the transaction so you know you are getting clear title to the property.

In all cases where inventory, fixtures, and other items are passing hands, check with the office of the secretary of state or an applicable state or county agency to determine whether or not a *Form UCC-1* has been filed. A *Form UCC-1* is a Uniform Commercial Code, which is signed by a debtor indicating that a creditor has a lien on certain enumerated items.

The secretary of state or an applicable state or county agency can also provide a *Form UCC-3*, which upon payment of a small fee, will result in the secretary of state forwarding copies to you of any financing statements — statements indicating liens — that are on file in the name of the particular seller or business entity.

If existing liens have not been revealed by the seller, the seller should be confronted with these forms, since liens are a cloud on your title to such items. There are some private agencies which, upon payment of an additional fee, will check the secretary of state's files or other appropriate state or county files for you in considerably less time than if you submitted a *Form UCC-3* to the secretary of state.

When checking the background of a seller, you may wish to use the checklist at the end of this chapter. This checklist will help you obtain some of the information discussed in this chapter.

Conclusion

To help ensure a good purchase of a local business, there are several tips you can follow.

- Determine what the seller is providing you for your money. Does this include a starting inventory, training, promotional advice, customer lists, and other such vital information necessary to your continued success?

- Check with competitors, and particularly with suppliers, to see if the seller has priced up the inventory to you, which, when you add your normal markup, will price you right out of the retail market. The suppliers can attest to the price that was paid for the inventory, as well as to what inventory prices will be in the future.

- Try to persuade the seller to allow you to watch him or her operate the business for a suitable period of time. You might be taking one giant step toward ensuring a good purchase.

- Encourage the seller to advise you fully as to whether or not his or her own personality has made the difference between success and failure. If it does, make sure you have a similar personality. A successful restaurant that attracts a multitude of people because of the outgoing personality of the owner might become a dismal failure to the purchaser who is much more introverted.

- Truly shop for your local business. Investigate several businesses and compare their profit and loss statements. Talk to other small business owners who are in the same line of endeavor, even if they are not direct competitors, and consider what they have to say. This may cost you a lot of lunches or dinners, but it could prove very beneficial.

- Determine whether or not the business will make a profit under your ownership. To help you do this, prepare a business plan. Such a plan will also be useful to your bank or investor if you are seeking funding. It also acts as a written confirmation of your long-term business goals. An excellent book to help you create the plan from start to finish is *No Money Down Financing for Franchising* by Roger C. Rule. To obtain your copy, contact:

The Oasis Press
(541) 479-9464
FAX (541) 476-1479

With this brief overview of what factors to consider when buying a local business, you will be better prepared to work with your attorney and accountant when investigating, evaluating, and negotiating the purchase of a small business.

Checklist of Information to Secure from the Seller of an Existing Business

- ☐ Obtain information on the background of the business and its owner.

- ☐ Obtain the seller's financials for the past three years.

- ☐ Obtain copies of all leases on location and equipment.

- ☐ Obtain an accurate list of all equipment, fixtures, inventory, and supplies.

- ☐ Determine the condition of equipment, fixtures, inventory, and supplies — particularly heating and air conditioning.

- ☐ Obtain copies of all maintenance agreements on equipment.

- ☐ Ask about potential or actual liability claims against the current business.

- ☐ Find out if a bulk sale law is applicable.

- ☐ Run a credit check on the seller.

- ☐ Question current and past employees on their views of the business.

- ☐ Check the seller's cash-flow analysis charts.

- ☐ Determine whether the seller's present prices for his or her products or services are competitive.

- ☐ Check with suppliers to verify actual prices of inventory and stock items.

- ☐ Prepare pro forma sales projections in the form of profit and loss statements for the next two years.

- ☐ Make sure the business' past success was not due to the personality of the seller.

- ☐ Secure a valid not-to-compete covenant from the seller.

- ☐ Make your own market study of the area or hire a qualified person to do this for you.

- ☐ Find out if any competitors, particularly high discounters, are looking for locations in your area. Make it a practice to contact local real estate and commercial brokers in your area as the source for this important information.

- ☐ Talk to the seller's customers and find out why they patronize the business and their thoughts on improving the business.

- ☐ Check with business owners of similar businesses as to their opinions on the merits of making money in their line of endeavor.

- ☐ Check with your bank regarding the availability of funds to you and the cost thereof.

- ☐ Find out if the seller's present lease is assignable on the same rental terms.

- ☐ Check county records for lawsuits and claims against the seller.

- ☐ Check with the local county or state agency where liens are filed — usually these are found in the secretary of state's office — and determine whether any liens against the seller and the seller's premises have been filed.

- ☐ Find out why the seller is selling his or her business.

Chapter 4

Buying a Local Franchise Operation

Introduction

Having read the previous chapters, you have a better understanding about purchasing a franchise from a franchisor or purchasing a business that is not a franchise from a local business owner. This chapter examines the scenario of purchasing an existing franchise business from a local franchisee.

The big difference between purchasing a franchise from a franchisor and purchasing a franchise from an existing franchisee is if it is truly a sale by the existing franchisee to the purchaser, the franchisee is not bound by restrictions on revealing actual or projected revenue figures. By the same token, the franchisee/seller is also not bound by any disclosure laws, such as the one issued by the Federal Trade Commission. Therefore, you should extensively review the previous chapters of this book regarding both purchasing a franchise and purchasing a business from a local business owner, and consult the checklists at the end of chapters 1–3 for additional information on what you need to know and research when purchasing a franchise or existing business.

In essence, ensure that you secure a written purchase agreement wherein the franchisee produces accurate, truthful financial statements and warrants their veracity. Because the business is also a franchise, familiarize yourself with the terms and conditions of the franchise agreement and with the information in the circular concerning the franchisor.

Reviewing the Disclosure Document

As stated above, the sale of a franchise that is strictly between the franchisee and the prospective buyer, and that does not involve the franchisor, does not require that the franchisee/seller provide you with the franchisor's disclosure document. However, since most franchise agreements provide that a franchisee can only transfer his or her franchise with the franchisor's consent, and upon the execution of a then-current franchise agreement by the purchaser, it is extremely wise for the franchisor to provide you with a disclosure document that contains the updated franchise agreement. Therefore, thoroughly examine the disclosure document, as indicated in Chapter 2. In addition, follow all of the suggestions made in Chapter 3 pertaining to the purchase of a nonfranchise business. Additionally, find out whether you must pay for training sessions required by the franchisor, or if your training can be obtained from the selling franchisee at no cost to you. This is extremely important to know.

You must realize that your relationship with the selling franchisee is only temporary and short-term, and that your assuming of the franchisee's franchise agreement or the execution of a new franchise agreement means a long-term relationship with the franchisor. Therefore, before you sign any documents or part with any money, familiarize yourself with the franchisor and contact other, nonselling franchisees to determine answers to the many questions you will have. In addition, find out why the existing franchisee is selling the franchise. In many instances, a selling franchisee places the business on the market because of an inability to make it profitable. This is why it is so important that you dig out all information available on the franchise you seek to buy, including the financials, the franchisee's reasons for selling the franchise, and the seller's relationship with, and opinion of, the franchisor.

Because the franchisee/seller could jeopardize any sale by being too frank about the shortcomings of the franchisor, information from the franchisee/seller is often slanted to avoid any criticism of the franchisor. Other franchisees of the same franchisor will not have this reservation when approached by you regarding the franchisor's performance with the franchisees.

Selling Price of an Existing Franchise Business

Since an ongoing business concern will be the subject of this particular type of purchase, along with a franchise, the transaction is going to be much more costly than buying a new franchise and starting it from scratch. There doesn't seem to be any set formula for determining a fair price for an existing franchise business.

Years ago, before inflation, a business would generally sell for three to five times its annual earnings, with all parties assuming that the investment could be recouped in three to five years. In more modern times, businesses generally are sold at one year's net earnings, plus the value of the equipment, fixtures, and inventory on the books. In reality, most businesses sell for a price the seller is willing to accept and the buyer is willing to pay. Anybody buying a business, however, should first consult an accountant or real estate agent familiar with the purchase and sale values of the business in question.

You may want to make arrangements to observe or work in the particular business for several weeks before making any written contractual commitment. However, if there are other prospective purchasers interested in the business, it is unlikely that the franchisee/seller of the business will entertain such an arrangement.

If the existing franchise you are thinking about buying is successful, be sure to find out why it has succeeded. If it is a service-oriented business, and the sales or technical ability of the franchisee/seller is the primary reason for the business' success, make sure you have some of the same qualities.

The success of the business may stem from competent employees. Therefore, although a franchisee/seller cannot "sell" his or her employees, the purchase agreement could be drafted with a warranty and representation by the seller that he or she will do everything within his or her power to convince the employees to stay on with you. In addition, a restriction that the seller will not compete with the you should also be incorporated into a written buy and sell agreement.

In any situation where an existing business is being purchased, you should make sure there is a long-term assumable lease in existence and the landlord will consent to the transfer. More businesses have been sunk when the purchaser took over a business only to find a few months later that the rent had been doubled or that the lease would shortly expire without any possibility of renewal.

Helpful Tips

Here are some tips for anyone interested in buying an existing franchise or business.

- Current federal and state franchise laws offer you what you need the most — information about the seller's franchisor. If you are interested in buying a franchise, utilize this source of information.

- If you are interested in buying a local nonfranchise business, read over the material in chapters 1 and 2 to get an idea of the type of information required of franchisors and ask for the same type of information from your local business owner interested in selling.

- The less information you get from the seller, the greater the risk you may be buying a "lemon."

- Remember to personally investigate the deal. Common sense is the key here. Why take a bigger risk than necessary? Check, check, and double-check.

- Anybody purchasing a business should seek out competent legal counsel versed in the practical business aspects of buying and selling a business.

- Use the checklists at the end of chapters 1–3 to evaluate every franchise or business you are seriously considering buying.

- Research and review all state and federal franchise laws and any state business opportunity laws. (See Appendix E.)

Conclusion

The following chapters contained in Part II, although written for the business owner who has an existing business and is considering franchising it, can also be viewed from the standpoint of purchasing a franchise. These chapters examine the factors that contribute to a good franchise business from a franchisor's viewpoint. The prospective franchisor will soon find that whatever makes the franchisee successful makes the franchisor successful as well.

If you are considering buying a franchise, compare the terms of your potential franchise purchase with the information in Part II to determine whether your potential franchisor has done his or her homework. In addition, remember that today's purchaser of an ongoing business may be tomorrow's franchisor.

Part II

Franchising Your Business

Chapter 5

Franchising Basics

Introduction

As a new franchisor, you need to realize that franchising is a method of marketing and therefore entails a business operation in and of itself. Before beginning the franchise process, you will need to know how to:

- Structure a workable franchise agreement with franchisees;
- Choose and train your franchisees; and
- Market not only the product or service the franchisee will sell, but the franchise concept itself to prospective franchisees.

Too often, many new, potential franchisors seek out an attorney — who perhaps has only worked on one or two franchise deals at the most — to draw up a franchise agreement for them. In most cases, these new franchisors are very successful in running their own businesses, but they don't know the first thing about franchising. For example, many first-time franchisors don't know some of the franchising basics, such as:

- What a franchisee is or what to expect from one;
- How to provide ongoing support to a franchisee;
- How much money is needed to capitalize the franchise venture; or
- How much to charge as an initial franchise fee and as an ongoing royalty.

Part II of this book — chapters 5–11 — provides you with this type of information so you can set up a franchising operation with some prior knowledge of the most common business mistakes made in franchising by inexperienced franchisors. As a result, you will hopefully avoid making the same mistakes and ensure a greater chance for success in your franchise endeavor. Before deciding if your business can be franchised, you may want to review some of the advantages and disadvantages of doing so.

Advantages of Franchising

When discussing the advantages of franchising for the franchisor, it is inevitable to discuss the advantages available to the franchisee as well. This is because many advantages attributed to one are also considered advantages to the other. So even though the following list specifies the advantage to the franchisor or franchisee, most of them are generally held to be advantages for both:

- There is a strong possibility for rapid maximum expansion with minimum capital expenditures.
- Direct managing responsibilities become the franchisee's obligation. and provide the franchisor with more freedom to do other things.
- The franchisee generally has pride of ownership and self-motivation because of his or her capital investment and stake in future profits. (This self-motivation generally results in the franchisee's lowering his or her costs, resulting in higher profit margins for the franchisee, and greater consumer markets for the franchisor not normally attainable by company employees.)
- A franchisee will generally have a minimum amount of line-management employees and a greater amount of staff advisory employees.
- National and local advertising fund dollars are available for franchisees at far greater amounts than could be generated by the franchisor or franchisee alone.
- There is increased buying power, resulting in a lower possible purchase price to the franchisee than for a company-owned entity.
- Research and development facilities are available to the franchisor through reports from franchisees.
- Steady cash flow from royalties is available to the franchisor.
- The franchisor enjoys greater control over franchisees through wise and fair contract provisions.
- Some limits of liability extend to the final consumer. (Franchisees generally are not held to be agents of the franchisor in the event of injuries due to negligence of the franchisee as opposed to sure liability to the company for injuries suffered in a branch store.)

Other advantages a franchisor may enjoy can be directly attributed to the advantages that a franchisee will enjoy. In short, if the franchisee is happy, you will be happy. For more on franchisee advantages, refer to Chapter 1.

Disadvantages of Franchising

Of course, as is the case with most things in life, there is usually a downside to every decision you make or every venture you pursue. And when it comes to franchising, you need to be aware of some of the disadvantages. This section of the chapter details some of the downsides of franchising so you are better informed and more prepared in making your franchising decision.

Decreased Net Receipts

Net receipts from franchisees could be less than net receipts from successful, company-owned operations. In reality, only a few new franchises break even immediately. Most franchises take six months to a year to break even. This is also true of most new company-owned retail outlets. Although the company-owned office retains 100 percent of its net profits, it has obligated itself to an initial capital indebtedness that would not be present if it were a franchise.

If you are relatively sure that company-owned retail outlets can produce an immediate profit and you have the capital and labor to staff them, you will certainly make much more money with company-owned outlets than if you franchised an equal number of franchises that made the same amount of profit. Your main problem will be to raise the necessary start-up capital and secure and retain qualified, hard-working managers and employees while hoping sales from the company-owned offices will immediately exceed the substantial start-up costs inherent in a company-owned outlet. Capital and qualified employees are very hard to come by, and the latter are even more difficult to retain.

Independence of Franchisees

As a franchisor, you will be dealing with independent operators rather than with company employees. The key is to treat all franchisees fairly. Franchisees should be subject only to enough control to ensure that your franchised service or product will be marketed to the consumer with the same quality that made you a success.

For example, if the franchisees feel they are overpaying for services they receive from you, or that the services are not what were represented to them, they will become disgruntled and eventually may group together, withholding payment of their franchise fees. Most franchisees who withhold payment of fees and sue are those who feel their contracts have been breached by the franchisor. And usually, these franchisees have experienced a personality conflict with someone in the franchisor's operation.

Be extremely careful in selecting a franchisee or allowing the initial franchisee to transfer his or her franchise to a succeeding transferee. Furthermore, continue to look upon each of your franchisees as an economical substitute for a company manager insofar as assisting and supporting that franchisee.

Many franchisors seem to have the attitude that they now are in the business of making money by selling franchises instead of selling their services or products. Their attention is more attuned to advertising and marketing the franchises rather than marketing the product or service to the consumer.

The primary goal of any franchisor is to sell his or her services or wares. The use of franchisees is a method of attaining this goal.

Difference in Required Business Skills

The business skills you will need for operating a franchisor system are entirely different from those you needed in running your original retail business. Most of the franchisors who fail in the franchising business are those who did not know what they were doing when they first started their franchisor corporation. They were experts at operating an initial retail business and tried to franchise because of their extensive trial-and-error experience in such a business; however, they did not know how to be a franchisor.

Overspending

Franchisors tend to spend too much money on show. There seems to be a tremendous temptation for franchisors to immediately "put on the dog." High-rise office buildings, overstaffing, company cars, expensive hotels, elaborate trade show booths, and costly classified advertising are some of the first mistakes many new franchisors make. Franchisors have a tendency to undercapitalize by not budgeting themselves.

No matter what your capital is, be it $20,000, $100,000, or $1,000,000, wisely budget the cost of your office, the marketing of your franchises, the training of your franchisees, and the maintenance and support of your franchise outlets.

Costs Can Be High

In the United States, franchisors are required to have written offering circulars containing copies of all proposed contracts that are to be entered into with the franchisees. (See Chapter 2 for more on offering circulars.) To prepare a circular, you will need to retain the services of an attorney and an accountant. As pointed out later in Chapter 11, the costs of preparing a circular and audited financial statements sometimes are not in direct proportion with the value given.

Try to get the most for your dollar, but be careful in your selection of attorneys and accountants. Rely heavily upon the references of a particular attorney's or lawyer's past clients. Under no circumstances should the costs of setting up the franchise be greater than the costs you would incur if you were to set up company-owned offices with qualified management personnel. When trying to control service costs of attorneys and accountants, complete the questionnaires in both Appendix C and Appendix D. You should complete these questionnaires before your first meeting with an attorney.

In addition to legal and professional fees, the cost of franchising in multiple states is high because of the individual legal costs for disclosure filings in the 14 states that have franchise registration laws. In these states, your legal requirements as a franchisor are governed by registration state rules. In 17 other states, your requirements are governed by business opportunity statutes. (See Appendix E, State Franchise Information Guidelines, for more on these state statutes.) In the remaining 19 states and

Washington, D.C., you will need to comply with the Federal Trade Commission's rules on disclosures.

Unfortunately, the registration states differ and one registration state will not allow an offering circular approved by another state without changes. The same is true in those states having business opportunity laws that require filing. Even the FTC rules require the circulars to differentiate regarding the individual noncompete, renewal, and termination laws of each of the FTC states; although, they are generally incorporated in one disclosure form.

This cost disadvantage can be minimized if you have a business plan of slow growth that concentrates on one or two states for the first few years and gradually expands to bordering states. By doing this, you will incur attorney fees and filing costs over a period of time rather than all at once. Thoroughly evaluate the particular advantages and disadvantages of franchising as compared to other alternatives of expansion before making the franchise decision. Refer to Chapter 6 for more on alternate expansion methods.

Can Your Business be Franchised?

If you already have a successful business that is susceptible to a regional or national system of marketing, and you do not wish to share control or risk the personality conflicts that come with bringing in investors who would become your equals in making decisions about the business, then franchising may be your best course of action. To help you determine if your business could be franchised, review some of the qualifiers and considerations described below.

Are You Franchisor Material?

Before you evaluate your business as a potential franchise, be sure to evaluate yourself as a potential franchisor. Often, a person who might successfully operate a business that is amenable to franchising may not be cut out to be a franchisor. Consider your qualities and remember franchising is more than the business of selling services and/or products to a consumer. In addition, as a franchisor, you will be an educator, trainer, psychologist, minister, and perpetual handholder to your franchisees. You will also be their Uncle Sam, extracting an initial fee to put them in a higher income tax bracket and then continually taxing them through the form of a royalty throughout their careers.

You will need to be aware of the franchisee-franchisor relationship and always remember to allow your individual franchisees to become their own person in having their own business, and always treat the franchisee as an independent business owner. It is important you carefully set forth the guidelines of this independent contractor relationship clearly in the **initial contract, the offering circular, and all further communications to the franchisee.**

Is There a Market for Your Particular Product or Service?

Do not consider franchising your business unless you have a known, local market for your product or service. Marketability is determined by need, and need is determined by competition. For example, if you are running a hamburger stand, your chances of finding a market for your franchise and a market for your franchisees are relatively small in today's business community.

However, if you have a unique way of running a hamburger stand, it is entirely possible to franchise it in today's market. Take the Wendy's operation, for example, which has gained steam by introducing the system of in-line preparation of hamburgers as the onlooking consumer waits for his or her order. This is in contrast to the traditional method of preparing hamburgers out of view and then setting them on a warming tray until someone places an order. Wendy's gives consumers the impression that it is making the hamburger to order right before their eyes.

Demand is the crucial force here. It is just as important as uniqueness. Your unique product or service must not only be desired by those who wish to buy franchises from you, it must also be desired by the American public, who will buy from the franchisees.

What Market Research Must You Complete?

If your product or service is relatively new and not extensively offered by anyone else but has proven extremely salable, your first task is to determine those sections of the country that would most likely buy your products or services, based on needs similar to those of your present customers. For example, a new type of thermal underwear would not go over well with residents of California's Palm Springs area; however, a successful gas-saving device might take hold anywhere in the world.

If your product or service is not relatively new, you can retain market research firms to prepare extensive reports concerning the types of consumers in various regions and their needs and buying power. This could be rather expensive, so another alternative is to do your own research by visiting the reference department of your local library. Study the Yellow Pages of phone books of the various cities in which you would like to offer your product or service to determine if any competition exists in those areas.

You will also want to interview existing franchisors and franchisees for their insight on franchising. People enjoy telling others of their business accomplishments, and this should be a particularly enjoyable aspect of researching your business' franchising potential.

Government agencies are also very helpful in providing demographic information and market research data. In particular, the U.S. Department of Commerce and the U.S. Department of Labor have conducted extensive studies on the regional consumer habits of Americans. You can use this information in your research.

An initial study of the existing demand for the products or services you are thinking of offering through a franchise system is always necessary. A more extensive study can be conducted by potential franchisees themselves. If you feel an initial market is out there, utilize potential franchisees by encouraging them to make their own market study as a prerequisite to receiving a license from you.

Do You Have a Registerable Trademark?

If you have a product or service that is unique or in demand, you must capture this uniqueness through the use of a trademark (if it is a product) or service mark (if it is a service). The idea is to get the American public to associate your product with a particular trademark.

For many years, purchasers of a certain type of transparent tape would not go into the local stationery store and ask for transparent tape but would instead automatically ask for the trademarked "Scotch" tape. In looking around, you will see that all of the big companies utilize this concept. The producers of various cola drinks do not want you to ask for a cola, thereby allowing the local dispenser of the product to make the choice for you. The Coca-Cola Company wants you to ask for a Coke, and the Pepsi-Cola Company wants you to ask for a Pepsi.

As a result, you will want to apply for a registered trademark or service mark on your particular product or service as soon as possible. You will most certainly want to do this before the first franchise agreement is negotiated and consummated. Keep in mind the trademark or service mark must be used in intrastate and interstate commerce before the owner can apply to the U.S. Patent and Trademark Office in Washington, D.C. for its registration.

Before spending any money in advertising or promoting a trademark or service mark, determine that no other entity has already secured the registered rights of that particular trademark or service mark. This determination can be done for less than $400 by contacting one of many existing trademark search firms. Be aware that some search firms will only provide their services to attorneys. Since your application for federal trademark or service mark registration will be reviewed and determined by a government attorney, you should retain a trademark attorney.

If you do not wish to utilize such a search, you can file an application to the U.S. Patent and Trademark Office for a trademark. Examiners will review your application and advise you as to whether or not there is an existing trademark that might be confused with yours. Thus, your next step after determining that you have a unique product or one that is in demand is to register your service mark or trademark with the U.S. Patent Office. This can be done by trademark attorneys who will normally charge between $750 and $1,000.

The filing fee for such an application is currently $380. For more information on trademark registration, obtain the publication, *General Information*

Concerning Trademarks and Trademark Rules of Practice with Forms and Statutes by writing:

Superintendent of Documents
U.S. Government Printing Office
Washington, DC 20402

If the examiner determines that your particular trademark will not cause confusion with the trademarked goods of others, your application will be published in the *Federal Register*, allowing third parties to object if they disagree with the examiner. If there are no objections, you will receive a certificate of trademark registration approximately three or more months after your application has been published in the *Federal Register*. Your registered trademark will be in effect for ten years before it needs to be renewed.

Once you have received your certificate of trademark registration, you should let the world know you have it. Remember that once you have obtained a certificate of registration, you are eligible to seek enforcement of your trademark or service mark against infringers through litigation in federal district courts. In addition, you may register your trademark with state agencies, although this is not necessary if you have a federal registration. Registration laws vary from state to state, but in most states, a nominal fee (less than $20) can secure registration of your trademark for a period of years, in many cases, for up to ten years.

The Final Decision to Franchise

Before you make your final decision to franchise, you need to know:

- You have what it takes to be a franchisor.
- Your product is unique and in demand, and your business is profitable and promising to a prospective franchisee.
- You have a market for your product or service.
- Your service or product is associated with a registerable trademark.

In addition, you have probably already decided you do not wish to share your control with any investors in the form of partners or shareholders, and you have investigated other business expansion alternatives. (See Chapter 6.) You should also have a strong idea of what to look for in your future franchisees. (See Chapter 7.)

Before you launch your plan to expand by franchising, prepare a thorough business plan so you can realistically look at what financial outlay each new outlet will require to get up and running, then compare that to what you can expect to receive in fees, royalties, and sales of ingredients and services.

Some of the items specific to franchising that you will want to build into your business plan are overhead costs of your franchise operation, such as salaries and benefits for you and employees in your head office, plus trainers and sales staff, as well as normal office expenses like rent, office equipment, car allowances, and travel. Plan in the cost of finding franchisees. This could include buying ads, traveling to franchise shows, preparing brochures and videos, and entertaining. In addition, add a healthy allowance for start-up and ongoing legal, accounting, and advertising fees.

Be overly conservative as you project the timing and amount of income you expect to receive back from your franchise outlets. You will have determined the mixture of franchise fees, royalties, and product sales that will bring you income from your franchisees. Pad your expectations of how soon these revenues will flow back to you instead of basing your predictions solely on how your business worked in the past.

Another important factor you should have investigated before making your franchise decision is the advantages and disadvantages of each legal form of business organization — the sole proprietorship, the partnership, or the corporation. By forming either a sole proprietorship or a partnership, your operation will be subject to unlimited liability — that is, if the sole proprietorship or partnership fails and its debts exceed its assets, the sole proprietor or the partners can be held individually liable for unpaid debts. Because of this aspect, most franchisors choose a corporate entity in order to limit their liabilities to the assets of the corporation. To find out more on legal forms of business organization, especially incorporating, consult an attorney and certified public accountant.

Conclusion

Franchising has grown in leaps and bounds in recent years, and so have the related state and federal regulations. Before making the final decision to franchise in your state, check what state and local regulations you will have to comply with. Refer to Chapter 8 and Appendix E for more on state and federal franchise laws.

Notes

Chapter 6

Franchising and Other Alternative Methods of Expansion

Introduction

During the last ten years in the United States, well-organized company programs, who are short of adequate expansion capital, have turned into efficient, highly profitable networks of franchised outlets. The desired end result of this popular marketing system called franchising is a highly motivated, cost-cutting, quality-conscious retailer who provides a product or service to the customer in a manner far more efficient and profitable than the often poorly managed, high-cost, poor-service marketing system known as the "company store."

Franchising, simply put, is a means of expanding a business operation by licensing a third party to engage in a franchise system under a required marketing plan or system using a common trademark, service mark, or trade name, for a fee. Franchising is available to businesses distributing both products and services and to those distributing services only. Today, the latter is by far the most popular category.

This chapter is written for the potential franchisor who has built a profitable business that craves expansion before it becomes stagnant or dies when an aggressive competitor captures the available expansion markets by franchising first. It is also aimed at the potential franchisor who wishes to set up the best operating franchise system at the lowest possible cost. This chapter is set up to help you explore your best expansion options, be it franchising or its alternatives, including the "as is" alternative, the company-owned outlet alternative, and the agreements of association alternative. As mentioned in the previous chapter, exploring all your expansion options before making your final franchise decision is a valuable activity. Take the time to review these alternatives and see if any seem applicable to you.

The "As Is" Alternative

The primary alternative to franchising is to let your business continue "as is," without franchising or expanding. This option, however, raises the possibility of your business being eliminated by the competition and you never reaching your full potential. Profits are limited to the amount of gross revenues that can be generated from one location. In many cases, unless a business expands, it dies. In addition, by choosing to stay "as is," your company's advertising budget remains minimal compared to that of a franchisor, whose local, regional, or national advertising fund is fed by a multiple number of franchise entities.

Above all, you must remain on the firing line. In other words, you are still the day-to-day manager and your life is spent hiring, firing, purchasing, and selling on the lower level. As a franchisor, you would direct a sizable operation with franchisees performing these duties. Franchising can give a business owner the opportunity to realize his or her full executive ability.

The sale of products or services through the Internet is an alternative to many businesses particularly those selling products in place of expanding by franchising. Of course the owner bears all the expenses involved in selling direct and receives no franchise fees or royalties but does not have possible difficult relationships with franchisees.

The Company-Owned Outlet Alternative

The second alternative — formerly considered the only method of expanding one's marketing system before the advent of franchising — is opening company-owned outlets. This normally requires a considerable capital investment and handling the difficult problem of securing capable, willing, and hard-working management personnel.

In addition to the amount of capital necessary to expand your own business through company-owned offices, the amount of time spent in such company expansion is likewise very demanding. Site location, general administration, lease negotiation, and interviewing and hiring managers and employees all require considerable time and money that are not anywhere near the amount required for franchise expansion.

When opening your own company-held retail distribution outlet, you spend money for a considerable time period while receiving little, if any, profit in return. In franchising, by comparison, you immediately realize a franchise fee at the outset, and possible royalties if the franchise can generate any type of sales during the first six months to a year. It is true you must train the franchisees conducting any franchise business but, by the same token, you would also have to train managers and employees of company-owned outlets; so franchising appears to have an advantage since as the franchisor, you do not have to pay the franchisees or their employees any type of wages or salary while they are being trained.

The Agreements of Association Alternative

A third and perhaps less followed alternative to franchising is association through dealerships, licenses, incentive programs, partnerships, and joint ventures. Most dealerships, partnerships, joint ventures, and licenses come about from negotiations between two parties having some adverse interest, resulting in a compromise-type of agreement. In most such cases, to satisfy the whims of both parties, control will be split, even though it should be centered in the hands of one. Often, when one party is supplying only the money, that party will insist upon some control over major decisions, even though he or she may be totally unqualified in management abilities. In many cases, the exercise of that control by the money provider will result in a decision based on money rather than on what is the most beneficial to the particular enterprise in the long run. This type of agreement is in contrast to the development of a franchising agreement, during which the franchisor unilaterally prepares his or her contractual arrangements from an objective standpoint without being pressed into compromises.

Associating with others is even more difficult since, in essence, only very loose agreements, exerting practically no marketing control, can be worked out without violating franchise laws. In most such relationships, the entities in a joint venture or partnership have equal control which, in many cases, may cause either a stalemate or compromised business decisions. A good business decision is never one that is the result of a compromise between two or more people. With a compromise, the best you will have is a partially correct arrangement that could easily result in the loss of quite a bit of money and loss of market share.

If an expanding entrepreneur in any joint venture or association intends to exert any type of control or even suggests certain marketing methods while receiving compensation for the right of the venture to use his or her particular trademark or service mark, he or she could easily put him or herself in danger of violating civil and criminal penalties of various state and federal franchise laws. These laws generally set forth the elements of a franchise as the existence of an agreement wherein one party licenses the other to use a trademark or service mark, exerts some type of control over the person using the trademark or service mark (usually in a form of suggested or required marketing methods), and then receives compensation for such rights.

In essence, many state regulators hold that if it looks like a franchise, it is a franchise. Thus, if you license another to use your trademark or service mark and set him or her up in a business which operates like your other licensees, you are most likely franchising your business. This is especially true if you receive any form of consideration for these rights or require compliance with your marketing plan. In some states, just the suggestion of such marketing procedures is sufficient for applicable government agencies to find a franchise law violation.

A partnership is a limited alternative to franchising, at best. If one partnership composed of one set of partners is the owner of all the retail stores, restaurants, or outlets operating under the partnership trademarks, the state registration authorities and FTC probably will not consider it a franchise. However, when a business entrepreneur enters into general partnership agreements with different partners for each additional outlet utilizing the entrepreneur's trademark at each outlet, the arrangement between the entrepreneurial partner and the different operating partners is, in essence, a franchise.

If you think about this, you will find that the new and different partner for each store generally will put some money into the partnership, pay the original entrepreneurial partner an initial and ongoing fee, salary, or draw for his or her expertise or supervision, or both, and the outlet will be operated under the trademark of the originating entrepreneur.

The same danger of violating franchise laws exists if the would-be franchisor decides to set up different corporate entities with the potential franchisor holding shareholder control of the separate corporations, each operating different outlets with different minority shareholders but with the same trademark. The key to a potential violation of the franchise laws is the trademark license agreement that must exist between the corporation holding the trademark registration and the sister corporations. These license agreements might constitute a franchise in the eyes of some state franchise legislation agencies. Such an arrangement should have prior clearances from the applicable state and federal franchise authorities.

Before any type of general partnership or majority-controlled, affiliated corporation or sister corporation is utilized, consult a competent franchise attorney.

Thus, anyone wishing to expand through company-owned offices, an association, or franchising must look first to available capital and then prepare a business plan that delineates the amount of capital needed to attain the desired level of expansion and the availability of efficient and loyal management personnel.

The expanding entrepreneur also must evaluate the efficiency of his or her own personnel since, in all probability, this personnel will be utilized by the entrepreneur through transfer to the expanded location. If available capital is limited and/or management personnel for company-owned offices or an association with third parties is insufficient, the expanding entrepreneur should then consider the advantages and disadvantages of franchising as compared to the alternatives just discussed.

Conclusion

Hopefully, these alternatives, as compared to franchising, have helped you get a better idea of how you will want to expand your business. Once you have made your final franchise decision, it will be time to begin searching for well-qualified franchisees.

Chapter 7 discusses some of the issues you will need to explore when recruiting prospective franchisees.

Chapter 7

Building a Strong Franchising Foundation

Introduction

As a would-be franchisor, you must realize that your existing management and present operating and marketing techniques probably are lacking in many ways from those required for a successful franchise operation. For instance, a good computer sales employee is not necessarily a good computer franchise salesperson. A good field manager is not necessarily a good franchise manager, particularly when it comes to the supervision of multiple independently operating franchisees. Company managers who have trained company employees on an informal, one-on-one basis might not be qualified to adequately train a group of potential franchisees who have a significant amount of their savings at stake.

In addition, present advertising media suitable for selling a product or service at the retail level is not necessarily suitable for attracting qualified people with adequate capital interested in purchasing franchises. In short, your previous experience and knowledge of your own business may not necessarily be the same experience and knowledge required to successfully operate a franchise business.

To be successful, a potential franchisor, no matter what size, must have built his or her own business on a sound foundation of well-trained personnel, good marketing techniques, and an adequate working capital structure. These foundation blocks are the same for a successful franchise operation as well, but as a franchisor, you will need to view them from a different perspective and utilize different skills.

Well-Trained Personnel

Your real success lies in your ability to recognize the required business insight necessary to operate a smooth-running, successful franchise. To help you do this, carefully review your existing management, marketing, training, advertising, and sales personnel to determine whether or not franchise-management training, specialized consultation for present personnel, or retention of new personnel is required. The capabilities of existing personnel — such as in the case of the very small entity, consisting of the founder and the founder's spouse — should be carefully reviewed and, where found lacking in franchise experience, such persons should be properly trained in franchise operating and marketing techniques.

Staffing a well-run franchise operation with knowledgeable, competent personnel can be achieved at a reasonable expense in one of four ways.

- Educating existing personnel;
- Hiring experienced franchise personnel;
- Subcontracting for franchise functions; and
- Retaining an all-purpose franchise consultant.

Educating Existing Personnel

First, if existing personnel are not only capable of performing franchising duties, but are also available for such duties without overextending themselves, franchise-oriented business seminars and literature should be sought out as educational tools. Many such courses are one or two days in duration and are offered by specific professional business symposiums or community colleges.

The courses and seminars are usually individual efforts presented by individual specialists with hands-on experience in their particular franchise fields and should not be confused with the all purpose franchise consultants discussed later in this section. Check the business opportunities section of your local Sunday newspaper regularly for listings of upcoming business events and seminars. These listings often contain goldmines of information for new franchisors and their inexperienced staff. The International Franchise Association (IFA) in Washington, D.C. can also provide you with a wealth of information regarding franchising.

International Franchise Association

(202) 628-8000

Hiring Experienced Franchise Personnel

The second method of ensuring adequate personnel familiar with current franchising methods is to hire experienced personnel who have worked for other franchisors. In addition to the applicant's franchise expertise, his or her character and knowledge of strict franchising laws should also be reviewed thoroughly. Pay particular attention to any substantial experience gained by an applicant before 1971. This is when the first franchise act was passed in California. This might indicate that the applicant's basic knowledge of franchising was formulated on methods now prohibited by franchise laws — methods such as providing actual or projected revenue and sales figures to potential franchisees and/or negotiating material terms of a franchise agreement without applicable government approval. Thus, ensure that employee applicants are familiar with current franchise marketing techniques, particularly the numerous legal restrictions franchises face.

Hiring additional experienced franchise personnel is costly and may be affordable, or even necessary, only for the larger franchisor. In many cases, the smaller franchisor will handle all the administrative, management, and marketing functions of his or her new franchise operation, at least initially. Therefore, if you will be a small or medium-sized franchisor, you may prefer educating existing personnel about franchising rather than hiring a high-priced new employee with previous franchise experience.

Subcontracting for Franchise Functions

The third and highly recommended way of educating yourself and your staff on the business aspects of franchising is to subcontract the job to individual franchise specialists in the fields of law, training, advertising, public relations, and marketing. These consultants will evaluate your needs and, instead of providing a complete package, will only give you what you actually need.

The one, outside professional always required is an experienced franchise attorney with vast experience not only in franchise law but in the everyday business aspects of franchising. Talk to the attorney's past franchise clients about the attorney's legal expertise and hands-on knowledge of franchising. Refer to Chapter 9 for tips on how to choose a franchise attorney.

When an advertising agency is selected, make sure it is one that specializes in franchising as well as general business. The same holds true with financing and marketing specialists. Carefully check each specialist's references.

Retaining an All-Purpose Franchise Consultant

The fourth method of obtaining franchise business guidance is to retain an "all-purpose" franchise-consultant entity — that is, an entity claiming to provide the franchisor with the entire "franchise package," from legal work to marketing and advertising, all under one roof.

Most such "package" and multi-purpose consultants do not do the actual selling of franchises but offer to train the franchisor's sales force. A multi-purpose consultant is one who offers so-called "complete services" to would-be franchisors, including preparation of the franchise circulars and other legal documents at costs ranging from $37,500 up to $150,000 or more for the complete package in phases. Such consultants require their clients to retain their own counsel to review the legal documents, and secure any required state registration thereof, at additional cost to the clients since a corporation or nonlawyer consultant, if he or she were to do so, would be illegally practicing law.

In addition, the all-purpose consultant provides operations manuals, video training films, and feasibility market and business plan studies that normally can be provided by individual local specialists in each field at much lower costs, often with a better final product. Never retain any consultant without thoroughly investigating his or her background and contacting his or her references and clients.

Individual franchise consultants who provide various individual functions, such as training, marketing, advertising, sales, business planning, or financing are generally far more likely not only to be better organized and informed, but less costly and much faster than an all-purpose, high-priced consultant. If you go the way of a consulting firm, compare the costs of all-purpose consultants with those of individual specialists in the legal and marketing franchise field. By farming out jobs to specialists, such as Kushell, who concentrate in individual areas, you might discover you can receive faster and better franchise work at a much lower price. Again, the best way to evaluate a consultant or marketing specialist is to thoroughly investigate the consultant's references, particularly business executives who have hired the consultant for assistance in franchising a similar business. Results, as explained by clients, and the price paid for such results weighed against the worth of such results, are vital.

Never retain a consultant just because the consultant was once a franchise executive. First, find out if he or she was a good executive, why he or she left his or her employment, and whether or not he or she is a good consultant. There are many former franchise executives who are out of work because of their lack of expertise. Evaluate the executive's versatility.

In a new and diversified industry, such as computer software and hardware franchising, the experience required might not be compatible with the background of a consultant who had a lifelong career in the restaurant business. A pennywise, but profit-motivated franchisor can retain various specialists as needed for specific functions and end up with less expensive, more suitable, and more extensive franchising services. An experienced, franchise-oriented consultant specializing in advertising will work perfectly with any experienced, franchise-oriented business planning or training consultant or employee. Both should be able to work effectively with an experienced, marketing-oriented attorney since they will all be somewhat of like minds.

Marketing Techniques

Once you have been licensed to sell franchises as required by registration states, or have obtained a suitable offering circular and disclosure for nonregistration states from your attorney, you must initiate advertising, sales, marketing, and public relations programs geared for the launching of your franchise operations. The sale of your product or service to the final user or consumer of that product or service is drastically different from selling a person on becoming a franchisee.

A small mom-and-pop franchise could easily be sold by a one-man franchisor operation where the franchisor has a built-in supply of good, qualified potential franchisees. An example of this would be the franchising of skilled trade services, via the franchising of skilled tradespeople, under a common trademark. The market consists of independent operators or skilled tradespeople working for a company engaged in that trade or business. Marketing, advertising, and public relations can consist of the franchisor contacting such individuals through trade papers or trade association meetings.

Even existing employees of the franchisor can be a good source of franchisees in a certain situation, depending on the financial status of the employees and cost of the franchise. A small franchisor capable of utilizing existing efficient staff could commence franchising at an initial outlay of amounts as low as $20,000. This amount encompasses:

- The costs of suitable brochures;
- An experienced, business-minded franchise attorney; and
- The use of the franchisor's existing facilities.

The cost of the existing facilities would be incurred as part of the franchisor's prevailing or existing business being franchised, making the original business a "pilot plant" and training facility. However, don't ever capitalize at this low amount unless you have carefully worked out a realistic estimation of your projected income and costs during the initial years of your franchise company.

The Ideal Franchisee

It is a growing trend among some franchisors not to sell a franchise to anyone who has not worked for the franchisor for at least one year. This is a company rule of one of today's leading franchisors, Domino's Pizza. However, if you are not in a position to offer franchises only to persons who have worked for you for at least one year, you must incur the cost of identifying the "potentially good franchisees" and establishing communications with them. In other words, you will need to formulate a profile of the type of franchisee who would have the best chance of succeeding in selling your product or service. The best franchisee is one who:

- Is a hard worker;
- Follows instruction;
- Will enjoy working in a particular type of business;
- Has a background suitable to it;
- Has adequate financial resources;
- Has a family that supports the new venture; and
- Is able to follow orders.

Generally, franchisees who continually wish to change systems or have suggestions for change based purely on theory do not make the best franchisees. The ideal franchisee should have advisory input abilities but not the stubbornness to insist upon changing the franchise system, at least until you have an opportunity to test market the franchisee's theories or can show, based on your experience, that such theories do not work.

Look for the same qualities that made you successful when you were operating your retail business in any would-be franchisee. There are business consultants who research and identify the profile of ideal franchisees for various industries and companies. If their clients have provided them with good references, it might be a good idea to retain such a consultant. In many ways, good common sense and an objective view of what is necessary, as determined by your past experience or your operational personnel, might be the ticket to determining the best profile for the ideal franchisee.

Selecting an Advertising Agency

In situations where the attraction of franchisees is not a simple matter and knowledge of the market for such franchisees is limited, an experienced, franchise-oriented advertising agency should be retained and a market survey initiated. The more difficult it is to attract the first franchisee, the more expensive the advertising will be. The more extensive the franchising program is in both number of franchisees sought and swiftness of the timetable of expansion, the greater the necessity for a good, experienced, franchise-oriented advertising agency.

The cost of such an agency's services normally runs on a monthly-payment basis constituting fees of $3,000 to $5,000 or more a month, according to the number of hours of work. Each franchisor is judged on an individual basis according to marketing needs, and the fee is set accordingly.

Remember to select an agency or hire an employee who has franchise business experience. Marketing products and services to the retail consumer is not the same as marketing a business to potential franchisees.

Most smaller franchisors initially will market their own franchises. This usually is done by advertising in the Thursday issue of the classified section of *The Wall Street Journal* or the Sunday edition of local metropolitan newspapers. Franchise trade shows, particularly those sponsored by the International Franchise Association are another good source for recruiting franchisees.

Working Capital Considerations

The costs involved in franchising will vary according to geographic areas, expansion time, and availability of potential franchisees, as well as the complexity of the product or service being sold.

A small one-man operation that has a profitable product or service with controlled lower costs and an ever-increasing market can franchise just as well as a larger competitor, provided the small business offers consistent services or products, or both, to its franchisee in a manner that will motivate the franchisee to remain in the franchise family. This usually constitutes either the franchisor's performing a service or selling a product to the franchisee that the franchisee cannot obtain elsewhere — or the franchisor's offering the product or service to the franchisee at a price lower than any price the franchisee could secure elsewhere, or at a quality unattainable anywhere else.

This is necessary at least until the franchisor's trademark attains the recognizability that will automatically result in continuing business for the franchisee based on the trademark's attraction alone, or until the common franchisee advertising fund grows big enough to enhance the franchisee's business through customer recognition.

As a would-be franchisor, you must have a "glue" or "hold" on the franchisee that will be strong enough to sustain the franchisee's interest in remaining a licensed franchisee. In addition to providing the lower selling prices and best available quality to the franchisee as described above, such additional holds include your ongoing support to the franchisee's success. To demonstrate such ongoing support, you can provide continued training sessions, co-op advertising, billing and accounting services, discounted inventory prices from third-party suppliers, and exclusive product distribution.

The amount of working capital you need to start a franchise operation will vary depending on your size, rate of expansion, complexity of training, necessity of site selection and architectural planning, extent of marketing, attractiveness of franchise, and required capital investment from franchisees, among other factors.

Carefully planned, slow expansion by a franchisor with a small, but efficient franchise-oriented staff or consultants, and a product or service attractive to potential franchisees, can be capitalized for as low as $20,000 to $50,000 by utilizing the existing franchise-trained staff.

Do not franchise your business without first developing a well-thought-out business plan. Realistic marketing goals should be set forth in this plan, along with expansion plans, advertising programs, capital outlay, and projected costs for a five-year period. Don't rely on initial franchise fees and royalties to support you in the first few years of your business.

Realistic financial forecasts and iron-clad budgets, including necessary ongoing support systems for the franchisees, should be the keys to any franchise endeavor.

Conclusion

To build a strong foundation for your franchise operation, ensure that you:

- Obtain well-qualified and well-trained personnel to run and operate the business efficiently as needed;
- Recognize the strategies for marketing your franchise opportunity to potential franchisees; and
- Determine the income and cash outlays of your first initial years as a franchisor so you understand the numbers behind the venture.

If you gather these resources and information in your franchising investigations, your franchise opportunity will have a much better chance for success.

Notes

Chapter 8

Franchise Laws – A Trap for the New Franchisor

Introduction

As discussed earlier in Chapter 6, many successful business owners decide to expand their businesses through distributorships, licensees, or joint venture/partnership arrangements to distribute and sell their products or services, and as a result, save themselves a considerable amount of capital investment in building or leasing company-owned and -backed outlets. The third parties, whether they are called distributors, licensees, partners, or joint venturers, all have one thing in common: They may constitute arrangements that are in violation of federal and state franchise laws.

These industrious and sincere business owners may, in their desire to adopt a successful marketing system and expand their businesses may very well be entering into a nightmare of litigation and government agency investigations resulting in considerable civil damages, as well as government penalties. In most cases, the business owner is unaware of the impending danger and perhaps has even consulted an attorney not experienced in or aware of the ramifications of federal and state franchise and business opportunity laws.

It is entirely possible that an entrepreneur may purchase — or an uninformed business owner may market — a company that is actually engaged in franchising without having registered it under applicable state law or without having followed the appropriate directives set forth in federal law.

A typical example of this is the business owner who has developed a new or improved product or service and has experienced a certain degree of success in marketing it. He or she must now decide whether or not to raise and risk additional capital to provide more marketing outlets for the expanding line of products or services, which would include hiring the necessary employment force to carry out his or her business in these new locations. All of this takes a considerable amount of time as well as money. In most cases, the money is either unavailable or interest rates are prohibitive, and finding additional competent employees who will properly market the product or service is almost impossible since the motivation of employees to succeed is not there. The business owner then decides that he or she will teach others to market the product or service and charge them for his or her expertise. The recipient of this training will, of course, want to have the right to use the name of the business owner which, in almost all instances, is an integral part of the sales success of the product or service. The business owner, by the same token, will want to exert some type of control or limitations on the third party's use of his or her name so that it can be used only under certain controlled circumstances, avoiding any chance of bringing the name into disrepute.

If any of these restrictions are violated, the business owner will want to call off the deal and revoke the right to use the trademark. In addition, in order for the fledgling business to become a success financially, it will be necessary for the business owner to teach the third-party licensee, distributor, or joint venturer methods of marketing the product or service that will bring a degree of success to the third party's operation. This marketing plan or scheme will be such as to correspond to the methods used by the business owner in gaining his or her initial success.

The end result desired by both the third party and the business owner is to maintain an operation engaged in marketing a common product or service that will look to the public as if it is one great big organization with a single identity and universal continuity of service. The business owner, of course, is going to want some type of remuneration for training the third party and allowing him or her to become part of what looks like a "big happy family." The consideration is usually in the form of an initial fee to cover the training and, in many cases, a percentage of future gross profits. In some cases it may be the outright sale of a facility, plus the right to use the name for a one-lump-sum payment. Such an arrangement is clearly a franchise under federal and state franchise law.

The realization of this franchise aspect is even less apparent to the business owner who is selling a product rather than a service to a third party, such as an image-engraving system or coin-stamping equipment.

Federal Law

The federal government entered into the regulation of franchises on October 21, 1979, when the Federal Trade Commission (FTC) published its *Interpretative Guides to the Agencies Trade Regulation Rules Regarding Disclosure of Requirements and Prohibitions Concerning Franchising and Business Opportunity Ventures*. In essence, the rules are an attempt to remedy the problems of nondisclosure and misrepresentation which arise when prospective franchisees purchase franchises without first obtaining reliable information about them. The rules thus require franchisors and franchise brokers to furnish prospective franchisees with information about the franchisor, the franchisor's business, and the terms of the franchise agreement in one single document — the basic disclosure document or offering circular.

Additional information must be furnished if any claims are made about actual or potential earnings. This is referred to as the earnings claim document. A copy of the proposed franchise agreement also must be furnished by the franchisor to the franchisee. The disclosures must include important facts in terms of the franchisor-franchisee relationship.

The FTC does not require registration but does require that you provide the potential franchisee with certain written disclosures which are given at the first face-to-face meeting of the two parties, at least ten days before taking any consideration for the franchise, and five days before the execution of any franchise agreement.

The FTC rule requires that your disclosure documents be updated at least quarterly when there is a material change in the franchisor's or subfranchisor's business during the quarter. Additionally, the FTC rule requires that disclosure documents be completely rewritten and updated once a year within 90 days of the fiscal year-end for distribution to prospective franchisees.

Due to the multi-faceted complexity of creating a disclosure document that meets all levels of legal requirements, it is not safe to attempt to complete this yourself. By following the sample franchise documents in the appendices, you can start to build the framework for your franchise documents that can be reviewed and completed by professionals. By doing this preliminary work, you most likely will reduce your attorney fees.

Prior to January 1, 1995, federal law preempted certain state laws where both had overlapping provisions. To prevent the duplication of disclosure requirements with state statutes, the FTC rules permitted use of a disclosure format known as the Uniform Franchise Offering Circular (UFOC) to comply with state registration laws on disclosure requirements. Under the new law, effective January 1, 1995, the same UFOC format is required by the FTC and state authorities. The revised and updated UFOC guidelines are reproduced in Appendix F of this book.

On October 22, 1999 the FTC formally requested public comment on proposed revisions to the existing franchise disclosure rule. It is doubtful that these proposed changes involving exclusion of applicability of the FTC Rules to Business Opportunities, time changes for making disclosures, clarification of application to foreign sales, certain additional changes regarding franchisor initiated lawsuits etc., electronic media disclosures, and expanding the rule's exemptions of sophisticated investors will become official for several years. (64 *Federal Register* 57293-57350). Your franchise attorney should keep you abreast of any formal changes.

A violation of the rules set forth by the FTC for failure to provide the required circular, or a misrepresentation, will constitute an unfair or deceptive act or practice within the meaning of Section 5 of the Federal

Trade Commission Act, and subjects the violator to civil penalty actions brought by the commission of up to $10,000 in fines per violation per day. The courts have held that the FTC rule does not create a private right of action in wronged franchisees. However, franchisees have successfully sought enforcement through "Little FTC Acts," which are state unfair practice acts.

Under federal law, as the franchisor, you must provide prospective franchisees with a circular that conforms to the law, but you do not have to send a copy to the FTC or register the same with the FTC. In states requiring registration, such as California, you must complete an application for registration that contains, among other things, information regarding the background of the salespersons authorized to sell the franchise. State registration fees vary from $50 to $750. See Appendix E for more specifics on filing fees of franchise registration states.

State Law

Fourteen states have also passed franchise registration or notice of filing acts. As a prospective franchisor, these acts require the filing and approval of an application that contains information about who you are, a copy of your proposed contract, and the preparation of a proposed circular that is to be given to the franchisee at least ten days before he or she purchases the franchise and pays any money for it.

As mentioned above, the offering circular required by the applicable state governments is referred to as a uniform offering circular and requires you to state:

- Background information regarding yourself, your predecessors, and affiliates;
- The identity and business experience of your key personnel;
- Pending franchisor litigation;
- Prior franchisor bankruptcies;
- Details of franchise fees and other fees;
- An outline of the franchisee's initial investment;
- Restrictions on sources of products and services;
- Territory;
- Trademarks;
- Patents, copyrights, and proprietary information;
- Obligations of the franchisee to participate in the actual operation of the franchised business;
- Restrictions on what the franchisee may sell;
- Renewal, termination, transfer, and dispute resolutions;
- Arrangements with public figures;
- Earnings claims;
- Identification of franchisees of the franchisor; and
- Financial statements of the franchisor.

In addition, a copy of the franchise agreement and an explanation of its more pertinent provisions are also required. Many of these topics are discussed in greater detail in Chapter 2.

You can also refer to Appendix B, which is a sample franchise agreement that is part of a circular that corresponds to the UFOC following the California Franchise Investment Act rules under certain restrictions.

In most cases, if you are in a registration state, you will submit your application with the franchise agreement and circular to a state official who will then determine whether or not it has any filing deficiencies from a state standpoint and will advise you accordingly.

In essence, these state statutes, like the federal statutes, require a complete disclosure of certain enumerated items. The states themselves do not determine whether or not the statements in the offering circular are true or false, but in the event that a stated item is not true, the state gives the franchisee an additional legal right for damages.

In some cases, a violation may result in administrative or criminal sanctions, or both, in addition to the civil remedies afforded to the franchisee. States having franchise investment laws have statutes that can be used in seeking damages through the courts or arbitration both for loss of profit and return of monies spent in the event these laws are violated. This is in addition to remedies for fraud that are available to any victimized business owner.

In addition, the states with franchise registration laws, and the FTC under its rule applying to franchising, have given government authorities certain powers to seek criminal remedies against franchisors violating the franchise acts and, in some instances, the power to order the franchisor to pay back franchise fees received in violation of the acts.

If you insist upon doing your own disclosure documents — which is not recommended by franchise experts — you should familiarize yourself with the laws of the state in which you intend to franchise. Or at the very least, contact the various state agencies to see whether or not you are required to comply by their laws if you are selling to a franchisee residing in that state or if you want to operate franchises in that state.

In all states with franchise registration laws, if the prospective franchisee is a resident of the state and the franchise is to be operated in that state, the franchise laws of that state will apply. Also remember that you can make no claims regarding existing franchisees' earnings or potential earnings unless you provide an earnings claim document. Those states with franchise registration laws also require an approved earnings claim document of a similar sort.

Conclusion

Before selling your business in any way that will involve third parties — such as distributors, licensees, or partners — be sure to review federal and state franchise laws so you are informed on their requirements. In particular, you are going to want to make sure your legal counsel is aware of these franchise requirements. It is amazing how many business attorneys are unaware of such requirements and legislation.

Ask your attorney if he or she is experienced with FTC Rule 436, as well as the franchise investment, business opportunities, and seller-assisted marketing plan acts in your state. These last two acts cover business ventures that are short of being franchises but are close enough to require a specific type of disclosure form. If your counsel is unfamiliar with these rules and regulations, seek counsel specializing in this area. Even if counsel is familiar with these laws, request the names of previous clients that he or she has helped franchise and call them for their opinion of his or her knowledge and ability.

For further information on state franchise laws and resources, refer to Appendix E, State Franchise Information Guidelines.

Chapter 9

Choosing a Franchise Attorney

Introduction

Throughout this book, you are advised to consult a competent attorney, who preferably specializes in franchise law, to assist you in the franchising arena — be it as a potential franchisor or prospective franchisee. Their assistance can range from putting together the required offering circular to researching federal and state franchise laws.

Because franchise attorneys have gone through the franchise process before, they can be of particular help to new franchisors who are not familiar with the training, marketing, administrative, and sales functions that are unique to a franchising operation.

Another important area where franchise attorneys can be of assistance is in the marketing of your potential franchise. For many potential franchisees, the offering circular is the first point-of-sale piece they see. Your offering circular introduces you, presents your background and those of your predecessors, and it relays to the potential franchisee all the services, products, and obligations you will provide to him or her. Having an experienced, business-oriented attorney help you in preparing your circular effectively and accurately could prove very valuable in terms of marketing and in terms of complying with federal and state franchise laws.

Select an Experienced, Business-Oriented Attorney

An offering circular must have provisions that are practical, time proven, business-oriented, workable and, above all, fair. Because most executives of a prospective franchisor entity, whether large or small, have no prior experience in operating a franchised business, nor much, if any, know-how in selling franchises, training franchisees, opening and servicing franchises, they are of little help to the franchise attorney from a business standpoint. Therefore, the situation arises in which the chosen attorney is required to know much more about franchising than his or her client does. This is in addition to knowing the legal requirements. Therefore, find out whether your franchise attorney is more than a legal technician whose only function is to file a legally acceptable document suitable only to get you a permit to sell franchises from the state authority.

When you and your experienced, market-oriented attorney begin work on the offering circular and franchise agreement, other business issues will have been decided, including among others, the franchise fee to be charged, the type of training to be given the franchisees, the continuing royalty and service fees to be charged, and the duties and obligations of both the franchisor and franchisee. All such business policies must be established on time-proven, practical terms that will work.

Failure on your part to properly prepare yourself for operating a franchise system, including the selection of either a business-minded, franchise-oriented attorney or an experienced, business-oriented franchise consultant, means that you may be launching your new franchise the same way you first started the business you intend to franchise, with absolutely no practical knowledge of how to operate it.

Chances are the attorney you have used in the past will be in the same boat when it comes to franchising the business. You both may have started out as novices in the business start-up world, but through trial and error, and working together, you have gained business know-how and developed proven procedures for business success. Now that you have reached the point of expanding your business through franchising, your past attorney may not be the one you want to rely on for determining such franchise factors as suitable franchise fees and royalties, how to actually set up and operate a franchise, and the franchise agreement. Trial-and-error methods of operating a franchise company do not succeed because such companies are operating with other people's money and lives, and on a limited time basis.

If you have knowledge of and experience in opening a franchise, or have guidance from a consultant or new employee who has actual experience in running a successful franchise company, you or your employee/consultant can tell the attorney what procedural rules are necessary for a workable franchise agreement.

Legal Fees — What to Expect

Attorney fees vary according to each attorney's overhead expenses and desire for profit. An experienced attorney who runs a cost-efficient operation can easily make a fair return on a $15,000 to $20,000 legal fee (depending on the business and knowledge of the franchisor) for the preparation and filing of a marketable, workable, and well-coordinated offering circular registration in the initial state of registration.

Attorneys should be able to complete their work within 30 to 40 days barring any unforeseen circumstances. Legal fees for each additional state (since the circular will have to be amended in certain states) will vary anywhere from $250 to $2,500, depending on the state. Filing fees range from $50 to $750. A complete fee quotation regarding the initial state, as well as additional states, should be obtained from the attorney, along with his or her scheduled date of completion. Completion of the franchisor-background questionnaires in Appendix C and Appendix D can help you save legal fees and expedite the timetable for completing the offering circular and franchise agreement. Refer to Chapter 11 for other tips on how to save on attorney fees.

Aside from legal costs, remember the cost of a certified audit, which is an initial necessity in certain states and an ultimate necessity in others. Generally, a good franchise attorney will have a client start a new corporation for the purpose of franchising and, therefore, the audited financials of the new corporation will be nominal — from $400 to $1,000, depending again upon the accountant and his or her cost-effectiveness.

Conclusion

As with any professional consultant, you cannot necessarily judge a good franchise attorney by his or her legal fees, but you can, however, judge franchise attorneys by what their franchise clients say about them, not only as an attorney complying with certain statutory laws but also as an attorney familiar with the time-proven and correct methods of operating a franchise in a particular industry. Insist upon references from the attorney and call each reference. Ask the client's opinion of the attorney's legal abilities and his ability to draft an offering circular and franchise agreement that are fair, marketable, and marketing-oriented — all of which are necessary elements of a successful franchise operation.

Notes

Chapter 10

Making Your Franchise Operation Work

Introduction

To make your franchise operation work more smoothly and succeed, you will want to ensure you do a couple of important activities. These activities include:

- Helping your franchisees find a suitable location for the franchise so it has a better chance of success;

- Preparing an operations manual to provide the franchisee with guidelines and instructions on how to operate the franchise on a day-to-day basis;

- Selecting a franchise office that is practical and economical; and

- Reviewing franchise agreement clauses regarding transfer, renewal, and terminating the franchise to ensure your franchise's reputation remains positive despite a potential franchisee's dissatisfaction and desire to leave your organization.

All of these activities are discussed in this chapter in hopes you, as the potential franchisor, will have much of this information and knowledge before dealing with potential franchisees, thus creating a better franchisee-franchisor relationship, and most likely, a more successful franchise operation.

Assisting Franchisees in Selecting a Site

If your franchise involves a restaurant or other business in which location is a key factor in franchise sales, you will want to have someone assist your franchisees in selecting sites. Most franchisors require their franchisees to conduct preliminary research regarding site selections. In most cases, real estate brokers or shopping-center managers can provide the demographics and other commercial information pertaining to each potential site.

The primary reason for making your franchisees responsible for site selection is not only to make the franchisee thoroughly familiar with the pros and cons of each potential site location, but also to help alleviate any liability you may face if you are the sole selector of the site and the franchisee subsequently fails. Many franchisees will blame their choice of site location as the primary reason for their franchise failure, even though the failure may be entirely the franchisee's own fault. Therefore, most franchisors require the franchisees to make their own site selection with the franchisor acting as the final approving authority.

To ensure that the franchisee has picked an appropriate site, however, you should have a qualified broker or other expert evaluate the suitability of the chosen site. This person should be qualified in real estate matters and have some experience in franchising and in the particular business being franchised. In some cases, a new franchisor may act as the site selection appraiser assisting the franchisee; however, most franchisors retain real estate consultants rather than hire full-time personnel, at least in the initial stages. These agents normally are compensated by brokers' fees from the landlord. Again, carefully checkout references and accomplishments of the brokers or individuals you hire to assist your prospective franchisee in finding a franchise location. For help in rating potential sites, use the Franchise Site Evaluation Form at the end of Chapter 2.

Site Selection Costs

If you are knowledgeable regarding the elements necessary for a good site for your business and conduct the site selection yourself, costs will be minimal. If contacts are made with local real estate brokers who are familiar with your franchisees' needs and territories, costs will also be minimal. Hiring a professional, full-time site selector could be expensive, depending upon your location. In most cases, an employee hired as a site selector will hold other positions in a franchise company, including marketing or training responsibilities. Again, try to keep your costs at a minimum without sacrificing the effectiveness of your organization.

Preparing the Operations Manual

As part of the operational function in a well-developed franchise system, you should prepare and provide an effective operations manual which, in essence, memorializes the functions of the franchise business on a written, chronological, step-by-step basis so that they can be easily followed by the franchisee after the initial franchise training program is completed.

You can have an all-purpose consultant prepare your operations manual, or if you are an experienced business owner, you can do it yourself by following the Operations Manual Outline on page 99 and merely listing, in chronological order — perhaps by talking into a tape recorder — the steps that complete the operations of your business. This account of basic business practices details the specific elements that made your business unique and successful in the first place. If you feel awkward in doing this, you can have someone else record and subsequently type up what you have said regarding the basic functions of the business. The operations manual is generally the framework that you will use for your training sessions. Thus, the substance of the training sessions will be based on whatever is in the operations manual.

In the event you feel you do not have the necessary dictation and writing skills required to create a training manual, and if you do not have a family member or employee who can do so, hire a qualified person to write one. Even individuals who specialize in writing manuals can be hired for fees ranging anywhere from $2,000 to $4,000. If any confidential information is to be contained in the manual, take steps to get a confidentiality nondisclosure agreement from the person retained to write and/or type the manual, and consider obtaining copyrights for the manual.

Contents of an Operations Manual

Each franchisor's operations manual is unique, because in a given industry, each successful franchisor has a quality that distinguishes his or her business from those of his or her competitors. For example, a Wendy's operation featuring orders made up as they are given to the cashier differs from a McDonald's, where food is prepared in advance. Another illustration of this is Subway's method of making sandwiches at the direction of the customer, who deals with the individual preparer instead of ordering through a cashier.

Some franchisors have two operations manuals. One might deal with site selection, the initial opening of the store, bookkeeping, accounting, advertising, and grand-opening procedures. The second manual may address the duties of individual employees and, in the case of a restaurant, preparation of the food. A second manual could also cover such everyday duties as opening and closing procedures, accepting checks, making daily reports, hiring new employees, preparing time sheets, receiving and transferring goods, preparing supply lists, and maintaining inventory procedures, security measures, and banking procedures.

Selecting Your Office

In many cases, one of the first things new franchisors do is commit themselves and their new franchise to a costly new office showplace. This can be fatal. You must do the same thing for yourself that you do for the franchisee: establish a highly capable, efficient organization at the lowest cost possible. You should have a pilot plant of the operation you are intending to franchise. Often, you can initially work from this location by using a back room and a new telephone number. If this workplace is not feasible because it does not present an attractive appearance, then you can rent, preferably on a month-to-month basis, a location and office furniture in an attractive, but economical building.

In many situations, executive suites that will provide services such as photocopying, faxing, telephone answering, and reception services can be rented on a monthly basis at an economical cost. It is suggested that this avenue be taken, at least initially, until the franchise business has taken hold.

Budget, budget, budget! Your success or failure can be determined in many instances on how well you plan your initial operation. Thus, plan your new business operation in the same careful way you have planned your original business and the future business operations of your franchisees.

Reviewing Transfer, Renewal, and Termination Clauses

You must carefully select each of your franchisees. Never sell a franchise to anyone you do not consider completely qualified for the job. The franchisee is also a manager of your business extension, so you should never choose a franchisee you would not hire as a manager. A good selection of franchisees will diminish the chance of franchise failure, especially early transfers and terminations. Treat the franchisee like a member of your team, and regard the franchising system as an extension of your marketing arm. It is your services or products that are being sold under your service mark or trademark. You would not hesitate to assist one of your company managers when in trouble or even to remove him or her if it were in the best interest of the company-owned office.

If you look upon the franchisee as a replacement for your company-owned office, your attitude will be positive when concentrating on assisting the franchisee. Your franchise agreement should allow for transfers, with your consent, which should not be unreasonably withheld. Examples of transfer and termination provisions are contained in the sample franchise agreement in Appendix B.

If you have a dissatisfied franchisee, the best procedure is to allow the franchisee to transfer, or for you to buy the franchisee out. Lawsuits are costly, time-consuming, and must be reported in the offering circular. Therefore, a lawsuit could be detrimental to the future sale of franchises since potential franchisees will be made aware of the dissatisfied franchisees who are suing or have been terminated, and probably will receive negative information from them about you.

Franchise agreements are generally drafted by an attorney with provisions that are applicable in the state where the franchisor and the attorney are located. In many cases, the termination and transfer provisions may be contrary to the laws of other states where the same franchise agreement is being utilized. The cost of tailoring each clause to abide by changing state laws on an individual-state basis is almost prohibitive. In addition, new state laws become effective from time to time after the initial franchise agreement has been drafted. Therefore, before any transfer is made, your attorney should check over the particular state law pertaining to transfers or terminations. This is true even if there is a clause in your agreement stating that the laws of the state of the franchisor apply.

State Renewal and Termination Laws

Clauses regarding the termination and transfer of franchisees are commonly referred to as "franchise relationship laws." Some of these termination and transfer laws are contained in state franchise investment or disclosure acts. Others are contained in a deceptive franchise act, pyramid scheme act, or retail franchising act, and in Wisconsin, the fair dealership law. For a complete list of such laws see Appendix E, State Franchise Information Guidelines.

Some of the state statutes require good cause for termination. In the absence of a state statute to the contrary, a fixed-term franchise that does not provide for general renewal will expire upon its expiration date. The good cause requirements in some of these franchise laws, however, may mandate renewal of a fixed-term agreement, even one that clearly states that no renewal is allowed, thereby resulting in the perpetual renewal of the agreement unless the franchisor can prove that the franchisee did something that constituted good cause for termination of the agreement. At the time of this writing, Arkansas, Connecticut, Delaware, the District of Columbia, Hawaii, Indiana, Iowa, Nebraska, New Jersey, Virginia, and Wisconsin require good cause for nonrenewal by the franchisor.

California permits nonrenewal upon receipt of 180 days' notice for several specified reasons including failure by the franchisee to agree to the standard terms of the renewal franchise. Some other states that affect the right to renewal are Arkansas, Connecticut, Indiana, Mississippi, Missouri, Nebraska, New Jersey, Minnesota, Illinois, Michigan, Washington, and Wisconsin. Mississippi and Missouri currently have notice requirements regarding nonrenewal of a franchise agreement.

Virginia passed an act which makes it unlawful for a franchisor to cancel a franchise without reasonable cause or to use undue influence to induce a franchisee to surrender any right given to him or her by any provision contained in the franchise agreement.

These laws change from time to time and, therefore, any franchisor who does not intend to renew or has a franchisee who is transferring his or her franchise should consult experienced legal counsel before issuing any communication to the franchisee.

Excessive Transfer Fees

Franchise attorneys have a tendency to draft provisions that require substantial transfer fees for the franchisee. Some of these high-figured transfer fee provisions have been attacked as unconscionable in court lawsuits. In fact, the states of Iowa and Washington prohibit a transfer fee in excess of an amount necessary to compensate the franchisor for expenses incurred as a result of the transfer. Therefore, it is recommended that transfer and renewal fees be geared more to compensate the franchisor for expenses rather than to make a huge profit. After all, a good franchisee who is renewing should bring additional royalties to the franchisor.

Conclusion

If you take the time to research and compile much of the information on or pertaining to this chapter's activities before organizing your franchise operation and recruiting potential franchisees, you will be much better off than many, other prospective franchisors who haven't done their homework.

The more knowledge you have on franchising — such as good site location data and resources for your particular business or writing a thorough manual on how to operate your particular type of franchise operation — the more secure and confident you will appear to potential franchisees. In other words, you will make a better impression on those you talk to when getting your franchise operation going.

In addition to creating a more confident appearance, your research will also make you more aware of the costly mistakes frequently made by new franchisors, such as spending money too extravagantly on new franchise headquarters or making fees too high so they backfire on you. You will be a much wiser franchisor by doing research and investigation on your own and in conjunction with potential franchisees or franchise attorneys.

Operations Manual Outline

I. Introduction

A. Welcoming Letter from Chief Operations Officer

B. Introduction to Manual

C. Biographical Information on Franchisor's Key Personnel

II. Pre-Opening Requirements

A. Preparation of Chronological Chart by Franchisee, with Franchisor's Assistance Setting Dates and Time Periods for:

    1. Selection of the site by franchisee

    2. Approval of site by franchisor

    3. Approval of the lease by franchisor

    4. Execution of a lease

    5. Commencement of construction within required number of days after execution of lease

    6. Finalization of construction

B. Preparation of Pro Forma Financial Statements by Franchisee and his Financial Advisers and Accountants

C. Checklist of All Necessary Permits and Registration Forms

D. Review of Franchisor's Specifications Regarding Construction and Decor

E. List of Equipment, Inventory, and Fixtures

F. Procurement of Necessary Documents, Items, and Services

    1. Suppliers

    2. Telephone systems

    3. Security systems

    4. Cleaning agencies

    5. Trash removal agency

    6. Pest control service

    7. Map services

    8. Fire extinguishers

    9. Background music installation

    10. Bank services

    11. Appropriate licenses

    12. Sales tax permit

    13. Minimum wage and equal opportunity literature

    14. Cleaning supplies

    15. Hand tools

    16. Office forms

Operations Manual Outline (continued)

III. Pre-Opening and Post-Opening Training Procedures

    A. General Daily-Business Operational Policies

    B. Product or Service to Be Sold

        1. Development of menu

        2. Specifications

        3. Purchase lists

    C. Preparation of Personnel to Sell Product or Service

    D. Decor and Dress Code of Restaurant Personnel

    E. Customer Service Procedure Deliveries

    F. Delivery Requirements and Techniques

    G. Preparation of Sales and Financial Reports

        1. Daily business forms

        2. Inventory strategy

        3. Preparation of daily, weekly, and monthly financial statements

    H. Security Procedures

    I. Cash Register Operation

    J. Store Policy on Tipping

    K. In-Store Promotion, Advertising, and Mandatory Direct Mailings

    L. Periodic Amendments to Operation Procedures

IV. Bookkeeping and Accounting Methods

V. Grand Opening Procedures

VI. Daily Operational Function

VII. Troubleshooting

VIII. Conclusion

Chapter 11

Final Thoughts on Franchising

Introduction

In this final chapter, you will find several helpful tips and information on franchising your business. Areas include subfranchising, saving on attorney fees, determining capital requirements, and avoiding litigation, among others. At this point, you hopefully have gained enough information to understand your responsibilities as a franchisor and perhaps have even began some of your research and investigation. Take the time here to learn ways to cover all your bases and save money at the same time.

Subfranchising or Area Franchising

Subfranchising is sometimes referred to as area franchising and is a procedure whereby a franchisor tries to clone him or herself. In other words, for a substantial fee, a franchisor sells to a third party, usually a group of investors, the right to use the original franchisor's trademarks; trade secrets; and training, administrative, and marketing procedures in designated regions of the United States and the world. Thus, the purchaser of a region will act in the place of the franchisor in that particular region. Before embarking upon this approach, however, thoroughly consider the positive and negative aspects of such an arrangement.

Usually, the consideration of subfranchising does not come up until a franchisor has successfully franchised in a particular area. A pioneer of subfranchising has been the Century 21 system. The cloned subfranchisees do not have to provide a great deal of training to his or her new franchisees since they are existing brokers who, for the most part, changed their coats and became part of the Century 21 communications system. The converted brokers knew how to sell real estate before they joined the nationwide Century 21 system.

Unlike franchisees, subfranchisees are usually a composite of wealthy individuals who are looking for a return on their investment. It is extremely difficult to get one or more investors of a subfranchisee to carry on the everyday activities required for a successful subfranchise company. Therefore, this avenue should be reviewed very carefully before any decision is reached. Selling a subfranchise territory is also expensive. The market for subfranchisors is limited to a person or persons who have a considerable amount of money — anywhere from a quarter of a million dollars to several million dollars.

Generally, this type of individual is looking for an investment and does not want to be taught the exhaustive, highly difficult job of marketing franchises and following through by providing supportive services to the franchisees. It is much easier to find qualified franchisees than it is to find qualified subfranchisors with huge capital resources. In addition, subfranchisors tend to make changes in the franchise system and often feel they are as competent or more so than the original franchisor, since they usually become more active than the original franchisor in the actual operation of the franchise.

In addition, in order to sell subfranchises, a franchisor must prepare an offering circular and a subfranchise contract detailing the terms and conditions of the arrangement between the franchisor and the subfranchisee, including the splitting of royalties and initial franchise fees, the delegation of someone as a trainer, and more. Once the subfranchisee has purchased a subfranchise that qualifies in the FTC states, he or she must in turn register his or her own circular before he or she can sell franchises in registration states. In nonregistration states, the subfranchisee must still provide prospective franchisees with an offering circular containing pertinent disclosure. If you are considering subfranchising as an option, take great care in selecting each subfranchisee and think through all the pros and cons.

Saving on Attorney Fees

As mentioned in Chapter 9, many new franchisors have little personal knowledge of how to run a franchise company; therefore, they have definite ideas of what they want to charge as franchise fees, royalties, and advertising fees. They generally base their ideas on what they would like, or what others have been doing — that is, seeking franchisees more as a method of making a lot of money rather than as a way to extend their marketing arm by adding franchised retail outlets.

It is the job of an experienced, knowledgeable franchise attorney to interview his or her franchisor clients and determine certain biographical information as well as their business desires, particularly those pertaining to royalties and franchise fees, and reconcile the information so he or she can give a more objective, realistic view of what a new franchisor should do. To help you in your first meeting with your franchise attorney, you will want to complete each questionnaire in appendices C and D, respectively.

Both of these background questionnaires make you think about what you want contained in the offering circular and the specific terms you want in the franchise agreement. By completing these questionnaires before your first visit to a franchise attorney, you may be able to convince him or her to lower the bill because of the time you have saved in securing such information.

In addition, if you can supply your attorney at this first meeting with further written documentation of the estimated costs of opening and operating one of your franchises, the number of such franchises that will be sold within the ensuing year, and a complete breakdown of what the franchisee will be required to spend in order to open one of your franchise outlets — including franchise fees, rent, fixtures, equipment, payroll, utilities, insurance, and working capital — you will hasten the preparation of your circular, and thus possibly reduce your legal expenses.

Determining Your Capitalization Requirements

One of the first items you, as a potential franchisor, must determine is the amount of money necessary to capitalize your franchise operation. From a registration state's standpoint, the minimum amount of capital that a franchisor should have is a sufficient amount of liquid cash (current assets) so that the franchisor can open the number of franchises he or she projected he or she would open in the forthcoming year. However, your capitalization amount should be equal to the amount you have projected to carry you to your break-even point — where income will begin to equal payables. In addition, the higher your capitalization, the easier it will be for you to sell franchises since your audited financials are part of your offering circular.

Impounds

In the event you are in a registration state and the attorney for the state examining your application for franchising determines you do not have sufficient capitalization to open the franchises you plan to open, you will generally be granted a permit to sell franchises by the applicable state agency. To do this, however, you must open an impound account in a bank chartered in that particular state for the direct deposit of all franchise fees. In essence, an impound is a trust account wherein the franchisor is required to have the franchisee write a check to the designated depository bank to be held in trust until such time as the franchisee provides a written declaration to the registration state that he or she is open and that the franchisor has performed all of his or her opening obligations under the franchise agreement.

Once this declaration is received, it is filed with the appropriate state registration agency and upon its approval, the agency will prepare an order allowing the removal of the franchisee's funds from the bank by the franchisor. The franchisor then receives this order, submits it to the bank, and the bank pays that particular franchise fee to the franchisor.

Unfortunately, there are not too many banks familiar with these trust account procedures, and most such escrow accounts are extremely expensive — $500 to $1,000 for each franchisee escrow account. In some instances, your franchise attorney may be able to convince the state authority that you will provide in your franchise agreement that you will not require payment of the franchise fee until the franchisee has opened his or her store and advised you that he or she agrees you have fulfilled all your opening obligations under the franchise agreement. Many registration states will allow this type of situation in lieu of impounds. Except for Hawaii, each of the registration states has impound conditions.

Franchise Taxes

As a franchisor, you will definitely need to retain the services of a competent accountant who is versed in franchise taxation. Presently, franchise income has generally been held not to be passive income if the franchisor has ongoing responsibilities. In addition, the Internal Revenue Service (IRS) places certain restrictions on the franchisor as to when he or she can report income as earned. Generally, the franchisor can report the franchise fee as earned only during the time the franchise is operating.

Besides the federal government's tax regulations on franchise income, many states have franchise tax regulations. To get more information on your tax obligations and reporting requirements, see an experienced accountant or certified public accountant. You don't want any nasty surprises that could cost you money. Be as informed as possible on franchise income taxation.

Franchisee Associations and Advertising Councils

Most registration states have laws that prohibit a franchisor from interfering with the right of franchisees to have their own associations. Franchisees can have an association, but that association should be formed by you, and you should be involved in its operations. Generally, a franchisee association will not be needed until seven to ten franchisees are operating in a given area.

A franchisee association should be an advisory body only, since you, as the franchisor, should still determine the specific procedures to be followed by the franchise system. Many successful franchisors, including McDonald's, have improved their systems by implementing suggestions from franchisees and instilling the changes within the entire system after they have been proven successful at one or two test-franchise operations.

Like franchisee associations, franchisee advertising councils can be effective too. Each franchisee usually has his or her own individual idea of what the ideal advertising media should be, and most of the ideas are cost-prohibitive. For instance, almost all franchisees want local, regional, and national television exposure, which is much too costly in most cases and clearly in excess of the advertising fund fees collected from franchisees. It would be better to poll the franchisees from time to time in order to get an idea of which local advertising media the franchisees have found effective in their operations.

A good franchise agreement should compel the franchisee to provide written reports of all types, particularly covering sales data. This information could then be compiled into meaningful results for each franchisee in the system. This is one of the major benefits of the franchise system — the experiences of each franchisee, rather than his or her theories, can be compiled, analyzed, and passed on for the benefit of the entire system.

Cost-Saving Tips for the Offering Circular

Do not indiscriminately pass out your disclosure document or offering circular because this document can be anywhere from 80 to 100 pages long and costly to reproduce. In addition, circulars shouldn't be easily disassembled, but you should not staple or bind these documents in any way, shape, or form. This is because you will be revising your disclosures quite often, particularly if you have registered in more than one state. You can save yourself the cost of completely replenishing your current supply of official circulars by substituting a revised page for the old page. A three-ring, loose-leaf binder might be a good alternative.

All franchise registration laws and the FTC rule require disclosure to be modified at least once a year or at any time a material modification is made, or both. Audited financials, for all practical purposes, must be updated yearly. To save on significant copying costs, screen your potential franchisees before sending out any offering circular.

Steps to Take before Sending the Circular

Following a prospective franchisee's initial inquiry, you should send him or her an informational brochure. Brochures can cost anywhere from a few dollars to thousands of dollars to prepare. Depending on your personal taste and budget, a simple letter-form brochure stating many of the items that are in the disclosure — but painting a nice picture of the attributes of the particular franchise system — may be preferable.

In California and a few other states where registration is necessary, the brochure, like any advertisement, must be submitted to the appropriate registration authority for prior approval. The ads generally are required to be submitted in duplicate anywhere from three to seven days before publication, with a duty upon the agency to disapprove it within such time, or the particular ad is deemed approved.

In addition to sending a brochure, you should make an attempt to find out if the franchisee is financially qualified to buy a franchise. Therefore, a franchisee application seeking background information and the net worth of the franchisee should be the first document forwarded to the franchisee. A sample of a Franchisee Business Application and Net Worth Form is located at the end of this chapter. This type of application seeks net worth financials of the prospective franchisee and should be tailored to your needs and reviewed by your legal counsel.

Acknowledgment Receipt

After a prospective franchisee has completed the background application and net worth financial form, use the document to assess the candidate's suitability to your franchise. If you determine a franchisee to have the necessary qualifications, the next step is to forward your disclosure document to the prospective franchisee or meet with him or her and present the circular at the first face-to-face meeting, as required by the franchise laws. The disclosure document is acknowledged by a document called an acknowledgment receipt. It should be signed by the franchisee and returned to the franchisor. At the end of Appendix A is an example of an acknowledgment receipt.

Always prepare two acknowledgment receipt forms, one signed copy for the franchisee and one signed copy for yourself. If the franchisee signs one and returns it to you but doesn't retain a copy for his or her own records, he or she may at some time in the future, particularly if he or she is bringing a lawsuit, contend that he or she didn't receive the disclosure at least ten business days before execution of the agreement or payment of any deposit or franchise fee. This initial accusation might be avoided if you provide the franchisee with a copy of the franchisee's acknowledgment receipt at the time it is executed.

Restrictions on Offer of Circular

In the 14 registration states, you are precluded from offering to sell a franchise to a prospective franchisee and discussing any of the substantive disclosure terms until the franchisee has received the disclosure document; however, the FTC rule does allow some discussion by telephone before actual receipt of the document by the franchisee. Keep in mind the FTC rule is quite nebulous as to the permitted extent and nature of this discussion. It is a much better practice to provide the potential franchisee with the required offering circular before any discussion about it.

If the franchisee is out of state and the franchise is to be operated in your registration state, the offering circular to be sent to the prospective franchisee would be your in-state offering circular. However, if the franchise is to be operated in another state, you will be required to register in the other state before offering your franchise.

Deposit and Lease Agreements

After the franchisee has reviewed the disclosure and indicated a desire to purchase the franchise, you may have the prospective franchisee execute a deposit agreement allowing the franchisee to make a partial franchise fee payment, called a deposit, while the franchisee evaluates possible franchise locations. Many franchisors prefer to have the franchisee sign the franchise agreement and immediately pay the entire franchise fee. The use of the deposit agreement, when a particular franchisee does not yet have a location and may be a little reticent, is one way to get your foot in the door. This is a marketing theory based on the premise that once a person pays something down, he or she is more likely to pay the remaining balance and not back out of the deal. A copy of the deposit agreement must be part of the circular.

You should be knowledgeable in lease negotiations or at least able to assist the franchisee in lease negotiations while making sure to inform him or her that final approval of his or her lease is at your discretion. In addition, certain information should be given to the franchisee, such as definite construction-completion and opening dates. Many franchisees have leased locations while signing leases that allowed the landlord to complete construction, for periods up to 18 months to two years, before the franchisee was allowed to cancel the lease.

Franchisee tenants should have an escape clause so they can cancel the lease if the particular building or structure is not completed within the time frame set by the franchisee. Depending on whether there is a seller's or buyer's market, it may be difficult to get a choice location under these conditions. One last warning: Never allow the franchisee and the franchisee's spouse to quit their jobs or sell their house and move until it is absolutely certain that their particular franchise will be opened shortly.

Some franchisors require that franchisees have their landlords execute a lease assignment agreement allowing the franchisor to take over the franchisee's location in the event the franchise agreement is terminated.

Avoiding Litigation and Arbitration

Avoid litigation if at all possible. Not only is litigation expensive — even though it is less expensive if an arbitration provision is included — but the facts of the litigation or arbitration must be reported in the franchise offering circular. This includes furnishing the name, address, and phone number of each litigating franchisee. It also makes the marketing of future franchises much more difficult since prospective franchisees can contact the listed litigating franchisees and, in all probability, will be the recipients of negative information about the franchise operation.

Breach of Contract

Some registration states do provide that if a franchisor fails to properly register an offering circular, the franchisee can automatically file an action for rescission and get his or her money back. However, many other states merely make this a possible criminal violation while upholding the validity of the franchise agreement. The general rules of agreement regarding substantial breach would then apply — that is, a franchisee would have the burden to prove to a judge, jury, or arbitrator that a franchisor made a specific written commitment and failed to follow through on that commitment. If this was proved, it would constitute a substantial breach of the franchise agreement. Again, there is a fine line between what is a "substantial" breach and an "insubstantial" breach, wherein a verdict for rescission would not be granted, but rather a judgment for whatever money damages the franchisee may have proven. In addition, most franchisors, in their franchise agreements, present a minimum amount of written obligations that apply after the franchisee has opened his or her operation.

If you are proven to have committed a fraud — making fraudulent promises that were not true which induced the franchisee to enter into the franchise agreement — the franchisee may seek to rescind the agreement based on what is called "common-law fraud." It is not the purpose of this book to be a franchise legal manual; therefore, you must take every precaution to make sure your employees, particularly your franchise salespeople, make no representations that are not set forth in the written circular. In addition, actively abide by all after-opening obligations to the franchisee as provided in the franchise agreement.

Pros and Cons of Arbitration

The positive aspect of arbitration is that you can generally select an arbitrator who has a firm knowledge of franchising from both the franchisor and franchisee standpoints, as opposed to a judge or jury who know little, if anything, about franchising. The ideal arbitrator is one who has a legal and a franchising background, because arbitrators who are businesspeople tend to give both parties some type of award. Therefore, neither party wins. As a straight legal rule in the judicial system, if a contract is breached or a franchisee has been defrauded, only one party should win with the losing party getting nothing. Three arbitrators may be selected in a major arbitration so as to eliminate the chance of selecting a totally outrageous sole arbitrator who will render a bad decision. The negative side of arbitration is that it is final and binding and, in most cases, cannot be appealed. However, most court appeals are won by the party winning at the lower level. In addition, court appeals are extremely expensive and time-consuming.

Franchise Fees and Royalties

Many franchisors fail because they expect to immediately profit by charging high initial franchise fees, high royalty fees, and high advertising fees. However, if you look at what is happening in the American market, you will find that discounters who charge lower fees and bank on volume to make profits have overtaken the retail market. Most franchisees cannot handle high initial franchise fees and even higher royalty fees based on their gross sales. As a result, keep your expenses at a minimum while maintaining a high level of services to the franchisee. The franchisee is the marketing arm of the franchisor, and if he or she can set up a franchisee by breaking even, he or she has already accomplished a great feat.

Many franchisors who set their fees higher are unable to sell many franchises. The franchises they do sell have such high fees that they soon go out of business, and in some states, where franchisees have brought lawsuits against franchisors with excessive fees and royalties the courts have sided with the franchisees! So having one thousand franchisees paying $50 a month is much more profitable than having ten franchisees paying

$1,000 a month. Always make detailed projections regarding how much profit you can make with a minimum amount of franchise fees and royalties, taking into consideration the profit you will make from the sale of your products and services to your franchisees. It will be time well spent.

Making the Decision

Now that you are more familiar with franchising in general, you are better prepared to make your final decision. Here are a couple of franchising factors to consider. Be sure:

- The advantages of franchising outweigh the disadvantages.
- Your business has a market and a registerable trademark.
- Your existing personnel or outside consulting personnel familiar with franchising are well qualified and available.
- You have no problem with site selection or manual preparation.
- You have the working capital necessary to start the franchising process.
- You have sufficient capital to market your franchise.
- You have prepared a realistic business plan and budget for your franchise entity.
- You have an attorney who is not only experienced in franchise law but is familiar with the business aspects of franchising and the necessary relationship with the franchisee.

If these statements apply to you, you are ready to move ahead to a new way of conducting business, and an exciting way of life.

Franchisee Business Application and Net Worth Form

This information is confidential. We will not contact your present employer without your consent.

Name of franchise and franchisor: _____

Name of applicant franchisee: _____

Personal Information on Potential Franchisee

☐ Single   ☐ Separated   ☐ Married   ☐ Divorced

Number of minor children: _____   Ages of children: _____

Other dependents: _____

☐ Own/buying home   ☐ Rent   ☐ Live with parents   ☐ Live with spouse   ☐ Live with relatives

Home Payments

Rental payments $ _____ per month

If buying, monthly payments $ _____   Paid to: _____

Applicant

Name: _____

Home telephone: _____

Business telephone: _____

Home address: _____

City/state/zip: _____

Social Security number: _____

Birthdate (day/month/year): _____

Physical Information

Height: _____   Weight: _____

Physical limitations or health concerns: _____

_____

_____

Educational Record

High school: _____

Last grade completed: 8 9 l0 ll l2 ___

College/university: _____

Major: _____

Degree received: _____   Year: _____

Applicant's Spouse

Name: _____

Home telephone: _____

Business telephone: _____

Home address: _____

City/state/zip: _____

Social Security number: _____

Birthdate (day/month/year): _____

Physical Information

Height: _____   Weight: _____

Physical limitations or health concerns: _____

_____

_____

Educational Record

High school: _____

Last grade completed: 8 9 l0 ll l2 ___

College/university: _____

Major: _____

Degree received: _____   Year: _____

Franchisee Business Application and Net Worth Form (continued)

Employment Record of Applicant

Current employer: _____

Address: _____

City/state: _____

Position: _____

Present salary: _____

Started (year): _____ to _____

Description of work: _____

_____

_____

Previous employer: _____

Address: _____

City/state: _____

Position: _____

Salary: _____

Started (year): _____ to _____

Description of work: _____

_____

Employment Record of Applicant's Spouse

Current employer: _____

Address: _____

City/state: _____

Position: _____

Present salary: _____

Started (year): _____ to _____

Description of work: _____

_____

_____

Previous employer: _____

Address: _____

City/state: _____

Position: _____

Salary: _____

Started (year): _____ to _____

Description of work: _____

_____

Previous Business Owned

Have you ever owned your own franchise or other type of business? If so, give the following details:

Business name: _____   How long owned? _____

Address: _____   How many employees? _____

Type of business: _____

Describe how the business changed over the time you owned it.

_____

_____

_____

Business name: _____   How long owned? _____

Address: _____   How many employees? _____

Type of business: _____

Describe how the business changed over the time you owned it.

_____

_____

_____

Franchisee Business Application and Net Worth Form (continued)

Financial Information *(Note: Additional financial information may be required upon request.)*

Net Worth Summary

	Current Assets			Current Liabilities
Cash in checking account	$ _____	Notes payable		$ _____
Cash in savings account	$ _____	Amount owed on real estate		$ _____
Total	$ _____	Total		$ _____

	Fixed Assets			Long-Term Liabilities
Real estate, home	$ _____	Describe: _____		$ _____
Other real estate	$ _____	_____		$ _____
Listed stocks and bonds	$ _____	_____		$ _____
Automobile(s)	$ _____	_____		$ _____
Your own business	$ _____	_____		$ _____
Money due you	$ _____	_____		$ _____
Insurance (cash value)	$ _____	_____		$ _____
Other assets (describe):		_____		$ _____
_____	$ _____	_____		$ _____
_____	$ _____	_____		$ _____
Total	$ _____	Total		$ _____
Total Assets	$ _____	**Total Liabilities**		$ _____

Net Worth
(assets minus liabilities) $ _____

How much capital can you allocate from the above sources to buy this franchise? $ _____

What is the cash down-payment you can make for a franchise? $ _____

If the required amount is not available, how would the investment be obtained? _____

If you own your home, do you plan to sell it?   ☐ Yes ☐ No   Equity $ _____

Do you plan to convert any of the above assets into cash?   ☐ Yes ☐ No

Do you plan to have a partner?   ☐ Yes ☐ No   If so, will the partner be active?   ☐ Yes ☐ No

Do you plan to have investors?   ☐ Yes ☐ No   If so, to what extent? _____

_____

Thoroughly explain your answers and any other strategies you have for obtaining the required funds. Use a separate sheet if necessary. _____

_____

What is the minimum income you need to maintain your family during the first year of business? $ _____

From what sources will it come? _____

Franchisee Business Application and Net Worth Form (continued)

References

Business References

Name	Address	Years Known

Character References (other than employers or relatives)

Name	Address	Years Known

Former Addresses for the Past Five Years

1. _____
2. _____
3. _____
4. _____
5. _____

Business Goals

In order of priority, list which specific types of business you prefer to become involved with.

1. _____
2. _____
3. _____
4. _____

Are you willing to relocate?   ☐ Yes ☐ No   If so, state locations in order of priority.

1. _____
2. _____
3. _____
4. _____

Franchisee Business Application and Net Worth Form (continued)

When do you want to start your franchise operation? _____

How did you happen to become interested in this particular franchise? _____

_____

_____

What are your realistic personal and professional goals:

Three years from now? _____

_____

_____

_____

Five years from now? _____

_____

_____

_____

Ten years from now? _____

_____

_____

_____

State your reasons for believing you will be able to successfully operate one of our franchises. _____

_____

_____

_____

Do there appear to be any disadvantages to owning one of our franchises? If so, please state your concerns.

_____

_____

_____

_____

I certify that the enclosed information as given is complete and correct.

_____   _____
Applicant's Signature   Date

It is understood that the purpose of this questionnaire is to gather general information and is in no way binding upon either the company or the applicant. It is, however, understood that the applicant supplies the information contained herein, to the best of his or her knowledge and ability, and that the company relies on this fact in assessing the desirability and qualifications of the applicant.

Part III

Appendices

Appendix A

Uniform Franchise Offering Circular

Introduction

This appendix contains a sample of the new Uniform Franchise Offering Circular (UFOC), effective January 1, 1995. This sample illustrates how the cover page and table of contents should appear, and how the many tables, outlining fees, investment costs, and obligations, might appear in a UFOC. Appendix F contains the UFOC Guidelines, which will give you further information about how to prepare or interpret a Uniform Franchise Offering Circular.

Most people, whether seeking to become franchisors or franchisees, initially have no idea what an offering circular looks like until they contact an attorney. Examine the sample circular, whether you are a potential franchisor or a prospective franchisee, and compare it with the information in chapters 2 and 8.

Pay particular attention to Item 11 of the circular entitled "Franchisor's Obligations." As a franchisee, you will receive important benefits from a good franchise agreement that you could not receive if you started the particular business on your own. For the franchisor, these obligations "glue" the franchisee to the franchise. For example, if the franchisee can purchase inventory at the lowest competitive price from the franchisor, this glues the franchisee to the franchisor for the term of the franchise agreement. The franchisee cannot purchase the inventory at that low price without the franchisor. Other benefits attractive to a franchisee, which serve as glue to the franchisor, may include the exclusive use of a patented process or product, low cost health plans, secret recipes, or access to national purchasing accounts.

Look for the "glue" when you review the following sample offering circular. Using the information you learned from this book, decide for yourself whether the UFOC you are signing is a good offering circular.

Lube N Latte®
is a trademark of Lube N Latte Franchise Company LLC. Further reproduction
or use of this registered trademark without the permission of
Lube N Latte Franchise Company LLC is prohibited.

*This Offering Circular is included for illustration purposes only with the consent of
Lube N Latte Franchise Company LLC.*

Lube N Latte SM

Franchise Offering Circular

Lube N Latte Franchise Company LLC
An Oregon Limited Liability Company
305 S.E. "G" Street
Grants Pass, Oregon 97526
(541) 479-4992

You will operate an independently owned professional LUBE N LATTE CENTER which will provide oil changes, replacement of filters, wiper blades, radiator caps, and various sensors, transmission maintenance services, differential maintenance services, radiator flushes, fuel injector cleaning, choke pull-offs and similar services as well as offering a variety of confectionery foods including freshly baked bagels, muffins, doughnuts, pastries, soup, snacks and a complete selection of aromatic, gourmet coffees, espressos, teas, smoothies and other drinks ("gourmet coffee"). The local franchisee may also perform state automotive inspections (smog checks) where allowed by state law and approved by us at our sole discretion.

The initial franchise fee is $ 35,000. The estimated initial investment ranges from $539,000 to $826,500 if the land is leased and $699,000 to $1,226,500 if the land is purchased rather than leased.

Risk Factors:

THE FRANCHISE AGREEMENT REQUIRES THAT ALL DISAGREEMENTS BE SETTLED BY ARBITRATION ONLY IN OREGON. OUT OF STATE ARBITRATION MAY FORCE YOU TO ACCEPT A LESS FAVORABLE SETTLEMENT FOR DISPUTES. IT MAY ALSO COST YOU MORE TO ARBITRATE WITH US IN OREGON THAN IN YOUR HOME STATE.

THE FRANCHISE AGREEMENT STATES THAT OREGON LAW GOVERNS THE AGREEMENT, AND THIS LAW MAY NOT PROVIDE THE SAME PROTECTION AND BENEFITS AS LOCAL LAW. YOU MAY WANT TO COMPARE THESE LAWS.

THERE ARE CERTAIN FEDERAL AND LOCAL HAZARDOUS WASTE REGULATIONS REGARDING OIL DISPOSAL THAT YOU MUST FOLLOW IF YOU DISPOSE OF YOUR OWN OIL AND CUSTOMARY LOCAL FOOD HEALTH ORDINANCES. THERE MAY BE OTHER RISKS CONCERNING THIS FRANCHISE.

Information about comparison of franchisors is available. Call the state administrators listed in Exhibit D or your public library for sources of information.

Registration of this franchise with the state does not mean that the state recommends it or has verified the information in this offering circular. If you learn that anything in this offering circular is untrue, contact the Federal Trade Commission and/or State authority.

Effective Date: NOVEMBER 5, 1999   California

TABLE OF CONTENTS

* Note: In your actual document, page numbers must be filled in, but they have been omitted in this publication to avoid confusion with the book's page numbers.

Item 1. THE FRANCHISOR, ITS PREDECESSORS AND AFFILIATES

To simplify the language in this offering circular, "we" or "Lube N Latte" means "Lube N Latte Franchise Company, LLC," the Franchisor. "You" means the person who buys the franchise and signs as an individual as well as any legal entities and their owners. We are an Oregon limited liability company that was organized on January 2, 1999 and does business as "Lube N Latte." Our principal business address is 305 S.E. "G" Street, Grants Pass, Oregon 97526. We have an affiliate owned by our same shareholders known as Arnesen Investment Corp. that operates a Lube N Latte unit in Grants Pass, Oregon.

Our agent for service of process is The Commissioner Of Corporations, 320 West 4th Street, Suite 750, Los Angeles, California 90013-1105.

We have not offered or sold this type of franchise before the effective date of this circular. Our Affiliate has operated this type of business since December 1, 1997. We have no other business activity. Neither we nor our predecessor and affiliate have offered or sold franchises in any other line of business.

You will be an independent operator providing motor vehicle lubrication, filter and other vehicle maintenance services to your shop customers and providing gourmet coffee, espresso, tea, smoothies, various other drinks and confectionery type services to your lube and oil customers and to the general public. Your gourmet coffee café is designed to incorporate an upscale gourmet coffee café look featuring indoor seating and take out service, custom designed interiors and furniture and fixtures, specially designed uniforms and wearing apparel for all employees to compliment the total gourmet café look with a modern lube facility. You will use our system including marketing techniques, trade secrets, and recipes in connection with one café and lube facility. You receive a comprehensive training program enabling you to operate both a gourmet coffee operation with your attached oil and lubrication facility. After your initial start up training, we provide you with free ongoing telephone technical and general consultation support.

Our Managing Partner has been involved with lube services since 1990 and espresso and coffee/tea service since 1993 and we will fully utilize his services and staff in your training and in your on going operations. Your business will be distinguished by the service mark "Lube N Latte."

We have no predecessor. Our system was developed by our founder to create a high quality duplicatable system to offer franchise opportunities to other potential business owners interested in a diversified business operation.

Both the lube and oil and the gourmet coffee café businesses are highly competitive. Your general market is anyone with a motor vehicle in need of oil and lube services that is aware of your location in addition to any person that likes to drink gourmet coffee and tea in an attractive café setting. Lube N Latte franchises are developed to meet both these modern day needs by offering the oil and lube customer the opportunity to join non lube and oil coffee/espresso drinkers in enjoying a gourmet coffee, at an attached, attractive gourmet coffee cafe occupying the same structure as the lube and oil facility. Our concept is unique to the market, giving our patrons the best of two worlds.

Your competition consists of other lube and oil centers such as large national franchise and chains including Jiffy Lube, Q-Lube, Oil Can Henry's etc. as well some small independents. Your "Latte" operation will compete with national coffee house such as Starbucks, Dietricks, etc., and numerous independent coffee houses.

There are no regulations specific to the industry other than waste disposal regulations and customary local health food ordinances.

Item 2. BUSINESS EXPERIENCE

MANAGING PARTNER: GLENN D. ARNESEN

GLENN has been our Managing Partner since its inception on January 2, 1999 to the present. From 1983 to the present, he has been the owner and president of our affiliate. From 1988 to present, Glenn has been involved in over 45 car wash projects as a consultant throughout the United States from the design, construction and providing and installing needed equipment. In addition, he has done extensive site selection consultations for these related car wash businesses. From 1991 to present, he has been involved in the design of several lube and oil facilities for Kim McGrew, Dough Parker and John Kim, among others, located in Truckee, California, Norco, California, and Oakland, California.

KEY INDIVIDUALS: THE FOLLOWING KEY INDIVIDUALS ARE EMPLOYEES AND CONSULTANTS BUT ARE NOT OFFICERS, CORPORATE DIRECTORS, FRANCHISE BROKERS OR MANAGEMENT PERSONNEL AND INCLUDE:

ADMINISTRATOR: NANCY ARNESEN

NANCY has been our Administrator since our organization on January 2, 1999. From 1982 to the present, she has been Secretary and Treasurer of our affiliate. In addition, she manages the Latte portion of our affiliates' shop where she designed the interior and created the menus.

FRANCHISE SALES AND MARKETING DIRECTOR: CHARLENE ARNESEN

CHARLENE has been our Franchise Sales and Marketing Director since our formation on January 2, 1999. From 1993 to the present, she has been the Sales and Marketing director for Clout, a company located in Medford, Oregon where her duties include customer relations and sales and advertising for the company.

FRANCHISE TRAINING MANAGER: JOE ARNESEN

JOE has been General Manager of our Affiliate's lube and oil facilities since 1993 and is the overall manager of our oil and lube franchisee training program since January 2, 1999. He also has been responsible for the operation of our affiliates' lube and oil unit in Grants Pass, Oregon.

Item 3. LITIGATION

No litigation is required to be disclosed in this offering circular.

Item 4. BANKRUPTCY

The Auto Massager, an Oregon partnership, in which Glenn D. Arnesen was a partner, filed a petition under Chapter 11 in Bankruptcy In The United States Bankruptcy Court For The District Of Oregon as Case No. 693-64453-Hil on November 8, 1993. The partnership had sought shelter in bankruptcy to gain additional time to pay off a sole creditor while continuing to operate its car wash. The partnership subsequently paid off the sole creditor in full and the action was the subject of an Order Of Dismissal filed on April 7, 1994. No other person previously identified in items 1 or 2 of this offering circular has been involved as a debtor in proceedings under the U.S. Bankruptcy Code required to be disclosed in this Item 4.

Item 5. INITIAL FRANCHISE FEE

You must pay us a uniform, non-refundable Initial Franchise Fee of $35,000 upon signing your Franchise Agreement.

Item 6. OTHER FEES

Name of Fee	Amount	Due Date	Remarks
Service fee	3% of gross sales (the term "gross sales" includes all sums or things of value received from your business from all sales of services, goods, and products for cash, check, credit, barter without deduction for failure to collect including. the sales and services where the orders originated at or accepted by you at one location but delivered or performance made from or at any other location. Gross sales do not include refunds or any sales taxes)	Due and payable by the 10th calendar day after the end of the previous month	The monthly service fee is uniform and non-refundable (includes billing services)

Name of Fee	Amount	Due Date	Remarks
Local advertising and possible future cooperatives costs	3% of gross sales	Due as required by media	All advertising to be approved in advance by us with proof of actual advertisement payment submitted to us 10 days after the end of the month
Transfer fees	$5,000	Upon any assignment, sale or transfer of the franchise except to a spouse or child	The transfer fee covers the training of the new transferee and may be increased to reflect increases in the local applicable Consumer Price Index
Renewal	$1,000	Upon renewal	You must be in good standing
Additional training	Reasonable (as determined by us) prevailing per diem rate plus travel, lodging and subsistence of our trainer when requested by you and approved by us	Prior to training	Your travel, lodging and meals are your responsibility if training is at location other than your location
Audit fee	Cost of audit plus legal interest rate from date of any underpayment	Upon billing	Payable only if understatement of at least 2% due. Late payments bear legal rate of interest

All these amounts payable to us except the local advertising are payable directly to us and are non-refundable.

Item 7. INITIAL INVESTMENT

Payment	Amount Low High	Method of Payment	When Due	To Whom Payment Is to Be Made
Initial franchise fee	$35,000	Lump sum	$35,000 upon signing Franchise Agreement	Us
Travel and living expenses while training, permits, organizational expenses	$1,000–$10,000	As incurred	During training	Airlines, hotels, and restaurants
Initial opening advertising	$10,000–$15,000 prior to opening (plus 3% monthly of your gross sales)	Lump sum	30 days prior to opening	Advertising supplier
Vehicle	Not required			
Site and floor plans; elevation and rendering	$5,000	Lump sum	Prior to receipt	Us (additional obligations are paid to architect, planner, city, county, or state building authority
Purchase of café and lube leasehold improvements including construction of building; landscaping, paving etc., but no land	$350,000–$500,000	Progress payments according to construction agreement until completion	Generally by agreement with contractor	General contractor
Alternate rental of real estate land for lube and oil facilities (approx. 20,000 sq. ft.)[1]	$4,000–$10,000 lease payment on ground itself	As incurred	Monthly	Landlord

Payment	Amount Low High	Method of Payment	When Due	To Whom Payment Is to Be Made
Business licenses	$0–$500	In full	Prior to opening	Applicable government agencies
Oil dispensing equipment [2]	$30,000–$50,000	Lump sum or as negotiated	Prior to opening	Designated supplier
Café equipment and furniture [3]	$20,000–$40,000	Lump sum or as negotiated	Prior to opening	Designated supplier
Signs (indoor and outdoor)	$20,000–$30,000	Lump sum or as negotiated	Prior to opening	Sign company
Opening lube inventory and supplies (coils, filters, windshield wipers, PC valves, breathers, etc.); computer hardware and software and maintenance and support fees	$20,000–$50,000	Lump sum or as negotiated	Prior to opening	Designated supplier
Opening café inventory and supplies (coffee, teas, fruit juices, confectionary, etc.)	$5,000–$10,000	Lump sum or as negotiated	Prior to opening	Designated supplier
Insurance for entire operation	$6,000–$10,000	Lump sum or as negotiated	Prior to opening	Insurance agent
Monthly Yellow Pages for entire operation	None. Initially $500–$1,000 to local phone directory for ad designed by us	Monthly installments	Prior to opening and monthly	Telephone company

Payment	Amount Low High	Method of Payment	When Due	To Whom Payment Is to Be Made
Working capital (additional funds for expenses including payroll, petty cash, and miscellaneous expenses necessary for first 3 months in addition to above expense)[4]	$30,000–$50,000	As required	As required	Suppliers, etc.
Security deposits, utilities, licenses, etc.	$3,000–$10,000	As negotiated	As required	Miscellaneous suppliers

ESTIMATED TOTAL INITIAL INVESTMENT AND INITIAL ADVERTISING REQUIREMENTS:

TOTALS   **$539,000–$826,500**   **(if land leased)**

                     $699,000–$1,226,500   **(if land is to be purchased)**

Note: The sources of funds listed above are amounts to be supplied from your own funds.

Note: No allowance has been made for inflation or debt service or interest payment on borrowed money but these should be considered by you especially if part or all of the startup costs are to be financed.

[1] Most leasing agents determine the monthly rental by the value of the land × 10% divided by 12 plus taxes and insurance (triple net lease). Although you will most likely choose to lease the business property and any related improvements, it is possible you might purchase the land. The above figures assume that you will lease the land and construct the building.

  If you purchases suitable land, your estimated acquisition cost could vary from $8.00 per square foot to $20.00 per square foot depending on desirability of specific location, local demographics, traffic count and region of the country.

[2] Varies depending on whether equipment is purchased, leased or is available on loan from suppliers. The oil vending company supplier approved by us will sign a supplier agreement with you. You may enter into equipment reimbursement arrangements with this oil supplier.

  We will negotiate with oil suppliers on your behalf. All oil suppliers must be approved in writing in advance by us. At present we work with Quaker State as our supplier.

[3] All Latte furniture, fixtures, glassware and similar items must be purchased from us or our designated supplier.

[4] Working capital does not include any draw or compensation for you as the owner but does include wages for 6 to 12 employees.

We do not provide direct or indirect financing.

The initial phase of your business is at least 3 months.

We rely on the demographics, your past work experience and that of your key employees, the local wage rates and standard of living expenses in setting additional funds required.

THERE ARE NO OTHER DIRECT OR INDIRECT PAYMENTS IN CONJUNCTION WITH THE PURCHASE OF THE FRANCHISE.

Item 8. RESTRICTIONS ON SOURCES OF PRODUCTS AND SERVICES

Our equipment and operation specifications may be modified as changes occur in the industry based on our research and made known to you by us in writing as the changes occur.

You must purchase numerically numbered Lube N Latte service orders from our designated supplier, Apex Business Forms of Medford, Oregon. Since the service orders are numerically numbered for auditing and control purposes, there are presently no alternative. It is estimated that the required purchase of these service orders will constitute less than 1% of the initial cost to establish your franchise, and an insignificant percentage of your future operating costs (Franchise Agreement – Paragraph 9.2).

You must purchase or lease, at your expense, a computer lube operation system from Innovative Control Systems (ICS) located in Pennsylvania. For a list of software, hardware and cash register requirements, see the Franchise Agreement's Schedule 1 (Exhibit A). ICS is the third party proprietary owner for the software program and supplies us with hardware. You must maintain support and updates with support included in updates. You must purchase this software and other equipment as we reasonably deem necessary from designated suppliers and pay all related reasonable fees and charges including $500 (which may be increased annually to be competitive) per year in software support and a 3 year prevailing maintenance agreement on the hardware. We will have independent access to all information and data generated on your computer programs and hardware to evaluate sales and services provided to the consumer and costs associated with your business. You must purchase an electronic cash register from our designated supplier list in the Franchise Agreement, Schedule 1 (Exhibit A). You also must purchase all Latte furniture, fixtures, glassware, equipment and similar items from us or our designated supplier. The goods and service provided by you to the general public must meet the quality standards necessary to uphold the reputation and public image of the Lube N Latte system. All goods, services, supplies, fixtures, equipment, inventory and real estate used to serve the public must meet the standards in the Confidential Operations Manual and other publications which may be changed.

If we sublease a premise to you, we, or our designated entity or affiliate, may derive revenue in excess of our costs.

We may derive income from your mandatory purchase of oil, filters and coffee/espresso/confectionery/smoothie ingredients, furniture and glassware etc. from us or our designated supplier based on cost and wholesale price with a maximum profit to us of 10% of your purchase price which will not exceed the average purchase price paid by your competitors. Your purchase of any of these items from others must be approved by us with a sample of the product or products provided to us by you before offer it for sale.

We only recently organized and had no total revenue from all sources for the last fiscal year end of December 31, 1998 and there were no revenues from required purchases and leases of products and services sold to our franchisees for the same period and no percentage of total revenues.

We estimate that the cost of equipment for lube, oil and coffee purchased according to our specifications represents 8% to 10% of your total purchases in connection with establishment of your franchise if none of these costs are reimbursed to you by the oil company.

We estimate that you will purchase or lease from us approximately 8% to 10% of all of the goods and services which you will need to establish and operate your franchise business.

We will use our best efforts to negotiate purchase arrangements on your behalf with potential suppliers of these products including price at our discretion for your benefit. We do not provide you with the right to purchase additional franchises or to renew based on your use of a supplier designated by us. There are no designated suppliers that make payments to us because of any transactions with you.

You may only offer those services and sell those products that have been designated by us in writing in order to be consistent with our theme. We will lend you a Confidential Business Operations Manual which will contain specifications and parameters developed by us and which are to be strictly followed.

You must submit all of your advertising to us for our approval of the contents, themes, materials and placement at least 5 business days prior to publication unless we specifically waive our consent in writing to each particular ad or advertising campaign and, if no action is taken by us within that time, the advertising will deemed to be approved.

We will supply you with our list of suggested and preferred suppliers which may be updated. We do not request nor will we accept any compensation from any of our suggested suppliers.

We evaluate, approve or disapprove suppliers who can reasonably demonstrate to us that they: (1) have an ability to meet our standards and specifications, (2) possess adequate quality control and the capacity to supply your needs promptly and reliably, and (3) have been approved by us in our manuals or in writing. You must submit to us a written request to approve your proposed supplier together with any information we may reasonably require including financials, total sales figures, written references, etc. We have the right to require that our representative be permitted to inspect the suppliers' facilities and that samples from the supplier be delivered for our evaluation and testing either to us or to an independent testing facility designated by us. You must pay a charge not to exceed the reasonable cost of the evaluation and testing whether or not the supplier is approved. We will notify you in writing of our approval or disapproval of the proposed supplier and the criteria for our approval and disapproval within 10 days after our receipt of your request and completion of the evaluation and testing. Designated suppliers do not make payments to us because of their transactions with you.

To insure uniformity and quality in all units, you must purchase supplies, materials and products including food and beverages or their components that are equal to or exceed the specifications established by us. All Lube N Latte service centers must meet the construction and appearance as well as equipment standards set forth in the then-current manual or written directive, however, you are not required to have construction services performed by any specific entity. Specifications set forth may include minimum standards for building size and style, sign(s), equipment types, products including food and beverages sold, inventory, quality, delivery, performance, warranties, logo and trademark design and compliance, appearance and other restrictions. These specifications are part of the Confidential Operations Manual issued to you and maybe changed. You must promptly comply with all changes. We may designate an affiliated entity as an approved supplier of items for the operation of the franchise business including products, materials, services, supplies, equipment and facilities, and, if the cost of these items is less than their sale price, we may realize a profit as a result of these sales. You are not required to purchase these items from us or our designated affiliate if another non-affiliate supplier is approved except for your required purchases of our "service orders" and specified hardware, software and cash register items.

We have the right to review or test all of your proposed equipment, products (food, beverage) materials and supplies to determine if they meet our standards and we may consider other factors including advertising contributions, marketing assistance, and equipment loan arrangements). Those items failing to meet our standards will be disapproved and you must replace these items with those meeting our requirements and standards. Approval of your proposed equipment, products, materials and supplies will not be unreasonably withheld, however, we reserve the right to require that you purchase and use specific brand name items in the operation of your center although you are free to purchase these items from sources identified by you and approved by us to obtain quality control, uniformity, and marketing and advertising contribution benefits for the system as a whole. If we have an approved brand name supplier who agrees to make advertising contributions or payments because of your or our use or sale of the approved product or service, all payments by the approved brand name supplier are generally made to us including an entity appointed by us and shall be spent by us consistent with any restrictions or conditions imposed by the approved brand name supplier. We reserve the right to require that all products used by you meet our quality standards and other reasonable requirements.

Item 9. FRANCHISEE'S OBLIGATIONS

THIS TABLE LISTS YOUR PRINCIPAL OBLIGATIONS UNDER THE FRANCHISE AND OTHER AGREEMENTS. IT WILL HELP YOU FIND MORE DETAILED INFORMATION ABOUT YOUR OBLIGATIONS IN THESE AGREEMENTS AND IN OTHER ITEMS OF THIS OFFERING CIRCULAR.

Obligation	Section in Agreement	Item in Offering Circular
a. Site selection and acquisition	Articles 8.1 and 8.5	Items 7, 11, and 12
b. Pre-opening purchases/leases	Articles 5, 6, 7, and 8.5	Items 7, 8, and 10
c. Site development and other pre-opening requirements	Articles 1.2, 2, 7.15, and 8.1	Items 7, 8, and 11

Obligation	Section in Agreement	Item in Offering Circular
d. Initial and ongoing training	Articles 5 and 8.11	Items 6 and 11
e. Opening	Articles 2, 5, 6, 7, and 9	Items 5, 7, 8, and 9
f. Fees	Articles 6.5, 6.6, 6.9, 6.10, 11.1, 11.8, and 15.2	Items 5, 6, and 7
g. Compliance with standards and policies/operating manual	Articles 1, 3, 4, 5, 6, 7, and 9	Items 8, 9, 11, 14, 15, 16, and 17
h. Trademarks and proprietary information	Articles 1, 2, 3, and 13	Items 8, 13, and 14
i. Restrictions on products/services offered	Articles 7.7 and 9	Items 8 and 16
j. Warranty and customer service	None	None
k. Territorial development and sales	None	None
l. Ongoing product/ service purchases	Articles 7 and 9	None
m. Maintenance, appearance and remodeling requirements	Articles 7.7, 9, and 11	Items 7 and 8
n. Insurance	Articles 6.11 and 6.12	Items 6, 7, and 8
o. Advertising	Articles 6.4, 6.7, 7.3, and 8.9	Items 6, 7, and 11
p. Indemnification	Articles 15.1 and 17	None
q. Owner's participation/ management/staffing	Articles 7.2, 7.4, 7.5, and 9.6	Item 15
r. Records/reports	Articles 6.16, 6.17, and 7.11	Item 6
s. Inspections/audits	Articles 6.9, 6.13, and 7.17	Item 6

Obligation	Section in Agreement	Item in Offering Circular
t. Transfer	Articles 6.5 and 11	Items 6 and 17
u. Renewal	Articles 6.6 and 11	Items 6 and 17
v. Post-termination obligations	Article 11.5	Item 17
w. Non-competition covenants	Articles 7.13, 12.1, and 12.2	Item 17
x. Dispute resolution	Article 23	Item 17
y. Other (describe)	None	

Item 10. FINANCING

We do not offer direct or indirect financing or guarantee your note, lease or obligation.

Item 11. FRANCHISOR'S OBLIGATIONS

Except as disclosed below, we need not provide any other assistance to you.

Before you open your business, we will:

1. Assist you in obtaining the necessary information and approve your base site within the territory (Franchise Agreement – Paragraph 8.1).

2. Loan you one set of the Confidential Business Operation Manual (Franchise Agreement – Paragraph 8.2).

3. Provide an initial training period of 15 business days of hands on training at a Latte and Lube center of our choice for you and 1 approved, other person and a minimum of 7 to a maximum of 15 business days at your location at opening (Franchise Agreement – Paragraphs 5.1, 5.2, 5.3, 5.4, and 8.3).

4. Provide you with a detailed list of all necessary equipment, supplies and inventory (Franchise Agreement – Paragraph 8.4).

5. For a mandatory fee of $5,000, we will provide you with site, floor, elevation and rendering (Franchise Agreement – Paragraph 8.5).

6. Within 60 days of your scheduled opening of your facility we will train you and one other person designated by you and approved by us at Grants Pass, Oregon, or a designated Lube N Latte location for 15 business days (8 hours per day for 120 hours) and a minimum of 7 business days to a maximum 15 business days (56 hours to 120 hours) at your location upon opening (a total of between 176 hours and 240 hours) as follows: (Franchise Agreement – Paragraphs 5.3 and 8.3)

Subject	Time Begun (Monday through Saturday)	Instructional Material	Hours	Instructor
Lube subjects: A. Equipment and tools B. Call system C. Procedures D. General operations	9 A.M. to 5 P.M. until a minimum of 120 hours expire	Manual and trainers; notes and knowledge	Minimum of 20 class and 100 on job	Glenn/Joe Arnesen
Coffee/Espresso subjects: Latte operations A. Equipment B. Recipes C. Food items D. Coffee items E. Procedures F. General operation	6 A.M. to 6 P.M. until at least 56 hours expire	Manual and trainers; notes and knowledge	0 class 56 hours to 120 hours on job	Nancy Arnesen/ staff

Glenn D. Arnesen has over 9 years of experience in the lube and oil business and over 5 years in the coffee and espresso business. Joe Arnesen has over 5 years of experience in the lube and oil business and over 4 years in the coffee and espresso business. Our trainers will have a minimum of 1 to 11 years experience in all facets of the lube and oil business and 1 to 5 years experience in all facets of the coffee/espresso/tea/smoothie/confectionery business.

Additional training will be at our sole discretion upon your written request at your expense. An annual inspection will be made by our personnel at your location.

We do not charge for this training but you must pay the travel and living expenses for you and your employees. All training occurs either at our Oregon headquarters or at location of our choice.

During the operation of the franchised business, we will provide:

1. Available general coffee/espresso/teas/smoothie service and product informational updates (Franchise Agreement – Paragraph 8.6).

2. A continuing non-technical consulting service (Franchise Agreement – Paragraph 8.7).

3. Technician support. If you request, We will supply a 1-800 number operated by a technician to assist you with technical lube and coffee business support for the first 12 months after you open. If you request assistance after the initial 12 months, you must pay a support fee at a nominal cost of $100 per year subject to annual increases in the local Consumer Price Index (CPI) (Franchise Agreement – Paragraph 8.8).

4. Available advertising material (Franchise Agreement – Paragraph 8.9).

5. Lube and oil maintenance updates (Franchise Agreement – Paragraph 8.10).

6. One week on site review course (Franchise Agreement – Paragraph 8.13).

7. Your Subsequent Franchise Training (Franchise Agreement – Paragraphs 5.6 and 8.11).
   (You and new assignees must attend training in Grants Pass, Oregon, or designated location.)

You must buy from us or our designated supplier any electronic cash registers or computer systems or any hardware and software in support.

You are not required to make contributions to an advertising fund operated by us. You must spend 3% of your monthly gross sales on local advertising approved by us including electronic media, print, radio or television. You may use your own advertising material if approved by us in writing. There is no advertising council and we are not planning to establish an advertising council. You must join a local or regional advertising cooperative if we should direct you at our sole discretion in the future. If you join a cooperative that is approved in the future, the 3% advertising fee can only be increased by a majority vote of the members of the cooperative. We cannot terminate or merge any cooperatives. Your software will collect customer billing information and connection to the Internet. We will have independent access to the information without limitation.

The typical length of time between your signing the franchise agreement and paying the initial franchise fee and your opening is 180 to 360 days. This schedule may be delayed because of vehicle lift instillation, pit construction, permits, plans, city requirements, weather conditions, time of year, availability of training, the time to select your location and acts of others beyond our control.

The table of contents of our Confidential Operations Manual and our Marketing Manual at the end of our last fiscal year including the number of pages devoted to each subject matter is:

OPERATIONS MANUAL

Chapter Title	No. of pages
I. Introduction	3
II. Latte operations	
A. Equipment	2
B. Recipes	3
C. Food items	3
D. Coffee items	4
E. Procedures	3
F. General operation	2
III. Lube	
A. Equipment and tools	4
B. Call system	2
C. Procedures	4
D. General operations	3
IV. Summary	2

Item 12. TERRITORY

We determine your territory primarily by the number of people in your area which must be a minimum of 20,000 people or more depending on the area and demographics including income and vehicles owned. We must pre-approve your operational site in your territory. If you proceed with a site not approved by us, you must sign a letter of understanding that we are not recommending the site. Your territory will be outlined on a map attached to the Franchise Agreement. We will not authorize another franchisee to operate a Lube N Latte location in your territory. However, some franchisees operating outside of your territory may use advertisements that are distributed in your territory in the ordinary course of their business. If we can not agree on your site for you within 60 days of receipt of your franchise payment, we will deduct our reasonable costs incurred in the site selection process and return the balance to you. The conditions under which we will approve a relocation include a lease of equal time, a minimum of 200,000 people, good demographics and in your area.

Item 13. TRADEMARKS

We grant you the right to operate your business under the principal service mark "LUBE N LATTE." Arnesen Investment Corp. has secured a Certificate of Registration on the Supplemental Register of "LUBE N LATTE" with the Commissioner of Patents and Trademarks on April 13, 1999 as Registration Number 2,240,019 and it has assigned us the service mark with a non-exclusive, revocable license back to it to use the service mark for its company stores.

By "trademarks," we mean trade names, trademarks, service marks and logos used to identify your business. By not having a Principal Register federal registration for "LUBE N LATTE," we do not have certain presumptive legal rights at this time granted by registration for this mark only.

You must follow our rules when you use these marks. You cannot use a name or mark as part of a corporate name or with modifying words, designs or symbols except for those which we license to you. You may use our service marks in your d.b.a. with our permission. You may not use our registered name in connection with the sale of an unauthorized product or service or in a manner not authorized in writing by us.

There are no agreements that limit our right to use or license the use of our trademark. You must make your own independent investigation of the demographics of your proposed area prior to making a final determination. In the event of a challenge to your use of our trademark, we will take the action we think appropriate. We, alone, have the sole right to control any legal action or proceeding including settlement involving service mark infringement or unfair competition against you or others. We will prosecute or defend an action at our sole discretion. You must notify us immediately upon learning about any infringement or challenge so we can take whatever action we deem is necessary. We may take over the defense of such claim at any time and settle it as we think fit.

You must modify or discontinue the use of a trademark if we modify or discontinue it. If this happens, we will reimburse you for your tangible costs of compliance for changing your signs, stationery or ads. You must not directly or indirectly contest our right to our trademarks, trade secrets or business techniques that are part of our business. We do not know of any infringing uses or litigation that could significantly affect the ownership or use of our principal trademark.

There are currently no material determinations of the Patent and Trademark Office, Trademark Trial and Appeal Board, the Trademark Administrator of this State or any court; pending infringement, opposition or cancellation; and pending material litigation involving the principal trademarks. We do not know of any infringing use or litigation that could significantly affect the ownership or use of a principal trademark.

Item 14. PATENTS, COPYRIGHTS, AND PROPRIETARY INFORMATION

No patents or copyrights are material of the Circular.

Item 15. OBLIGATION TO PARTICIPATE IN THE ACTUAL OPERATION OF THE FRANCHISE BUSINESS

You must devote your best efforts and dedicate a minimum of 25 hours per week to the onsite management of your franchised business. If you are a corporation or partnership, you must designate an individual upon whom we may rely for the personal and direct onsite management of the franchised business.

Item 16. RESTRICTIONS ON WHAT THE FRANCHISEE MAY SELL

You may offer for sale to the public only those goods and services which comply with our standards for kind and quality designated in the operations manual or directives in writing provided by us. All products and services used or offered must be from an approved vendor.

To ensure the uniformity and high quality product of the cafe food, you must prepare and serve only those items on the café menu as approved by us (Franchise Agreement – Paragraph 9.6). All café menu drink items will be selected for their wholesome and nutritional food value. All café menu items will be formulated, designed, and enhanced by us (Franchise Agreement – Paragraph 9.6). (See requirements on sources of products in Item 8.) You will not be prevented from creating and test running new beverage items with our prior written approval. You must operate the café facilities continuously from 6 A.M. to 6 P.M. minimum (minimum 7 A.M. to 5 P.M. closing on Saturday and minimum 9 A.M. to 4 P.M. on Sunday is permissible) seven days per week unless different hours have been approved by us (Franchise Agreement – Paragraph 9.6). You must operate the Lube facility from Monday through Friday a minimum of 8 A.M. to 6 P.M. with 8 A.M. to 6 P.M. on Saturdays and 9 A.M. to 4 P.M. on Sundays (Franchise Agreement – Paragraph 9.6). You must set all prices and include appropriate sales tax on each item although we may recommend certain prices to assist you in securing the proper price structure for our products. (Franchise Agreement – Paragraph 9.7). You must adequately stock your café and lube center with product. Vending or other operated machines are permitted only with our prior written consent (Franchise Agreement – Paragraph 9.8). Depending on your location, we set the days and hours of operation which may vary from location to location and from time to time.

Item 17. RENEWAL, TERMINATION, TRANSFER, AND DISPUTE RESOLUTION

This table lists important provisions of the franchise and related agreements. You should read these provisions in the agreements attached to this offering circular.

Provision	Section in Franchise Agreement	Summary
a. Term of the Franchise Agreement	Sections 6.6 and 10.1	Term is 10 years from the date of execution of the Franchise Agreement
b. Renewal or extension of the term	Sections 6.6 and 11.1	You can renew for unlimited additional periods of 10 years each providing: (1) you are not in default or in violation franchise agreement or any other agreement with us; and, (2) upon execution of the then current franchise agreement, under the terms in effect at that time including new royalty rates, advertising fees, etc., with the exception that the length of term or renewal terms shall not change your territory. You must pay a $1,000 renewal fee
c. Requirements to renew or extend	Sections 6.6 and 11	Sign new agreement, pay fee, be in good standing
d. Termination by you	Section 11.2	You may terminate the franchise for good cause only if we have immediately breached the franchise agreement, provided however, prior to your terminating the franchise agreement for good cause, you must serve a written notice of default upon us specifying the grounds for default and granting us a reasonable opportunity, but in no case less than 30 days in which to cure the default or in which to commence diligent efforts to cure the default (if the default cannot reasonably be expected to be cured within 30 days)
e. Termination by us without cause	Sections 11.3 and 11.4	We can terminate only if you default
f. Termination by us with cause	Sections 11.3 and 11.4	We can terminate only if you default

Provision	Section in Franchise Agreement	Summary
g. "Cause" defined — defaults which cannot be "cured"	Sections 11.3 and 11.4	No days to cure: Attachment of involuntary lien over $1,000; adverse conduct affecting goodwill; default of franchise agreement; failure to make timely payments after 5 days notice or as Guarantor; conduct damaging to goodwill; transfers without our prior consent; failure to cure a default within 10 business days; failure to pay for or conduct an audit after 10 days notice; failure to supply reports on gross sales; failure to use our techniques; failure to put in hours managing during such days and hours as may be specified in accordance with the franchise agreement; failure to keep accurate business records; failure to maintain good conduct standards; failure to maintain confidential information; operating out of territory; failure to participate in a cooperative ad group and failure to pass training or open within scheduled time after training
h. "Cause" defined — defaults which cannot be "cured"	Sections 11.3 and 11.4	Judicially declared insolvent; abandons business for 5 consecutive days; we mutually agree in writing; material misrepresentations; your failure after 10 day notice to comply with laws; engage in same conduct after cured or not; repeated failure to comply with terms; franchised premises are seized and judgment unsatisfied for 30 days; conviction of felony or any criminal misconduct; failure to pay franchise fees within 5 days after notice; we determine danger to public health
i. Your obligations on termination non-renewal (also see r, below)	Section 11.5	Obligations include complete de-identification and payment
j. Assignment of contract by us	Section 11	No restriction on our right to assign
k. "Transfer" by you — definition	Sections 11.8 and 11.9	Includes transfer of contract and sole assets or ownership change

	Provision	Section in Franchise Agreement	Summary
l.	Our approval of transfer by franchisee	Sections 11.8 and 11.9	We have the right to approve all transfers but will not unreasonably withhold approval
m.	Conditions for our approval of transfer	Sections 11.8, 11.9, and 11.11	New franchisee qualifies, transfer fee paid, purchase agreement approved, training arranged, and release signed by you and current agreement signed by new franchisee
n.	Our right of first refusal to acquire your business	Section 11.6	We can match any offer
o.	Our option to purchase your business	Section 11.6	We have the right of first refusal except the transfers to approved qualified children and/or spouse exercisable within 30 days of receipt of your notice to us. We can purchase the franchise at any time that you attempt to cause a transfer to any other person
p.	Your death or disability	Section 11.9	The franchise must be assigned by estate to approved buyer in 3 months
q.	Non-competition during the term of the franchise	Sections 7.13, 11.5(8), and 12.1	You cannot directly or indirectly operate a business similar to your franchised business
r.	Non-competition after the franchise is terminated or expires	Sections 7.13 and 11.5(8)	No competing business for 2 years following the termination and within 10 mile radius from another of our franchises or company unit or at your location
s.	Modification of the agreement	Section 18	No modifications generally but Operation Manual subject to change
t.	integration/merger clause	Sections 24.1, 24.2, and 25.2	Only the terms of the franchise agreement are binding (subject to state law). Any other promises may not be enforceable
u.	Dispute resolution by arbitration or mediation	Section 23.3	Except for certain claims, all disputes must be arbitrated in Oregon before Franchise and Mediation or American Arbitration Association
v.	Choice of forum	Section 19	Arbitration must be in Oregon
w.	Choice of law	Section 19	Oregon law applies

These states have statutes which may supersede the franchise agreement in your relationship with the franchisor in checking the areas of termination and non-renewal of your franchise:

Arkansas (Stat. 70-807), California (Bus. & Prof. Code Sections 20000–20043), Connecticut (Gen. Stat. Section 42-113e *et seq.*), Delaware (Code, tit.), Hawaii (Rev. Stat. Section 482E-1), Illinois (Rev. Stat. Chapter 121-1/2, Par. 1719–1720), Indiana (Stat. Section 23-2-2.7), Iowa (Code Sections 523H.1–523.17), Michigan (Stat. Section 19.854(27)), Minnesota (Stat. Section 80C.14), Mississippi (Code Section 75-24-51), Missouri (Stat. Section 407.400), Nebraska (Rev. Stat. Section 87-401), New Jersey (Stat. Section 56:10-1), New York (N.Y. Gen. Bus. Law Art. 33, Section 87-401), Rhode Island (Section 19-28, 1-14, Juris. & Venue, R.I. Franchise Investment Act), South Dakota (Codified Laws, Section 375A-51), Virginia (Code 13.1-557–574-13.1-564), Washington (Code, Section 19.100.180), Wisconsin (Stat. Section 135.03). These and other states may have court decisions which may supersede the franchise agreement in your relationship with us including the areas of termination and renewal of your franchise. The laws of the state where you will operate regarding termination of franchises should be checked thoroughly by your attorney.

Item 18. PUBLIC FIGURES

We do not use any public figure to promote our franchise.

Item 19. EARNINGS CLAIMS

We do not furnish or authorize our salespersons to furnish any oral or written information concerning the actual or potential sales, income or profits of Lube N Latte franchised or company owned units. Actual results vary from unit to unit and we cannot estimate the results of any particular franchise

Item 20. LIST OF OUTLETS

Franchised Site Center Status Summary for Last Three Calendar Years (1998/1997/1996)[1]

State	Transfers	Cancelled/ Terminated	Not Renewed	Reacquired by Franchisor	Left the System/ Other	Total from Left Columns[2]	Franchises Operating at Year End
Oregon	0/0/0	0/0/0	0/0/0	0/0/0	0/0/0	0/0/0	0/0/0
Total	0/0/0	0/0/0	0/0/0	0/0/0	0/0/0	0/0/0	0/0/0

[1] Note: All numbers are as of December 31st for each year.

[2] The numbers in the "Total" column may exceed the number of centers affected because several events may have affected the same center. For example, the same franchised center may have had multiple owners.

Please refer to Exhibit C entitled franchisee list.

There have been no transfers, cancellations or terminations or not renewals or reacquired franchises.

Status of Company Owned Centers for the Last Three Years (1998/1997/1996)

State	Sites Closed During Year	Sites Opened During Year	Total Sites Operating at Year End
Oregon	0/0/0	0/0/0	0/0/0

Projected openings as of January 1, 2000

State	Franchise Agreements Signed but Site Center Not Opened	Projected Franchised New Site Centers in the Next Fiscal Year	Projected Company Owned Center Openings in the Next Fiscal Year
Oregon	0	2	0
California	0	2	0
Washington	0	2	0
Totals	0	6	0

ITEM 21. FINANCIAL STATEMENTS

THE FINANCIAL STATEMENTS ATTACHED AS EXHIBIT A: AUDITED BALANCE SHEET AND RELATED STATEMENT OF INCOME AS OF JANUARY 2, 1999.

ITEM 22. CONTRACTS

ATTACHED AS EXHIBIT "B" IS A COPY OF THE FRANCHISE AGREEMENT PROPOSED TO BE USED IN THIS STATE.

ITEM 23. RECEIPT

THE LAST PAGE OF THE OFFERING CIRCULAR IS A DETACHABLE DOCUMENT ACKNOWLEDGING RECEIPT OF THE OFFERING CIRCULAR BY YOU AND IS ATTACHED AS EXHIBIT G.

EXHIBIT A

FINANCIAL STATEMENTS

[Financial Statements are omitted. This circular is not an offering, but included for illustration purposes only.]

EXHIBIT B

FRANCHISE AGREEMENT

[*Please see Appendix B of this book for a full illustration of a Franchise Agreement*]

EXHIBIT C

LIST OF FRANCHISEES

OF THE OFFERING CIRCULAR FOR LUBE N LATTE SHOPS

Franchisee # Number	Location	Owner	Address/ Phone
None			

EXHIBIT D

STATE ADMINISTRATORS AND AGENCIES

Listed here are names, addresses and telephone numbers of state and federal agency personnel having responsibility for franchising disclosure/registration laws and selected business opportunity laws.

California
Commissioner of Corporations
Department of Corporations
Los Angeles
Suite 750
320 West 4th Street
Los Angeles, California 90013-1105
(213) 576-7500

Connecticut
[Business Opportunity Investment Act]
Cynthia Antanaitis
260 Constitutional Plaza
Hartford, Connecticut 06106
(860) 240-8233

Florida
[Sale of Business Opportunities Act]
Bob James
Senior Consumer Complaint Analyst
Department of Agriculture and Consumer
  Services
Division of Consumer Services
Mayo Building, Second Floor
Tallahassee, Florida 32399-0800
(850) 922-2770
FAX: (850) 921-8201

Hawaii
Business Registration Division
Securities Compliance
Department of Commerce and Consumer
  Affairs
1010 Richards Street
Honolulu, Hawaii 96813
(808) 586-2727

Director, Department of Commerce and
  Consumer Affairs
Kathryn S. Matayoshi

Illinois
Robert A. Tingler
Chief
Franchise Bureau
Office of Attorney General
Room 12-178
100 W. Randolph Street
Chicago, Illinois 60601

Registration and Materials Inquiries:
500 S. Second Street
Springfield, Illinois 62706
(217) 782-4465

Attorney General
Jim Ryan
Commissioner of Commerce
David B. Gruenes

Indiana
Patrick Sanders
Chief Deputy Commissioner
Franchise Section
Indiana Securities Division
Secretary of State
Room E-111
302 West Washington Street
Indianapolis, Indiana 46204
(317) 232-6681

Securities Commissioner
Bradley W. Skolnik

Iowa
[Business Opportunity Promotions Law]
Dennis Britson
Director of Regulated Industries Unit
Iowa Securities Bureau
340 East Maple
(515) 281-4441
FAX: (515) 281-6467

Maryland
Peggy Jones
Franchise Examiner
Maryland Division of Securities
20th Floor
200 St. Paul Place
Baltimore, Maryland 21202
(410) 576-7042

Assistant Attorney General
Dale E. Cantone
Securities Commissioner
Robert N. McDonald

Michigan
Marilyn McEwen
Franchise Administrator
Consumer Protection Division
Antitrust and Franchise Unit
Michigan Department of Attorney General
670 Law Building
Lansing, Michigan 48913
(517) 373-7117

Minnesota
Ann Hagestad
Franchise Examiner
Minnesota Department of Commerce
133 East Seventh Street
St. Paul, Minnesota 55101
(612) 296-6328

Nebraska
[Seller-Assisted Marketing Plan Law]
Karen Reynolds
Security Analyst
Department of Banking and Finance
1200 N Street
Suite 311
P.O. Box 95006
(402) 471-3445

New York
Joseph J. Punturo
Special Deputy Attorney General
Bureau of Investor Protection and Securities
New York State Department of Law
23rd Floor
120 Broadway
New York, New York 10271
(212) 416-8211
FAX: (212) 416-8816

Assistant Attorney General in Charge
Andrew Kandel
Attorney General
Dennis C. Vacco

North Dakota
Diane Lillis
Franchise Examiner
Office of Securities Commissioner
Fifth Floor
600 East Boulevard
Bismarck, North Dakota 58505
(701) 328-4712

Securities Commissioner
Syver Vinje

Oregon
Dick Nockledy
Department of Consumer and Business Services
Division of Finance and Corporate Securities
Labor and Industries Building
Salem, Oregon 97310
(503) 378-4140

Rhode Island
Thomas Corrigan
Securities Examiner
Division of Securities
Suite 232
233 Richmond Street
Providence, Rhode Island 02903
(401) 277-3048

South Dakota
Katie Hofer
Franchise Administrator
Division of Securities
c/o 118 West Capitol
Pierre, South Dakota 57501
(605) 773-4013

Director, Division of Securities
Debra M. Bollinger

Texas
[Business Opportunity Act]
Dorothy Wilson
Statutory Document Section
Secretary of State
P.O. Box 12887
Austin, Texas 78711
(512) 475-1769

Utah
[Business Opportunity Disclosure Act]
Francine A. Giani
Division of Consumer Protection
Utah Department of Commerce
160 East Three Hundred South
P.O. Box 146704
Salt Lake City, Utah 84114-6704
(801) 530-6601
FAX: (801) 530-6001

Virginia
Stephen W. Goolsby
Chief Examiner
State Corporation Commission
Ninth Floor
1300 E. Main Street
Richmond, Virginia 23219
(804) 371-9051

*Director, Division of Securities and
   Retail Franchising*
Ronald W. Thomas

Washington
Deborah Bortner
Acting Administrator
Department of Financial Institutions
Securities Division
P.O. Box 9033
Olympia, Washington 98507-9033
(360) 902-8760

Wisconsin
James R. Fischer
Franchising Administrator
Securities and Franchise Registration
Wisconsin Securities Commission
P.O. Box 1768
Madison, Wisconsin 53701
(608) 266-8559

Administrator, Division of Securities
Patrica Struck

Alberta Canada
R.J. (Rudy) Palovic
Director of Industry Standards
Department of Municipal Affairs
Housing and Consumer Affairs Division
16th Floor, Commerce Place
10155-102 Street
Edmonton, Alberta T5J 4L4
Canada
(403) 422-5201

Federal Trade Commission
Division of Marketing Practices
Bureau of Consumer Protection
Pennsylvania Avenue at 6th Street, NW
Washington, D.C. 20580
(202) 326-3128

EXHIBIT E

COPIES OF NOTICES OF NEGOTIATED SALES

NOTICES FILED IN CALIFORNIA IN THE LAST 12 MONTHS OF THE OFFERING
CIRCULAR FOR LUBE N LATTE FRANCHISE COMPANY LLC.

NONE

EXHIBIT F

CALIFORNIA APPENDIX

SECTION 31125 OF THE CALIFORNIA CORPORATIONS CODE (THE CALIFORNIA FRANCHISE INVESTMENT LAW) REQUIRES US TO GIVE YOU A DISCLOSURE DOCUMENT APPROVED BY THE COMMISSIONER OF CORPORATIONS BEFORE WE ASK YOU TO CONSIDER A MATERIAL MODIFICATION TO YOUR FRANCHISE AGREEMENT.

IN ADDITION TO THE INFORMATION REQUIRED BY ITEM 3. C., NEITHER THE FRANCHISOR, NOR ANY PERSON OR FRANCHISE BROKER IN ITEM 2 OF THE UFOC IS SUBJECT TO ANY CURRENTLY EFFECTIVE OF ANY NATIONAL SECURITIES ASSOCIATION OR NATIONAL SECURITIES EXCHANGE AS DEFINED IN THE SECURITIES EXCHANGE ACT OF 1934, 15 U.S.C.A. 78a et.; SUSPENDING OR EXPELLING SUCH PERSONS FROM MEMBERSHIP IN SUCH ASSOCIATION OR EXCHANGE.

CALIFORNIA BUSINESS AND PROFESSION CODE SECTIONS 20000 THROUGH 20043 PROVIDE RIGHTS TO THE FRANCHISEE CONCERNING TERMINATION OR NON-RENEWAL OF A FRANCHISE. IF THE FRANCHISE AGREEMENT CONTAINS A PROVISION THAT IS INCONSISTENT WITH THE LAW, THE LAW WILL CONTROL.

THE FRANCHISE AGREEMENT PROVIDES FOR TERMINATION UPON BANKRUPTCY. THIS PROVISION MAY NOT BE ENFORCEABLE UNDER FEDERAL BANKRUPTCY (11 U.S.C.A. SECTION 101 *ET. SEQ.*)

THE FRANCHISE AGREEMENT CONTAINS A COVENANT NOT TO COMPETE WHICH EXTENDS BEYOND THE TERMINATION OF THE FRANCHISE. THIS PROVISION MAY NOT BE ENFORCEABLE UNDER CALIFORNIA LAW.

THE FRANCHISE AGREEMENT REQUIRES BINDING ARBITRATION. THE ARBITRATION WILL OCCUR AT GRANTS PASS, OREGON WITH THE COURT COSTS AND REASONABLE ATTORNEY FEES BEING BORNE BY THE FRANCHISEE. THIS PROVISION MAY NOT BE ENFORCEABLE UNDER CALIFORNIA LAW.

THE FRANCHISE AGREEMENT REQUIRES APPLICATION OF THE LAWS OF OREGON. THIS PROVISION MAY NOT BE ENFORCEABLE UNDER CALIFORNIA LAW.

THE FRANCHISE AGREEMENT CONTAINS A LIQUIDATED DAMAGES CLAUSE. UNDER CALIFORNIA CIVIL CODE SECTION 1671, CERTAIN LIQUIDATED DAMAGES CLAUSES ARE UNENFORCEABLE.

YOU MUST SIGN A GENERAL RELEASE IF YOU RENEW OR TRANSFER YOUR FRANCHISE. CALIFORNIA CORPORATIONS CODE SECTION 31512 VOIDS A WAIVER OF YOUR RIGHTS UNDER THE FRANCHISE INVESTMENT LAW (CALIFORNIA CORPORATIONS CODE SECTIONS 31000 THROUGH 31516).

THE CALIFORNIA FRANCHISE INVESTMENT LAW REQUIRES THAT A COPY OF ALL PROPOSED AGREEMENTS RELATING TO THE SALE OF THE FRANCHISE BE DELIVERED TOGETHER WITH THE OFFERING CIRCULAR (CALIFORNIA CORPORATIONS CODE SECTIONS 31000 THROUGH 31516).

RECEIPT

THIS OFFERING CIRCULAR SUMMARIZES PROVISIONS OF THE FRANCHISE AGREEMENT AND OTHER INFORMATION IN PLAIN LANGUAGE. READ THIS OFFERING CIRCULAR AND ALL AGREEMENTS CAREFULLY.

IF LUBE N LATTE FRANCHISE COMPANY LLC OFFERS YOU A FRANCHISE, IT MUST PROVIDE THIS OFFERING CIRCULAR TO YOU BY THE EARLIEST OF:

(1) THE FIRST PERSONAL MEETING TO DISCUSS OUR FRANCHISE; OR

(2) TEN BUSINESS DAYS BEFORE SIGNING OF A BINDING AGREEMENT; OR

(3) TEN BUSINESS DAYS BEFORE ANY PAYMENT TO US.

YOU MUST ALSO RECEIVE A FRANCHISE AGREEMENT CONTAINING ALL MATERIAL TERMS AT LEAST FIVE BUSINESS DAYS BEFORE YOU SIGN ANY FRANCHISE AGREEMENT.

IF WE DO NOT DELIVER THIS OFFERING CIRCULAR ON TIME OR IF IT CONTAINS A FALSE OR MISLEADING STATEMENT, OR A MATERIAL OMISSION, A VIOLATION OF FEDERAL AND STATE LAW MAY HAVE OCCURRED AND SHOULD BE REPORTED TO THE FEDERAL TRADE COMMISSION, WASHINGTON, D.C. 20580.

We authorize The Commissioner of Corporations,State of California,3700 Wilshire Blvd.,Sixth Floor, Los Angeles, California 90010-3001 to receive service of process for Lube N Latte Franchise Company LLC., an Oregon Limited Liability Company

I have received a Uniform Franchise Offering Circular dated November 5, 1999. This Offering Circular included the following exhibits:

A. Financial Statements

B. Franchise Agreement

C. List of Franchisees

D. State Administrators and Agencies

E. Copies of Negotiated Sales

F. California Appendix

G. Receipt

Date _____   Franchisee _____

Franchisor's Copy

Appendix B

Franchise Agreement

Introduction

A sample document of an actual franchise agreement is included in this appendix to illustrate typical terms and restrictions contained in most service franchise agreements.

As either a potential franchisor or a prospective franchisee, acquaint yourself with the evaluation pointers discussed in Chapter 2, Learning about Franchise Documents, and other portions of this book, and make your own evaluation of the sample franchise agreement.

As a franchisor, be aware of your franchisee's needs, because if the franchisee fails, so will you. You will want to supply all the support necessary to ensure the possibility of your franchisee's success.

FRANCHISE AGREEMENT
Lube N Latte Franchise Company LLC
An Oregon Corporation
305 S.E. "G" Street
Grants Pass, Oregon 97526
(541) 479-4992

TABLE OF CONTENTS

* Note: In your actual document, page numbers must be filled in, but they have been omitted in this publication to avoid confusion with the book's page numbers.

LUBE N LATTE FRANCHISE CORPORATION

FRANCHISE AGREEMENT

THIS FRANCHISE AGREEMENT is entered into and effective this _____ day of
_____ 200__ by and between LUBE N LATTE FRANCHISE COMPANY,
LLC, an Oregon limited liability company, 305 S.E. "G" Street, Grants Pass, Oregon. 97526
(hereinafter called "we," "us," etc.) and _____
_____
_____ (hereinafter
called "you").

WHEREAS, you hereby acknowledge that this franchise agreement was accompanied by a
uniform franchise offering circular which you received at the earlier of: 1) the first personal
meeting with us; 2) 10 business days prior to the signing of any franchise agreement; or 3)
10 business days before any payment by you. In addition, you acknowledge receipt of this
franchise agreement containing all material terms at the time of the delivery of the uniform
franchise offering circular.

WHEREAS, you are desirous of obtaining a franchise for the purpose of joining a network
of independently owned professional businesses known as LUBE N LATTE shops which
will provide motor vehicle owners with oil changes, replacement of filters, wiper blades,
radiator caps, and various sensors, transmission maintenance services, differential maintenance services, radiator flushes, fuel injector cleaning, choke pull-offs and similar services
as well as offering the motor vehicle owner and the general public a variety of confectionery foods including freshly baked bagels, muffins, doughnuts, pastries, soup, snacks and
a complete selection of aromatic, gourmet coffees, espressos, teas, smoothies and other
drinks. The local franchisee may also perform state automotive inspections (smog checks)
where allowed by state law and approved by us at our sole discretion.

Each franchisee receives a comprehensive step-by-step customer-oriented training program
enabling him or her to provide the highest quality, most consistent, modern
coffee/espresso/latte/smoothie/confectionery cafe in conjunction with an attached, attractive, oil change and lubrication facility. The Franchisees are distinguished by the service
marks "Lube N Latte SM," and other trademarks, service marks, trade names, logotypes,
commercial symbols, unique forms and materials, a possible central telephone number, cen-
trally coordinated advertisements, low overhead operating expenses as well as our true commitment to customer service.

NOW THEREFORE, we and you, intending to be legally bound, for and in consideration of
the mutual covenants hereinafter following, do mutually covenant and agree:

Article 1. GRANT OF FRANCHISE LICENSE

1.1 License Rights. We hereby grant you the right, during the term of this agreement, to use the service marks "Lube N Latte SM." You are licensed to operate the franchised business under such name and such other trademarks, service marks, trade names, logotypes, commercial symbols and copyrights as we may designate from time to time solely for the purpose of identifying and advertising the franchised business. You are designated as a participant in our system while operating your franchise.

1.2 Single Site. We grant you the right to use and operate from a single, approved site under the service mark "Lube N Latte SM." Such business shall be conducted by you from your approved site which may feature our trademarks, service marks, trade names, logotypes or commercial symbols and approved materials within a designated exclusive territory. You have no right to delegate, franchise or subfranchise the right to use the marks or to authorize independent contractors or any third party with whom you transact business to use the marks.

1.3 Use of Marks. You shall use the marks in signage, business cards, stationery, promotional materials and advertising only in the form, manner and extent required or permitted as set forth herein, or by the Confidential Business Operation Manual or by us. You shall not use any of the marks as part of your trade or corporate name but may file appropriate notices required under an applicable fictitious or assumed name law (see also Paragraphs 3.2 and 3.3). You may not use our registered name in connection with the sale of an unauthorized product or service or in a manner not authorized in writing by us. You must notify us immediately upon learning about any infringement or challenge so we can take whatever action we deem is necessary. You must not directly or indirectly contest our right to our trademarks, trade secrets or business techniques that are part of our business (see also Paragraphs 3.4 and 3.5).

1.4 Trade Practices. You agree that we have the sole rights to certain trade practices pertaining to our business practices and procedures and that no goodwill associated with any of the trade practices shall inure to you. It is further agreed that the items of this trade practice constitute our trade secrets which are revealed to you in confidence and you will not, at any time during the term of this Agreement or any time thereafter, use or attempt to use the trade practices in connection with any other entity or business in which you have an interest, direct or indirect, nor shall you disclose, duplicate, reveal, sell or sublicense the trade practices or any part thereof or any way transfer any rights in the trade practices except as authorized by us.

1.5 Reservation of all Rights. We reserve all rights, except as precisely provided herein, including the right to offer or open additional company owned sites and additional franchises.

Article 2. EXCLUSIVE AREA OR TERRITORY

2.1 Exclusive Territorial Aspects and Minimums. The franchise territory is exclusive in that we will not designate or allow a franchise or a company-owned site to be physically opened and operated from an approved site location within your territory if you are in good standing under your franchise agreement. Each franchised territory includes an estimated number of at least 20,000 people. We will not open or operate company-owned or franchised center in a similar business under your trademark or a different trademark in your designated territory if you are in good standing in your territory.

2.2 Franchisee's Exclusive Territory. The Exclusive Territory boundaries shall be as follows:

Territory: _____

_____

_____

(SEE OUTLINED MAP OF YOUR TERRITORY BOUNDARIES ATTACHED AS SCHEDULE 1)

Article 3. TRADEMARKS, SERVICE MARKS, TRADE NAMES, LOGOTYPES, AND COMMERCIAL SYMBOLS

3.1 Federal Service Mark Registration. We grant to you the right to operate and use one location featuring the "Lube N Latte.SM" service mark as well as other service mark designs that we may develop for your business at your chosen site.

3.2 Restrictions on Use. You are restricted to use the name and service marks in your "d/b/a" in such a format and with such suffix as the law and/or we may from time to time designate including such designation as "Lube N Latte SM" of _____ (name of city, town or county where you are is located).

3.3 Fictitious Name Filing and Presently Effective Determinations of the Trademark Administrator. You are required to file the necessary fictitious name affidavit applicable to your county or state. You can not use our trademarks or service marks in your corporate or business trade name.

3.4 Service Mark Protection. We are not required to protect you against claims of infringement or unfair competition arising out of the use of our trademarks, service marks or logos or defend you in any legal action arising therefrom. However, we will take such action that we think is appropriate under the circumstances provided you have promptly notified us in writing of the facts of such claims or challenges and if you have used such service mark, trademarks or logos in strict accordance with the provisions of the franchise agreement and all rules, regulations, directives and procedures provided by us. We may take over the defense of the action at any time if we initially declined to take over the defense.

3.5 Control of Actions and Service Mark Usage. We alone have the sole right to control any legal actions or proceedings including settlements involving service mark infringement or unfair competition against you or against others using our marks without our permission. We may, at our sole discretion, prosecute or defend any infringements or unfair competition involving our marks or any other actions or proceedings which we deem necessary or desirable for the protection of our service marks, trademarks or logos and you agree not to contest our right, title or interest in such marks and logos. If it becomes advisable at any time in our discretion to modify or discontinue the use of any such logos, names or marks or institute the use of one or more additional or substituted names or marks, we will reimburse you for the reasonable cost of changing your necessary signs, stationery and ad copy. Any other costs shall be your obligation.

Article 4. CONFIDENTIAL BUSINESS OPERATION MANUAL

4.1 Confidential Business Operation Manual. You will be supplied with an Confidential Business Operation Manual which will contain specifications, instructions and specified parameters developed by us which are to be strictly followed.

4.2 Receipt Acknowledgment. You acknowledge receipt of copies of the Confidential Business Operation Manual and our systems and agree to abide by all policies and rules set forth therein and to require any employees to abide by all such policies and rules. The Manual and systems remain our property and all rights therein and must be returned to us promptly upon expiration or termination of this franchise agreement. The Manual and systems are considered to contain proprietary information and our trade secrets.

4.3 Additions and Modifications. We may, in our reasonable business judgment, add to or otherwise modify the Manual and systems, from time to time, for all franchisees uniformly and on a non-discriminatory basis, if possible, whenever we consider such additions or modifications desirable to improve or maintain the standards of our franchise system and to effectuate the efficient operation, or to protect or maintain the good will associated with the marks, or to meet the demands of competition.

Article 5. TRAINING

5.1 Training. We shall provide you and 1 designated person with training in operating the franchise as set forth in the following paragraphs and Article 8 to enable you to independently operate your franchised business.

5.2 Training Programs. We will provide initial, mandatory and optional training programs. We will conduct training programs at our designated training facilities in various locations and at various times to be named by us.

5.3 Initial Training. Within 60 days of your schedule opening, we will provide to you and 1 acceptable designated person an initial training period of 15 business days at Grants Pass, Oregon, or a designated Lube N Latte location for 15 business days which will consist of at least 8 hours per day (including 1 hour for lunch) for 120 hours prior to the opening of the franchise and a minimum of 7 business days to a maximum 15 business days (56 hours to 120 hours) at your location upon your opening as further specified in Article 8. The initial training will cover all aspects of the franchise operation and will include on-site training and some classroom training.

5.4 Failure to Complete Initial Training or Open. If you and your designated manager fail to complete the initial training program to our satisfaction or to open by your scheduled opening date after training, we may terminate this agreement.

5.5 Training Program Completion. It is at our sole discretion as to whether or not you and/or your designated manager have successfully completed a training program.

5.6 Mandatory and Optional Training Programs. We, at our discretion, will also provide from time to time mandatory and optional training programs on selling techniques, services, preferred suppliers, management skills, subscriber service standards and other aspects of business operations which we believe are useful to franchisees. These programs are conducted for various lengths of time and at various locations selected by us. Certain programs will be offered at no charge, while others may require a fee. All franchisees and new assignees must attend initial training in Grants Pass, Oregon, or designated location) (see also Paragraph 8.11).

5.7 Additional and Special Training. Additional, mandatory, optional or special training may be requested by you. If you request additional or special training, and we agree, a charge for the special training may be required.

5.8 Franchisor's Initial Training Expenses. We provide and pay only for the training instructors, facilities and training material in connection with our initial training programs.

5.9 Franchisee Training Expenses. You must pay all expenses incurred by you, your designated manager and your employees in connection with all training programs including, without limitation, the cost of travel, entertainment, room, board and wages for the duration of all training programs.

Article 6. FRANCHISEE'S FEES AND OTHER PAYMENTS

6.1 Initial Franchise Fee. You will pay us a uniform, non-refundable Initial franchise fee of $35,000 payable upon signing the Franchise Agreement.

6.2 Monthly Service Fee and Minimum Payment. In consideration of the franchise granted, you are required to pay us a continuing Monthly Service Fee of 3% of your gross monthly sales for each month or portion thereof during the term of the franchise agreement. The Monthly Service Fee is due and payable by the 10th calendar day after the end of the previous month based on Gross Sales for the previous month. The Monthly Service Fee is uniform and non-refundable for all franchisees.

6.3 Gross Sales Defined. The term "gross sales" is defined to include all sums or things of value received by you in and from your business from all sales of services, goods, and products whether for cash, check, credit, barter or otherwise without reserve or deduction for inability or failure to collect same including, without limitation, such sales and services where the orders thereof originated at or accepted by you at one location but delivered or performance thereof made from or at any other location. Gross sales do not include refunds to customers or the amount of any sales taxes or any similar taxes collected from subscribers to be paid to any federal, state or local taxing authority. All such items, including non-collectible accounts which are claimed as deductions to gross sales, must be supported by proper documentation.

6.4 Local Advertising and Possible Cooperatives. You are also required to spend a minimum sum equal to 3% of your monthly gross sales on local advertising enhancing the reputation of your service on a local level. All local advertising must be approved by us. You are required to substantiate the minimum advertising required by supplying such written information as we may require on a weekly, monthly, quarterly, annual or other basis. We, at our sole discretion, may establish areas of local or regional cooperative advertising and all franchisees are required to become active members with maximum contributions determined by a majority vote of the cooperative members but in no event less than 3% of your monthly gross sales. Once an advertising cooperative is established, all participating franchisees will contribute their 3% local advertising fee to the cooperative fund as managed by at least a person chosen by each cooperative with our approval. A regional cooperative must have a minimum of two (2) franchisees at all times in order to qualify for approval as a cooperative by us.

All advertising by you shall first be approved by us in writing, and our consent will not be unreasonably withheld. Failure to participate in such cooperative advertising shall be deemed cause for termination.

6.5 Transfer Fee. You shall be required to pay a non-refundable transfer fee (except where a transfer is to your spouse, your adult child [18 years or older], or your corporation or entity in which you own the majority of stock or interest), of $5,000 upon any assignment, sale, or transfer of the franchise to cover our costs of research, administration and, where we deem necessary, the cost of training the new franchisee in our system. This transfer fee may be increased to reflect increases in the local applicable Consumer Price Index.

6.6 Renewal Fee. The term of the franchise commences from the date the franchise agreement is executed for a ten (10) year period. The renewal fee is $1,000 for each renewal period. You can renew for unlimited additional periods of ten (10) years each providing you are not in default or in violation of the franchise agreement and upon execution of our then-current franchise agreement. under the terms in effect at that time including new royalty rates, advertising fees, etc., with the exception that the length of term or renewal term shall not change nor shall your territory change without your consent.

6.7 Yellow Page Advertising by Franchisee. In addition to spending 3% of your gross monthly sales on local or cooperative advertising, each franchisee may be required, at our option, to have a local advertising listing in the yellow pages of your dominant telephone book in your territory according to our specifications as to copy and size, which shall be a minimum of a single column ad measuring approximately one and one-half inches by one and three quarter inches in such directory.

6.8 Training Expenses and Graduation. We will conduct training programs at our designated training facilities in various locations at various times to be designated by us including:

A. **Initial And Mandatory Training Expenses:** We will provide initial and Mandatory training programs. We provide and pay only for the training instructors, facilities and training material in connection with our initial and mandatory training programs. You are required to pay all personal expenses for yourself and/or your designees including travel, meals and lodging (see Paragraph 5.6 above).

B. **Special or Additional Training Program Expenses:** Special or additional training programs may be implemented by us at the special request of you, but at our sole discretion, to help you effectively succeed in the franchised business where we deem a particular franchisee or franchisees are in need of such training. The expenses for special or additional training programs will be borne by you including all expenses for instructors, facilities and training manuals in addition to you, or your designees's personal expenses including travel, meals or lodging. These expenses will not be uniform, but will vary according to your location or in relation to the training facilities and other variables.

6.9 Audit and Late Payment Fee. The franchise agreement grants us the right to verify the information contained in your reports to us by inspecting and auditing your records. If any such inspection or audit discloses a deficiency in payments exceeding 2% due to us under the franchise agreement, you must immediately pay the deficiency and you must also pay travel, lodging, meals, salaries and reasonable professional service fees and other expenses of the inspecting or auditing personnel. Such payments are not refundable under any circumstances. If any such inspection or audit discloses an overpayment, we will credit the overpayment to your account. Any payment owed to us but not paid when due bears interest at a rate equal to the maximum contract rate allowed by the governing state law.

6.10 Delinquent Payments and Fees. Any payment or fee not received on time payable from you to us shall bear interest at the rate equal to the maximum contract rate allowed by governing state law from the date due until the date received by us.

6.11 Insurance. At all times during the term of the franchise agreement, you shall maintain in effect a policy or policies of insurance naming us as an additional insured on the face of each policy at your sole cost and expense subject to change from time to time including:

1. Professional public liability policy that includes comprehensive general liability, errors and omissions coverages in the amount of $1,000,000 per occurrence.

2. Any additional insurance including worker's compensation insurance and unemployment compensation for any employees you may choose to hire.

3. All insurance coverages required by city, county, state or federal agencies.

6.12 Acceptable Insurance Companies. All insurance shall be with insurers acceptable to us. Insurance amounts may be changed from time to time upon receipt of written demand from us. All policies of insurance shall be renewed timely and copies of all policies and certificates together with evidence of payment of premiums shall be delivered to us at least 30 days prior to the expiration of such policies by certified mail or by hand delivery with receipt.

6.13 Customer Disputes. You shall use your best efforts to resolve satisfactorily any subscriber disputes and refund any amounts disputed by the subscriber for services that the subscriber deems unsatisfactory.

6.14 Reports, Agencies, and Organizations. You are also required to compile and report certain information to us as required by our written directives or the Confidential Business Operation Manual (see also Paragraph 7.11). You also must maintain any membership and/or filing requirements with agencies and organizations necessary to enable your continued functioning as a franchisee. You must file duplicate copies of reports with us when filed with any agency or organization.

6.15 Monthly Financial Statements. You are required to submit monthly profit and loss statements to us. You must submit to us, no later than the 10th day of each month during the term of the franchise agreement, a monthly profit and loss statement on forms prescribed by us accurately reflecting all gross sales during the preceding month and such other data and information regarding the operation of the franchised business as we may require.

6.16 Annual Financial Statements. Annually within 60 days after the close of your fiscal year, you are required to submit to us an income and expense statement and a balance sheet for your business as it stands at the end of the fiscal year, setting forth in each case corresponding figures in comparative form for the preceding year and compiled by you or by your accountant. All statements must be in reasonable detail and in accordance with generally accepted accounting practices and accompanied by a declaration from you that same are true and correct to the best of your knowledge. We will supply you with reports of information required by us each year for completion by you.

6.17 Franchisee's Tax Returns. Annually within 60 days after the close of your fiscal year, you are required to submit to us a copy of your federal and state tax returns and all amendments thereto prepared for the franchised business and a letter from you or your accountant stating as applicable whether or not (1) all payroll tax returns have been filed and payroll taxes paid to the end of the fiscal period, (2) all federal income tax returns have been filed and taxes paid, and (3) all state income tax returns have been filed and any payments due have been paid.

6.18 Cost of Accounting Services. The cost of accounting services are your responsibility and may vary substantially depending upon your size and location, but the requirements are imposed uniformly on all franchisees.

Article 7. OBLIGATIONS OF FRANCHISEE

Your obligations include:

7.1 Franchisee Services. You shall render the services of selling motor vehicle owners with oil changes, replacement of filters, wiper blades, radiator caps, and various sensors, transmission maintenance services, differential maintenance services, radiator flushes, fuel injector cleaning, choke pull-offs and similar services as well as offering the motor vehicle owner and the general public a variety of confectionery foods including freshly baked bagels, muffins, doughnuts, pastries, soup, snacks and a complete selection of aromatic, gourmet coffees, espressos, teas, smoothies and other drinks and such other services and products as specified in this franchise agreement, Confidential Business Operation Manual and by our written directives. You shall offer services and products to the general public, shall maintain the highest professional and ethical standards, shall observe any preferred suppliers program requirements, and shall conduct no other business under our marks without our consent.

7.2 Full Time Effort. You are obligated to devote your best efforts and dedicate a minimum of 25 hours per week to the management of the franchised business unless a designated manager is approved and accepted by us in writing. Corporate or partnership franchisees must designate an individual upon whom we may rely for the personal and direct management of the franchised business.

7.3 Advertising Approvals. You shall not permit any advertising to be published unless such material is furnished by or approved by us in writing. Any advertising request will be expedited by us within 10 days. We do not currently grant you the right to use the name of a public figure or celebrity in your promotional efforts or advertising.

7.4 Employees. If you hire employees, you shall use your best efforts to properly train or procure qualified and competent personnel in keeping with the standards established by us through your Confidential Business Operation Manual and our periodic directives, including the standards set for all services and products sold by you.

7.5 Central Telephone Number. If required by the us, you will be required to use a single central telephone number for the franchised business. The central telephone number would be maintained by us for your support, your customer's support and customer leads would be dispersed by us to the appropriate franchise territory.

7.6 Administrative Codes. You and your employees shall adhere to any and all administrative codes at all times when serving a customer.

7.7 Quality Control and Purchases from Franchisor. You shall operate the franchised business in accordance with our standards of quality, production, appearance, cleanliness and service as prescribed by us and the Confidential Business Operation Manual. You may be required to purchase certain proprietary marketing materials from us.

7.8 Customer Service Policies. You shall conform to our customer service policies as set forth in the Confidential Business Operation Manual or as may be changed from time to time by us.

7.9 Customer Complaints. Any complaints from dissatisfied customers shall receive prompt attention. Whenever possible, you will initiate contact within 24 hours after a complaint is received. Should you be unable to equitably resolve the complaint within 7 days after the complaint, you will contact us for assistance in handling the complaint.

7.10 Permits and Licenses. You shall maintain all permits and licenses required for the operation of the franchised business.

7.11 Records and Reports. You shall maintain all county, state and federal records and reports and file them with the appropriate agency and provide copies of same to us. Also, all records and reports including monthly statements of sales, costs of operation, suppliers, and such records and reports as are required in this agreement and by the Confidential Business Operation Manual must be filed expeditiously with us.

7.12 Annual Conventions. Each year an annual franchisee convention may be held to provide additional and current updates for the benefit of the franchisees and to award franchisees who have operated exceptional franchises. Franchisee attendance is mandatory at all annual conventions..

7.13 Agreement Not to Compete. You agree that during the term of this agreement or any extension hereof you will not compete with us. You further agree that for 2 years after the termination hereof, you will not, without our prior written consent, either directly or indirectly as principal, agent, servant or otherwise carry on or engage in or have a financial interest in, the same or similar business as in this agreement at your location or within a 10 mile radius from any other company owned outlet or one of our franchisees. You acknowledge and agree that the damage caused to us by your violation of this Section shall constitute irreparable injury and accordingly, acknowledge and agree that we may enforce this section by applying for a temporary and/or permanent restraining order, temporary and/or permanent injunction and any such other legal or equitable relief as may be appropriate.

7.14 Adherence to Franchisor's Policies and Procedures. It is understood and agreed that a material part of our consideration granting your license to you, without which we would not execute this agreement, is that you agree to adhere strictly to the specifications, methods; practices and systems established by us in our matters and written directives for the management, marketing and operation of the franchised business.

7.15 Timely Fees Payable and Site Development. You are required to pay all fees herein and develop your site in a timely manner.

7.16 Alternate Supplier Qualifications. In the event that you desire to purchase your required equipment and materials from someone other than us or our approved suppliers, you must submit a complete description of the history and credit rating of the supplier and a description of such items together with specifications and tests which will prove to us, at our satisfaction, that the equipment and materials are of equal or superior quality to those which we or our designated supplier may offer for sale to you at reasonable prices (see also Paragraph 9.5).

7.17 Independent Access. You agree that we will have independent access to all information and data generated by you and your computer.

Article 8. OBLIGATIONS OF FRANCHISOR

Our obligations prior to opening or shortly thereafter of the franchised business are:

8.1 Territorial and Site Assistance. We will assist you in obtaining the necessary information and assist you in the selection of your base site within the territory. The final selection is your primary responsibility subject to our approval of your choice.

8.2 Confidential Business Operation Manual. We will loan you one set of the Confidential Operations, Manual covering our operational procedures consisting of suggested marketing tool descriptions, market identification and penetration, maintenance and follow up programs, suggested media, accounting procedures, hiring and training, publicity and subscriber services, among others.

8.3 Franchisee Training. It is our obligation, within 60 days before your opening, to provide you and 1 acceptable designated person approved by us, an initial training period of at least 15 business days which will consist of at least 8 hours per day (including one hour for lunch) at Grants Pass, Oregon or a designated Lube N Latte location. Upon your opening, we will provide a minimum of 7 business days to a maximum of 15 business days (if we deem additional 8 days are necessary) of on site training at your location. The initial training will cover all aspects of the franchise operation including but not limited to administration, marketing and operation and will include classroom, and some on-site training (see Paragraph 5.3 above).

8.4 List of Supplies and Equipment and Negotiations of Supply Agreements. We will provide you with a detailed list of all necessary equipment, supplies and inventory and negotiate oil supply and equipment reimbursement on your behalf.

8.5 Site and Floor Plans; Evaluation and Renderings. We will provide you with site and floor plans and elevation and Renderings at an additional cost which at this time is $5,000.

The obligations performed by us during the operation of your business are:

8.6 Informational Updates. We will provide service and product information updates regarding our industry which we feel are necessary to your operation of your franchise as such information becomes available to us.

8.7 Franchisor Non-Technical Consultations. We will provide, according to the extent required by us in our sole judgment, a continuing advisory service which shall include consultation on promotional, business or operation's problems, an analysis of your services, sales, marketing and financial data at times and places and, to the extent designated by us partly based on required reports from each franchisee regarding such areas as advertising performed and results thereof, a description and number of leads, completed services rendered, follow-up services required and type of errors, etc., following the opening of your LUBE N LATTE shop.

8.8 Technician Support. If you request it, we will supply a 1-800 number operated by a technician to assist you with technical lube and coffee business support as requested by you. The cost of this service shall be paid by us for the first 12 months after you open. If you request technical assistance after the first 12 months, You must pay a nominal cost of $100 per year for this service subject to annual increases in the local Consumer Price Index (CPI).

8.9 Advertising Materials. We will provide you with all existing and available advertising slicks (camera ready art) for copying for all E-mail, Internet, newspaper and direct mail advertising or similar advertising. Costs of copies of such advertising slicks (camera ready) and similar items shall be at your expense and credited to your local advertising fee obligation.

8.10 Lube and Coffee Business Maintenance Updates. We will update you on any changes in the lube and coffee industry that we feel are important to your operation and you agree to update your operation accordingly.

8.11 Subsequent Franchisor Training. We may provide subsequent training classes, both mandatory and non-mandatory to you, offered from time to time with you also required to pay all costs of travel, lodging and subsistence unless any such mandatory training classes exceed two (2) per calendar year wherein we shall then reimburse you for the air fare of the required attendee. If you request special training, and we agree, a charge for the instructor may be added (see also Paragraph 5.6 above).

8.12 Newsletter. We, at our discretion, will provide you with monthly newsletters regarding current industry trends and marketing updates as well as business recognition.

8.13 Annual One Week Review Course. We will conduct a yearly one week review course at your facility and you agree to assist us in our on site review of your business operation.

Article 9. RESTRICTIONS ON GOODS AND SERVICES OFFERED BY FRANCHISEE

9.1 Restrictions. You may sell or offer for sale to the public only services and goods of the kind and quality which comply with the reasonable standards designated in the Confidential Business Operation Manual or directives in writing provided by us from time to time. You may not use our name, trademarks, service marks, trade names, logotypes or commercial symbols in any business other than the franchised business. All products and services used or offered must be from an approved vendor (see Articles 1 and 7 above).

9.2 · Required Service Orders and Special Equipment, Software and Hardware. You agree o to purchase numerically numbered Lube N Latte Service Orders from our designated supplier for use at your oil Change and Service Center. You will be required to purchase or lease, at your sole expense, a computer lube operation system from Innovative Control Systems (ICS) located in Pennsylvania or the subsequent supplier of our choice. A list of software, hardware and cash register requirements is attached as Schedule 1, Part 2 to this Franchise Agreement. Support and updates are required to be purchased by you with support included in your updates. You also will be required to purchase such software and other equipment as we reasonably deems necessary from designated suppliers and to pay such reasonable fees and charges as may be appropriate in connection therewith including $500 per year (subject to competitive price increases) in software support and a 3 year prevailing maintenance agreement on the hardware subject to competitive increases. You agree that we will have independent access to all information and data generated on computer programs and hardware in order to evaluate sales and services provided to the consumer and costs associated with your business. You also are required to purchase an electric cash register from our designated supplier listed in Schedule 1, Part 2 attached to this Franchise Agreement.

9.3 Latte Furniture, Equipment, Fixtures, Glasswares, etc. All Latte furniture, fixtures, equipment, glassware and similar items must be purchased from us or our designated supplier.

9.4 Required Quality. Each of the goods and services supplied by you to the public are subject to the quality standards necessary to uphold the reputation and public image of the Lube N Latte system. All goods, services, supplies, fixtures, equipment, inventory and real estate used to serve the public must meet the standards as set forth in the Confidential Business Operation Manual and other written publications and as subject to change from time to time. You may only offer such services and sell such products as may be designed by us from time to time in writing in order to be consistent with our theme.

9.5 Approved Suppliers and Advertising. You may only offer such services and sell such products as may be designed by us from time to time in writing in order to be consistent with our theme. You will be supplied with a Confidential Business Operation Manual and/or written directive which will contain specifications and parameters developed by us and which are to be strictly followed.

We reserve the right to designate or consent to the content, themes, materials and placement of all advertising programs by you. All such advertising shall be submitted to us for our approval at least five business days prior to publication unless specifically waived in writing by us as to each particular ad or advertising campaign.

You will be supplied with our list of suggested and preferred suppliers by us, which may be updated by us from time to time. We do not request nor will we accept any compensation from any of our suggested suppliers.

We evaluate, approve or disapprove suppliers based on suppliers who demonstrate to us with continued reasonable satisfaction: (1) an ability to meet our standards and specifications, (2) possess adequate quality control and the capacity to supply our franchisees' needs promptly and reliably, and (3) who have been approved by us in our manuals or otherwise in writing. You are required to submit to us a written request to approve a proposed supplier together with such information as we may reasonably require including financials, total sales figures, written references, etc. We also reserve the right to require that our representative be permitted to inspect the suppliers' facilities and that samples from the supplier be delivered for our evaluation and testing either to us or to an independent testing facility designated by us. A charge not to exceed the reasonable cost of the evaluation and testing is required to be paid by the franchisee whether or not the supplier is approved. We will notify you in writing of our approval or disapproval of the proposed supplier and the criteria for our approval and disapproval within 10 days after our receipt of your request and completion of the evaluation and testing.

To insure uniformity and quality in all units, you are required to purchase supplies, materials and products including food an beverages or components thereof that are equal to or exceed the specifications established by us. All Lube N Latte service centers must meet the construction and appearance as well as equipment standards set forth in the then-current Confidential Business Operation Manual or written our written directives, however, you are not required to have construction services performed by any specific entity. Specifications set forth may include minimum standards for building size and style, sign(s), equipment types, products including food and beverages sold, inventory, quality, delivery, performance, warranties, logo and trademark design and compliance, appearance and other restrictions. Such specifications are part of the Confidential Business Operation Manual or written directives which are issued to the you and are subject to change from time to time. You must promptly comply with all such changes. On occasion, an affiliated entity may be an approved supplier of items relating to the operation of the franchise business such as products, materials, services, supplies, equipment and facilities. You are not required to purchase such items from an affiliate, if another supplier is approved by us, except the required purchases by the Franchisee of "Service Orders" and specified hardware and software items with information relating to all such required purchases being contained in this agreement and/or the Confidential Business Operation Manual or our subsequent written directives.

You agree that we have the right to sample, review or test all equipment, products (food, beverage, oil or otherwise), materials and supplies to determine compliance with our standards and conformity (as well as other factors such as advertising contributions, marketing assistance, and equipment loan arrangements). Those items failing to meet such standards will be disapproved and it will be your responsibility to replace such items with those meeting our requirements and standards. Our approval of your equipment, products, materials and supplies will not be unreasonably withheld, however, we reserve the right to require that you purchase and use specific brand name items to be used in the operation of the franchise center (although you are free to purchase such items from sources identified by you and approved by us as meeting our reasonable requirements) to obtain quality control, uniformity, and marketing and advertising contribution benefits. Where we have designated an approved brand name supplier and such supplier has agreed to make advertising contributions and/or other payments with respect to such approved product or service conditioned on use, sales or otherwise by us or you, all such payments by such approved brand name supplier are generally made to us or an entity appointed by us and shall be spent by us or such entity provided that any expenditure or other handling of such payments must be consistent with any restrictions or conditions imposed by such approved brand name supplier. We reserve the right to require that all products used by you meet our quality standards and other reasonable requirements.

9.6 Menu Items and Hours of Operation. You are required to prepare and serve only items on the menu as approved by us in advanced in writing. You shall submit in writing to us for approval all contemplated menu changes and additions to or deletions from the items presently approved for sale. All café menu items will be formulated, designed and enhanced by us. You may create and test new beverage items with our prior approval. You shall adequate stock the cafe with sufficient supplies of approved food and beverages and comply with all applicable health and sanitation ordinances.. You are required to operate the cafe facilities continuously from 6 A.M. to 6 P.M. minimum (minimum 7 A.M. to 5 P.M. closing on Saturday and minimum 9 A.M. to 4 P.M. on Sunday is permissible) seven (7) days per week unless different hours have been approved by us. (Franchise Agreement.) You are required to operate the Lube facility from Monday through Friday a minimum of 8 A.M. to 6 P.M. with 8 A.M. to 6 P.M.

on Saturdays and 9 A.M. to 4 P.M. on Sundays. Depending on your location, we set the days and hours of operation which may vary from location to location and from time to time.

9.7 Your Prices. All prices are set by you and include appropriate sales tax on each item although we may, from time to time, suggest certain prices so as to assist you in securing the proper price structure for its products.

9.8 Vending Machines. Vending machines or other operated machines are permitted only with our prior written consent.

Article 10. TERM

10.1 Term. The initial term of the franchise agreement is 10 years from the date of execution of this agreement.

Article 11. RENEWAL, TERMINATION, REPURCHASE, MODIFICATION AND ASSIGNMENT OF THE FRANCHISE AGREEMENT AND RELATED INFORMATION

11.1 Renewal. The franchise agreement provides for unlimited additional renewal by execution of a new franchise agreement at the end of the initial 10-year term for additional 10 year periods providing: (1) you are not in default or in violation of the franchise agreement or any other agreement with us; and, (2) upon execution of the then current franchise agreement, or if no current agreement is in effect, extension of the last agreement executed by the parties within the applicable state, under the terms in effect at that time including new royalty rates, advertising fees, etcetera, with the exception that the length of term or renewal terms shall not change nor your territory. The renewal fee charged to you by us is $1,000.

11.2 Termination by Franchisee. You may terminate the franchise agreement by obtaining our written consent, which consent we are not obligated to give. You may terminate the franchise agreement for good cause only if we have materially breached the franchise agreement, provided that, prior to your terminating the franchise agreement for good cause, you must serve a written notice of default upon us specifying the grounds for default and granting us a reasonable opportunity, but in no case less than thirty (30) days in which to cure the default or in which to commence diligent efforts to cure the default (if the default cannot reasonably be expected to be cured within thirty (30) days).

11.3 Franchisor's Termination Rights After Failure to Cure. The conditions under which we may terminate, subject to a thirty (30) day notice to cure, unless otherwise specified include:

1. The attachment of any involuntary lien in the sum of $1,000.00 or more upon any of your business assets or property, which lien is not promptly removed.

2. Conduct of the franchised business in such a manner so as to affect materially and adversely your goodwill or reputation or your products and services.

3 Default by you of any provision of the franchise agreement or under any other agreement between you and us not subject to earlier termination as agreed by the parties.

4. Any purported assignment, transfer, or sublicense of the franchise, or any right hereunder, without our prior written consent.

5. Failure to make timely payment to us of any and all sums payable to us pursuant to the franchise agreement after five (5) days' written notice of such failure to pay.

6. Failure to make timely payments upon any obligation of you upon which we are acting as a guarantor or default upon or a breach of any provision of any promissory note or other evidence of indebtedness or any agreement relating thereto.

7. Failure to cure a default under the franchise agreement, within ten (10) business days after receipt of notice thereof, which default materially impairs the goodwill associated with our trade names, trademarks, service marks, logotypes or other commercial symbols.

8. Failure to pay for or conduct any audit required by us or failure to secure and maintain the required insurance, including but not limited to public liability and worker's compensation insurance after ten (10) days' written notice requiring such deficiency to be cured.

9. Failure to supply reports on gross sales receipts and business activities or other information required in such reports, including but not limited to, advertising performed and results thereof, description and number of leads.

10. Failure to use the techniques, training, and methods promulgated by our manuals or attend seminar sessions required by us which are limited to one required session per calendar year.

11. Failure to put your full efforts into the franchised business of at least 20 hours per week or, in your excused absence, to have the franchised business managed by someone who has the proper training and aptitude in the procedures and systems as prescribed by us.

12. Failure to keep true and accurate business records and books in accordance with our procedures or failure to make available those items deemed necessary for inspection or provide federal and state income tax returns as requested by us or upon discovery of a deficit of two percent (2%) or more in any audit of your business.

13. Failure to maintain the standards of good conduct and appearance designated by us for the success of the franchise in order to assure continuity of quality, appearance and professionalism.

14. Failure to maintain confidential any information designated as confidential by us.

15. Operating any business center from a permanent base point location other than the location address approved herein by us.

16. Personally operating in another franchisee's territory after notice to cease and desist.

17. Failure to participate in any approved cooperative advertising group or to advertise in the dominant telephone directory in your territory.

18. Failure to participate in any approved cooperative advertising group or to advertise in the dominant telephone directory in your territory.

19. Failure to pass our training or to open the business within the scheduled time after completing training and and securing an approved location.

11.4 Franchisor's Termination Rights Without Notice. If during the period in which the franchise is in effect, there occurs any of the following events which is relevant to the franchise, immediate notice of termination without an opportunity to cure, shall be deemed reasonable:

1. Insolvent or all or a substantial part of the assets thereof are assigned to or for the benefit of any creditor, or you admit your inability to pay your debts as they become due;

2. You abandon the franchise by failing to operate the business for 5 consecutive days during which time are required to operate the business under the terms of the under the facts to conclude that you do not intend to continue to operate the franchise, unless such failure is due to fire, flood, earthquake or other similar causes beyond your control;

3. We and you agree in writing to terminate the franchise;

4. You make any material misrepresentations relating to the acquisition or operation of the franchise or you engage in conduct which reflects materially and unfavorably upon the operation and reputation of the franchise system;

5. You fail, for a period of 10 days after notification of noncompliance, to comply with any federal, state or local law or regulation applicable to the operation of the franchise;

6. You, after curing any failure in accordance with Article 11.3, above, engage in the same conduct or noncompliance whether or not such conduct or noncompliance is corrected after notice.

7. You repeatedly fail to comply with one or more requirements of the franchise agreement whether or not corrected after notice;

8. The franchise business or business premises of the franchise are seized, taken over or foreclosed by a governmental official in the exercise of his duties, or seized, taken over or foreclosed by a creditor, lienholder or lessor, provided that a final judgment against you remains unsatisfied for thirty (30) days (unless supersedes or other appeal bond has been filed); or a levy of execution has been made upon the license granted by the franchise agreement or upon any property used in the franchised business, and it is not discharged within five (5) days of such levy;

9. You are convicted of a felony or any other criminal misconduct which is relevant to the operation of the franchise;

10. You fail to pay any franchise fees or other amounts due to us or our affiliate within five (5) days after receiving written notice that such fees are overdue;

11. We make a reasonable determination that continued operation of the franchise by you will result in an imminent danger to public health or safety.

11.5 Obligations of Franchisee After Termination. In the event of termination of the franchise agreement for any reason:

1. You lose all rights to all fees paid and may no longer use our trademarks, service marks, trade name, copyrights, systems, manuals, displays, your telephone numbers or any other property connected with the franchise.

2. You must immediately cease use of all trade names, systems, service marks, trademarks, training manuals, and other proprietary property of ours which must be returned to us immediately upon written notice.

3. We have the right to enter the premises of the franchised location and to recover and remove training material and all other proprietary property of ours.

4. Any amounts due or owing to us by you including unpaid royalties and fees remaining on the unexpired portion of your franchise agreement when terminated by you without our permission shall be paid immediately.

5. You, in executing the franchise agreement, agree to assign all right, title and interest to all of your business telephone numbers upon termination, for any reason, of your franchise and to execute any further documents or instruments or instructions necessary to further effect such transfer.

6. You, after termination of the franchise agreement, will have no interest in the franchised business and all rights and privileges are terminated.

7. All Confidential Manuals and Systems must be returned to us by you within 24 hours after notice.

8. You will abide by the non-compete provisions in Paragraph 7.13.

11.6 Franchisor's Right of First Refusal. We have the right of first refusal exercisable within thirty (30) days after receipt of notice by us from you of the proposed sale or assignment, in which we may repurchase the franchise at any time that you attempt to transfer to any other person or entity except a qualified spouse or child. This also includes a transfer by will or intestate upon the death of a sole proprietorship, partner or shareholder. Any attempt to transfer the assets and/or business without assigning the franchise agreement to the potential purchaser shall constitute a default and a breach of the franchise agreement.

The purchase price is determined by the amount of a bona fide offer from a third party in the event of a sale or transfer. Such repurchase price will recognize goodwill and other intangibles associated with the normal sale of a going business if same is included in the bona fide offer of a third party.

On any termination due to your default or breach of the Franchise Agreement or an attempted cancellation by you, we shall have the right, at our option, for thirty (30) days after such termination, to purchase your interest in all or a portion of equipment, inventory, supplies or fixtures at a purchase price equal to the fair market value of such items. If the parties do not agree to any such purchase price within such thirty (30) day period, such prices shall be set by an independent appraiser designated by us.

11.7 Provisions of Applicable Law. The provisions herein shall be subordinated to and conformed with the provisions of any valid applicable law or regulation affording you any more favorable rights or remedies.

11.8 Franchisee Assignment. You may not sell, assign or transfer, in whole or in part, your interest in the franchise agreement without first obtaining our written consent, which consent will not be unreasonably withheld subject to our rights set forth herein. We will require, as a condition to any transfer, that you deliver to us the complete financial statements of the proposed transferee, and make payment in full for all obligations outstanding or accruing to us through the date of such sale, assignment or transfer. You must pay us a transfer fee (Paragraph 6.6) and the transferee (new Franchisee) must assume your complete obligations under the franchise agreement and complete our training as a condition precedent to our approval. The new Franchisee's net worth must be sufficient enough, in our sole discretion, to pay all current liabilities out of current assets and to have a reserve necessary for the continued operation of the franchise.

11.9 Transfer of Franchise Agreement and Death of Franchisee. A transfer or attempt to transfer your interest in this franchise agreement, without our written consent and the payment of the transfer fee, constitutes abandonment of this franchise agreement by you. If you, a sole proprietor, or a partner or a shareholder of a corporation dies, your estate may sell the franchise to a transferee acceptable to us within three (3) months after the death of the original franchisee. If the franchise is stalled in probate for more than three (3) months, we have the right to place our personnel in your area and all necessary support systems required to maintain the franchise as we deem necessary on a cost plus twenty percent (20%) basis to the deceased franchisee's estate.

11.10 Resignation, Removal, Non-Performance. The resignation, removal, non-performance, death or permanent disability of you or your designated manager is treated as a proposed assignment by you of your rights and obligations, and you or your estate must promptly request approval of a replacement franchisee or designated manager.

11.11 Current Standards on Transfer. The purchaser or assignee will be required to update the franchised business to our then current standards and will be required to fulfill all training and testing requirements at the assignee's or purchaser's expense for travel, lodging and meals. The new owners may be required to participate in our training program.

11.12 Assignment by Franchisor. This franchise agreement may be assigned in whole or in part by us without your consent or prior approval and such assignment shall not modify or diminish your obligations hereunder.

Article 12. CONFLICTS OF INTEREST

12.1 Affiliations. To maintain our confidentiality of marketing and operational plans and programs, commission rates and other information, you shall not during the term of this agreement (1) be a member of, or otherwise be associated with, any consortium or other organization engaged, directly or indirectly, in the purchase or arranging for the purchase of a competing business for or on behalf of its members, or (2) personally, directly or indirectly or through a family member, partner or affiliate, maintain any ownership or leasehold interest in or business affiliation with any franchise system other than our franchise operated under a direct franchise agreement from us, without our prior written consent, which consent may be withheld at our discretion with or without cause, or (3) authorize or allow independent contractors or any third party with whom you transact business to use or have access to our confidential marketing and operational plans and programs, without our prior written consent, which consent may be withheld with or without cause. However, you may be a member of, or otherwise be associated with trade associations or an association among you and us.

12.2 Confidentiality. You shall keep strictly confidential our marketing and operational plans and programs, suggested pricing, commission rates, proprietary materials or information access, retrieval, storage and management systems and other information contained in the Confidential Business Operation Manual or otherwise conveyed to you by us. If requested by us, you shall cause your officers, directors and employees to execute written agreements to keep such information strictly confidential.

Article 13. COPYRIGHTS

13.1 Copyrights and Patents. We do not own any rights in or to any patents which are material to the franchise. We presently have proprietary rights in numerous items, such as your manuals, systems, advertising designs, and the like relating to the operation of our business which are suitable for copyright protection. We reserve to ourselves or our designee any and all rights which we have in and to such items. We may obtain copyright registration on our confidential Confidential Business Operation Manual and any future manuals and may, at our discretion, obtain copyright registration for any now unregistered items that are a part of this agreement.

Article 14. RIGHT OF OFFSET

14.1 Right Of Offset. You authorize us to retain monies received by us on your behalf or due to you to offset amounts owed to us by you.

Article 15. INDEMNIFICATION

15.1 Indemnify. You shall indemnify and save us harmless from and against all costs, damages, expenses, claims and other losses and liabilities, in tort or contract and including reasonable legal and accounting fees, incurred directly or indirectly out of or in connection with, or alleged to have been caused by, the operation of your business or arising or alleged to have arisen against you, including all costs incurred as a result of claims or suits against us arising therefrom, unless such claim is due to our negligence or willful act or that of our agents, employees or representatives. We may take steps we deem necessary to protect ourselves from such claims or suits, and you shall reimburse us for all expenses incurred in connection therewith, including reasonable attorneys' fees, within 10 days from the date of an invoice from us to you for such expense.

15.2 Attorneys Fees. If any provision of this agreement is enforced at any time by us or if any amounts due from you to us or our affiliates are at any time collected by or through an attorney at law, you are liable to us for all costs and expenses of enforcement and collection, including court costs and reasonable attorneys' fees.

Article 16. NOTICES

16.1 Written Notices. Any notice required or permitted by this agreement shall be deemed given if sent postage prepaid, registered or certified mail, or overnight express service and addressed to the following address or to such other address as may be provided by either party upon written notice to the other party or published in the Confidential Business Operation Manual.

FRANCHISOR: LUBE N LATTE FRANCHISE COMPANY LLC
ATTENTION: PRESIDENT
305 S.E. "G" Street
Grants Pass, Oregon 97526

FRANCHISEE: _____
_____
_____

Article 17. INDEPENDENT CONTRACTOR

17.1 Franchisee is an Independent Contractor. Nothing in this agreement is intended to constitute you as our agent, legal representative, subsidiary, joint venturer, fiduciary partner, employee or servant for any purpose whatsoever. You are an independent contractor and are in no way authorized by this agreement to make any contract, warranty or representation, or to create any obligation, express or implied, on behalf of or in the name of us. All your employees are your responsibility and not ours.

17.2 Franchisee Disclosure of Independence. In all of your dealings with third parties including customers, employees and suppliers, you shall disclose in an appropriate manner acceptable to us that you are an independent entity. This agreement does not create a relationship of fiduciary standards or of special trust or confidence.

17.3 Third Parties. The parties intend to confer no benefit or right on any person or entity not a party to this agreement and no third party shall have the right to claim the benefit of any provision hereof as a third party beneficiary of any such provision.

Article 18. MODIFICATIONS

18.1 Modification of Agreement. The franchise agreement may be modified only with the written consent of both parties except as stated herein.

18.2 Franchisor's Modification Rights. We expressly reserve the right to modify our Manuals and Systems, the composition of the package of services offered to you and/or to change our trademarks, service marks, trade names, logotypes, commercial symbols and specifications without your consent.

18.3 Additional Actions. The parties agree to execute such other documents and perform such further acts as may be necessary or desirable to carry out the purposes of this agreement.

Article 19. GOVERNING LAW AND PUBLIC POLICY CHANGES

19.1 Applicable Law. This Agreement shall be governed by and construed in accordance with the internal laws of the State of Oregon however, if this agreement concerns a franchisee located in a state other than such state and the laws of that state require terms other than those or in addition to those contained herein, then this agreement shall be deemed modified so as to comply with the appropriate laws of such state, but only to the extent necessary to prevent the invalidity of this agreement or any provision hereof; the imposition of fines or penalties, or the creation of civil or criminal liability on account thereof. To the extent permitted by applicable law, you waive any provision of law which renders any provision of this Agreement prohibited or unenforceable in any respect.

Article 20. SEVERABILITY

20.1 Severability. If this agreement is held to violate any law, regulation or ordinance of the United States, any country, any state or any municipality, the relevant portion is severable and the balance of this Agreement shall be enforced as if such provision had not been included herein. All rights and remedies provided herein or by law are cumulative and not mutually exclusive, and may be exercised serially.

Article 21. FAILURE TO ENFORCE

21.1 Failure to Enforce. Failure of either party to enforce any of the terms and conditions of this agreement shall not constitute a waiver of the right subsequently to enforce such provisions or to enforce other provisions of this agreement.

Article 22. SUCCESSION OF BENEFITS

22.1 Succession of Benefits. In the event that you should become deceased or incapacitated, the provisions of this agreement shall inure to the benefit of and be binding upon the parties thereto, their heirs, executors, administrators and assignees. The transferee must assume your obligations under this agreement and must meet our standards including training.

Article 23. MISCELLANEOUS

23.1 Headings, Table of Contents, Gender and Language Usage. The headings, table of contents, gender and language usage used herein are for purposes of convenience only and shall not be used in constructing the provisions hereof. As used herein, the male gender shall include the female and neuter genders, the singular shall include the plural, and the plural, the singular.

23.2 Injunctive Relief. You recognize the unique value and secondary meaning attached to our franchised business system, our trade names, service marks, trademarks, logotypes, commercial symbols, standards of operation and the trade practices and agree that any non-compliance with the terms of this agreement or any unauthorized or improper use will cause irreparable damage to us and our franchisees. You therefore agree that if you should engage in any such unauthorized or improper use, during or after the period of this franchise, we shall be entitled to apply for both permanent and temporary injunctive relief from any arbitration panel or court of competent jurisdiction in addition to any other remedies prescribed by law.

23.3 Arbitration. A. Except as specifically modified by this Article, any controversy or claim arising out of or relating to this agreement or its breach, including without limitation, any claim that this agreement or any of its parts is invalid, illegal or otherwise voidable or void, shall be submitted to arbitration before and in accordance with the arbitration rules of Franchise Arbitration and Mediation, Inc. ("FAM") or, upon mutual consent of us and you, or, if FAM is unable to conduct said arbitration, then before the American Arbitration Association in accordance with its Commercial Arbitration Rules. We and you agree that arbitration shall be conducted on an individual, and not a class-wide basis and that there shall be three neutral arbitrators that are recognized franchise attorneys.

   A. The provisions of this Article shall be construed as independent of any other covenant or provision of this Agreement; provided that if a court of competent jurisdiction determines that any such provisions are unlawful in any way, such court shall modify or interpret such provisions to the minimum extent necessary to have them comply with the law. Notwithstanding any provision of this agreement relating to under which state laws of this Agreement shall be governed by and construed, all issues relating to arbitrability or the enforcement of the agreement to arbitrate contained herein shall be governed by the Federal Arbitration Act (9 U.S.C. Section 1 *et seq.*) and the federal common law of arbitration.

B. Judgment upon an arbitration award may be entered in any court having competent jurisdiction and shall be binding, final and non-appealable. We and you (and our respective owners and guarantors, if applicable) hereby waive to the fullest extent permitted by law, any right to claim for any punitive or exemplary damages against the other and agree that in the event of a dispute between us and/or them each shall be limited to the recovery of any actual damages sustained by it.

C. Prior to any arbitration proceeding taking place, we or you may, at our respective option, elect to (1) have the arbitrator(s) conduct, in a separate proceeding prior to the actual arbitration, a preliminary hearing, at which hearing testimony and other evidence may be presented and briefs may be submitted, including without limitation a brief setting forth the then applicable statutory or common law methods of measuring damages in respect to the controversy or claim being arbitrated, or (2) submit the controversy or claim to non-binding mediation before FAM or other mutually agreeable mediator, in which event both parties shall execute a suitable confidentiality agreement.

D. This arbitration provision shall be deemed to be self-executing and shall remain in full force and effect after expiration or termination of this agreement. In the event either party fails to appear at any properly noticed arbitration proceeding, an award may be entered against such party by default or otherwise notwithstanding said failure to appear. Arbitration and/or mediation shall take place at Grants Pass, Oregon, unless otherwise agreed by us and you.

E. The obligation herein to arbitrate or mediate shall not be binding upon either party with respect to claims relating to our trademarks, service marks, patents, and copyrights; claims related to any lease or sublease of real property between the parties or their affiliated entities; requests by either party for temporary restraining orders, preliminary injunctions or other procedures in a court of competent jurisdiction to obtain interim relief when deemed necessary by such court to preserve the *status quo* or prevent irreparable injury pending resolution by arbitration of the actual dispute between the parties.

Article 24. ACKNOWLEDGMENT BY A PROSPECTIVE FRANCHISEE

24.1 Acknowledgment. You, by executing this Agreement, acknowledge receipt of our Uniform Franchise Offering Circular (UFOC) and Franchise Agreement including all exhibits required by various states, at least 10 business days before signing this agreement and that the agreement received, is substantially the form being executed this date, has been in your possession for at least 5 business days.

24.2 Further Acknowledgment. You further acknowledge that you have entered into this agreement in reliance upon the information set forth in this agreement and the Uniform Franchise Offering Circular and have relied on no promises, no representations, no statements or no undertakings made by us or our representatives or others which are in conflict with any statements or representations made and not set forth in this agreement or in the uniform franchise offering circular.

24.3 Independent Counsel. You expressly acknowledge that you have conducted an independent investigation of the contemplated association with us and have been advised by your independent counsel.

24.4 Business Risk. You expressly recognize that the contemplated association with you involves business risks making the success of the association largely dependent upon the business abilities of you and external economic forces. You acknowledge that neither we nor any other person can guarantee the success of your franchised business.

24.5 No Financial Projections or Representations. You expressly acknowledge that you have not received or relied upon any warranty or assurance, expressed or implied, as to the potential sales volume, profits or success of the association with our franchise system.

Article 25. ENTIRE AGREEMENT

25.1 Additional Provisions. Please indicate any representations or provisions orally made that are not contained herein. If none, write: "None"

_____

_____

_____

_____

_____

25.2 Entire Agreement. This agreement constitutes the entire agreement of the parties into which all prior negotiations, commitments, representations and undertakings are merged and no modification or termination of this agreement shall be binding unless executed in writing by all parties hereto. This agreement is binding on the parties and their heirs, successors and assigns.

THE UNDERSIGNED ACKNOWLEDGES THAT THEY HAVE READ THIS AGREEMENT IN FULL AND HAVE BEEN SUPPLIED WITH A UNIFORM FRANCHISE OFFERING CIRCULAR IN ACCORDANCE TO FEDERAL AND STATE LAW.

IN WITNESS WHEREOF, the parties hereto have caused this Agreement to be duly executed in duplicate as of the day and year written herein.

FRANCHISOR:
LUBE N LATTE FRANCHISE COMPANY, LLC
An Oregon Limited Liability Company

By: _____   Date: _____

_____
(Typed or printed name and title)

FRANCHISEE:

_____
(Name of Entity)

_____   Date: _____
(Signature of Sole Proprietor if a Sole Proprietorship)

_____   Date: _____
(Signature of a Partner if a Partnership all Partners must sign)

_____   Date: _____
(Signature of any additional Partner if a Partnership)

_____   Date: _____
(Signature of any additional Partner if a Partnership)

By: _____   Date: _____
Title (This line to be used if a corporate entity is involved)

_____
Secretary (to be used if corporate entity is involved)

SHAREHOLDERS OF FRANCHISEE
(If Corporate Entity is Involved —
all Shareholders must sign and date
and by signing hereunder agrees to
be individually bound by all of the
terms and conditions this Agreement)

Dates: _____   _____

_____   _____

_____   _____

_____   _____

(SEE TERRITORY MAP ATTACHED HERETO AS SCHEDULE 1)

SCHEDULE 1

MAP WITH TERRITORY OUTLINED IN COLOR TO BE ATTACHED HERE

SCHEDULE 1 PART 2

LIST OF SOFTWARE, HARDWARE AND CASH REGISTER REQUIREMENTS
(ITEM 8)

Appendix C

Background Questionnaire for Offering Circular

Introduction

As a franchisor, you will be required — either by federal or state laws — to prepare and use an offering circular when offering a franchise for sale. This offering circular incorporates certain required information concerning such items as:

- The description of your business to be franchised;
- Your business' litigation and bankruptcy history;
- Your background and that of your principals as franchisors; and
- The extent of the support you plan to give your franchisees.

To help you gather this information and other important facts and figures for your offering circular, complete the background questionnaire in this appendix. When you have filled out this questionnaire, you will not only have learned more about you and your business, you will also have helped to facilitate the offering circular process. By saving time on this critical information gathering, you could even possibly reduce your attorney fees for preparing the first draft of your offering circular.

When answering the questions, be sure to attach additional sheets if needed.

This questionnaire is to be used in gathering required due diligent information from the franchisor for insertion into the new Uniform Franchise Offering Circular as adopted by NASAA on April 25, 1993, effective on or before January 1, 1995.

1. (a) Franchisor's name, principal business address (home office in the United States) and telephone number (if a franchise corporation is to be formed, insert the name of the proposed new corporation); (the business address cannot be a post office):

    _____

    _____

    _____

    (b) Name, principal business address and telephone number of international home office:

    _____

    _____

    _____

2. If the franchisor had a predecessor, i.e., a person from whom the franchisor acquired during the past 10 years or will acquire directly or indirectly the major portion of the franchisor's assets, give the name, address and telephone number of the predecessor:

    _____

    _____

    _____

3. If the proposed franchisor has an affiliate defined as a corporation or entity other than a natural person controlled by, controlling, or under common control with the franchisor which is offering franchises in any line of business or is providing products or services to the franchisee of the franchisor, give the name, address and telephone number:

    _____

    _____

    _____

4. The name under which the franchisor does or intends to do business:

    _____

    _____

5. The name, address and telephone number of person who will be listed as agent for service of process:

    _____

    _____

    _____

6. State of incorporation or business organization and the type of business organization (corporation, partnership, sole proprietorship):

_____

_____

_____

7. (a) Does the franchisor operate a business of the type being franchised? Yes ☐ No ☐
If yes, give a brief description of the location and type of business.

_____

_____

_____

(b) Does or has the franchisor sold or granted franchises? Yes ☐ No ☐
If yes, please describe when, where and to whom:

_____

_____

_____

_____

8. List the franchisor's other business activities:

_____

_____

_____

9. Please give a brief description of the business to be conducted by the franchisees:

_____

_____

_____

10. Describe briefly the general market for the product or service to be offered by the franchisee. Is it a relatively new product or service or is the market fairly saturated? Will the goods or services by seasonal or offered primarily to a certain group of purchasers?

_____

_____

_____

_____

11. Are there any regulations specific to the industry in which your franchise business will operate? (Include any special licenses or legal restriction on operations set by statutes.)

   _____

   _____

   _____

   _____

12. Give a brief description of the competition that will be faced by your franchisees.

   _____

   _____

   _____

13. Give the prior business experience of the franchisor including (1) the length of time the franchisor has conducted a business of the type to be operated by the franchisee; and (2) the length of time the franchisor offered franchises for the same type of business as that to be operated by the franchisee and in which states the franchises were offered:

   _____

   _____

   _____

   _____

   _____

   _____

   _____

14. Describe whether the franchisor has offered franchises in any other lines of business including:

   a) A description of each other line of business: _____

   _____

   _____

   b) The number of franchises sold in each other line of business: _____

   _____

   _____

   c) The length of time the franchisor has offered each other franchise: _____

   _____

   _____

15. Briefly describe the business experience of any predecessor and/or affiliate of the franchisor including (1) the length of time each predecessor or affiliate has conducted a business of the type to be operated by the franchisee; and (2) the length of time each predecessor and affiliate offered franchises for the same type of business as that to be operated by the franchisee:

_____

_____

_____

_____

_____

_____

16. Describe whether or not each predecessor and affiliate offered franchises in another line of business and if so, include:

a) The description of each other line of business: _____

_____

_____

_____

_____

b) The number of franchises sold in each other line of business: _____

_____

c) The length of time each predecessor and affiliate offered each other franchise: _____

_____

_____

17. List by name and position all of the directors of the corporation or general partners of a partnership or trustees if a trust and include each person's principal occupation and employers during the past five years with the beginning date and departure date for each job so designated as well as the location of the job:

Director, Trustee, General Partner (strike inapplicable words): _____

_____

_____

_____

Director, Trustee, General Partner (strike inapplicable words): _____

_____

_____

_____

Director, Trustee, General Partner (strike inapplicable words): _____

_____

_____

_____

Director, Trustee, General Partner (strike inapplicable words): _____

_____

_____

_____

(NOTE: Questions 1–17 should cover only the last 10 years.)

18. List by name and present position, the principal officers and other executives who will have management responsibility relating to the franchises offered by this offering circular (include jobs for the last five years with beginning and departure dates):

Chief Executive Officer: _____

_____

_____

_____

Chief Operating Officer: _____

_____

_____

_____

President: _____

_____

_____

_____

Treasurer or Chief Financial Officer: _____

_____

_____

_____

Franchise Marketing Officer: _____

_____

_____

_____

Franchise Training Officer: _____

_____

_____

_____

Franchise Operations Officer: _____

_____

_____

_____

Director: _____

_____

_____

_____

Director: _____

_____

_____

_____

Director: _____

_____

_____

_____

Other employees or consultants having management responsibilities: _____

_____

_____

_____

19. Does the franchisor have a franchise broker, i.e., an independent firm that specializes in selling franchises? Yes ☐ No ☐

If yes, please briefly state the names, addresses and telephone numbers of the franchise broker's directors, principal officers and executives with management responsibilities to market or service the franchisor including your beginning and departure dates of employment for the past five years:

_____

_____

_____

20. State whether or not the franchisor, its predecessor, a person identified in Item 2 or an affiliate operating franchises under the franchisor's principal trademark has been involved in any of the following:

(a) Pending Actions

Has an administrative, criminal, or material civil action pending against that person alleging a violation of a franchise, antitrust, or securities law, fraud, unfair or deceptive practices, or comparable allegations. In addition, include actions other than ordinary routine litigation incidental to the business which are significant in the context of the number of franchisees and the size, nature or financial condition of the franchise system or its business operations.   Yes ☐ No ☐

If yes, disclose the names of the parties, the forum, nature and current status of pending action:

_____

_____

_____

(b) Please state whether or not such person(s) or entity(ies) have, during the 10 year period immediately before the date of this questionnaire, been convicted of a felony or pleaded nolo contendere to a felony charge; or have been held liable in a civil action by final judgment, or been the subject of a material action involving a violation of franchise, antitrust or securities law, fraud, unfair deceptive practices, or comparable allegations.   Yes ☐ No ☐

If yes, disclose the names of the parties, the forum and date of conviction or the date the judgment was entered, penalty or damages assessed and/or terms of the settlement including the name of the court and the number of the action.)

_____

_____

_____

c) Please state whether or not during the last 10 years the above-named person(s) or entity(ies) are subject to a currently effective injunctive or restrictive order or decree relating to the franchise or under a federal, state or Canadian franchise, securities, antitrust, trade regulation or trade practice law resulting from a concluded or pending action or proceeding brought by a public agency.   Yes ☐ No ☐

If yes, disclose the names of the person, the public agency and court, a summary of the allegations found by the agency or court and the date, nature, terms and conditions of the order or decree.)

_____

_____

_____

(NOTE: For the purposes of the aforementioned, "franchisor" includes the franchisor, its predecessors, persons identified in Item 2 and affiliates offering franchises under the franchisor's principal trademarks. Furthermore, the definition of an "action" includes any complaints, cross-claims, counter claims or third party claims in a judicial proceeding and their equivalent in administrative action or arbitration proceeding. The franchisor may disclose its counter claims. Please omit actions that were dismissed by final judgment without liability of injury of an adverse order against the franchisor. The definition of "material" is an action or an aggregate of actions that a reasonably protective franchisee would consider important in making a decision about the franchise business. It should also be noted that settlement of action does not diminish its materiality if the franchisor agrees to pay material consideration or agrees to be bound by obligations which are materially adverse to the franchisor's interest. Also note that "held liable" includes a finding by final judgment in judicial binding arbitration or administrative proceeding that the franchisor, as a result of claims or counterclaims must pay money or other consideration, must reduce an indebtedness by the amount of the award, cannot enforce its rights, or must take action adverse to its interest. Remember the title of each action and state the case numbers or citations along with the filing date, the opposing party's name and the opposing party's relationship with the franchisor. "Relationship" includes the editor, supplier, lessor, franchisee, former franchisee or class of franchisees. You should also have summarized the relief sought or obtained. "Conviction" involves the title of the action and state citation in parentheses with the title underlined. Include the name of the person convicted or held liable and state the crime or violation and date of conviction as well as disclose any sentence or penalty.

21. Please state whether the franchisor, its affiliates, predecessor, officers or general partner during the 10 year period immediately before the date of this questionnaire:

a) Filed as a debtor (or had filed against it) a petition to start an action under the U.S. Bankruptcy Code?   Yes ☐ No ☐

b) Obtained a discharge of its debts under the Bankruptcy Code?   Yes ☐ No ☐   or

c) Was a principal officer of a company or a general partner in a partnership that either filed as a debtor (or had filed against it) a petition to start an action under the U.S. Bankruptcy Code or that obtained a discharged of its debts under the Bankruptcy Code within one year after the officer or general partner of the franchisor held the position in the company or partnership?   Yes ☐ No ☐

If yes, disclose the name of the person or company that was the debtor under Bankruptcy Code, date of the action and the material facts including the name of the party that filed or had filed against it. If the debtor was an affiliate of the franchisor, state the relationship. If the debtor in the bankruptcy proceeding is unaffiliated with the franchisor, state the name, address and principal business of the bankrupt company.)

_____

_____

_____

_____

d) Did the entity referred to in subparagraph c) file bankruptcy or reorganization under the bankruptcy law?   Yes ☐ No ☐

If so, identify the date of original filing while identifying the bankruptcy court, the case name and number, the date the debtor obtain a discharge in bankruptcy (including a discharge under Chapter 7 and confirmation of any plans of reorganization under Chapters 11 and 13 of the Bankruptcy Code?

NOTE: Remember, cases, actions, or other proceedings under the laws of foreign nations relating to bankruptcy proceedings should be included in answers where responses are required.)

22. a) State what you think would be the initial franchise fee (includes all fees and payments for services or goods received from the franchisor before the business opens) and how you arrived at this figure: _____

_____

_____

   b) State whether or not the initial franchise fee includes all fees and payments whether payable in a lump sum or installments before the franchisee's business opens. If no, please describe fees not included: _____

_____

_____

_____

   c) Is the initial franchise fee uniform?   Yes ☐ No ☐

   If no, disclose the formula or range of initial fees paid in the previous fiscal year, if any, before the application date and the factors that determined the amount of these initial fees.)

_____

_____

_____

   d) If the initial franchise fee is payable in installments, disclose the installment payment terms in this portion of the questionnaire as well as in the following portion which is dedicated to information regarding Item 10 of the offering circular, i.e., the financial arrangements.

_____

_____

23. Other Fees:

Name of fee	Amount	Due Date	Remarks[1]
Royalty	_____	_____	_____
	_____	_____	_____
	_____	_____	_____
Advertising Fund	_____	_____	_____
	_____	_____	_____
	_____	_____	_____
Cooperative Advertising	_____	_____	_____
	_____	_____	_____
	_____	_____	_____

Name of fee	Amount	Due Date	Remarks[1]
Local Advertising	_____	_____	_____
	_____	_____	_____
Additional Promotional Fees	_____	_____	_____
	_____	_____	_____
Initial Training	_____	_____	_____
	_____	_____	_____
Additional Training	_____	_____	_____
	_____	_____	_____
Transfer Fee	_____	_____	_____
	_____	_____	_____
Renewal Fee	_____	_____	_____
	_____	_____	_____
Audit Fee	_____	_____	_____
	_____	_____	_____

[1] Be sure to indicate, in the remarks column, answers to each of the following questions:

Is the fee imposed and collected by franchisor?

Is the fee non-refundable?

At what point in time does interest begin?

Are the fees collected by the franchisor? If no, indicate those that are and those that are not and who collects the ones that are not collected by the franchisor:

Are all of the fees listed in the above chart non-refundable? If no, which fees are refundable?

Will the franchisor-owned outlets (company-owned office) have voting power on any fees imposed by cooperatives? If yes, disclose a range for the fee.

(NOTE: when listing fees as in the above chart, please remember that fees are royalty, lease negotiation, structure and remodeling, additional training, advertising, additional assistance, audit and accounting, inventory, transfer and renewal fees. These are fees that are paid either to you as franchisor or your affiliate or fees that you or an affiliate collect in whole or part on behalf of the third party.)

24. Initial Investment: Disclose in the following chart the expenditures including high and low to the best of your ability. If columns "Method of Payment", "When Due", and "To Whom Payment Is To Be Made" are different from that stated below, cross out reply and write in applicable wording:

Payment	Amount	Method of Payment	When Due	To Whom Payment Is to Be Made
Non-refundable Initial Franchise Fee	$ _____	$_____ upon signing Deposit Agreement and $ _____ upon signing Franchise Agreement	Upon execution of Franchise and Deposit Agreements	Franchisor
Area Development Option Fee	$ _____ to $ _____ (each additional franchise option fee within territory is $ _____)	Lump sum	Upon execution of Area Development	Franchisor
Leasehold[1, 2] Improvements	$ _____ to $ _____	Progress payments according to construction agreement until completion	Generally by agreement with contractor	General contractor
Equipment, furnishings and fixtures[2]	$ _____ to $ _____	As required by vendor	As required by vendor	Vendor
Complete Signage (Interior and exterior)	$ _____ to $ _____	As required by vendor	As required by sign vendor	Sign Vendor
Blue Prints, Plans, Permits	$ _____ to $ _____	As required by architects and authorities	As required by architects and authorities	Architect, Planner, City, County, or State
Rental approximately _____ sq. ft. and up	$ _____ to $ _____ per month	Lump sum (non-refundable)	Monthly	To particular landlord
Initial Inventory and Operating Supplies	$ _____ to $ _____	Lump sum	As required by supplier	Supplier
Security Deposits (including lease deposit, utilities, licenses, etc.)	$ _____ to $ _____	Lump sum	As required by Landlord	Landlord

Payment	Amount	Method of Payment	When Due	To Whom Payment Is to Be Made
Insurance	$ _____ to $ _____ per month	Lump sum	Normally at time of coverage	Insurance agent
Initial Advertising and Promotions (includes $ _____ and opening promotions expenses)	$ _____ to $ _____	Lump sum	As required by media	Supplier
Miscellaneous (travel and living expenses while training, permits, organizational expenses, etc.)	$ _____ to $ _____	Lump sum	As needed	Airlines, restaurants, motels, governmental agencies, etc.
Additional Funds necessary to commence or continue operation for 3 months[3]	$ _____ to $ _____	Lump sum	As needed	Employees, utilities, vendors, suppliers; does not provide living expenses for Franchisee
Other	$ _____ to $ _____			

TOTALS $_____ (Including Initial Franchise Fee)
to
$_____ (Including Initial Franchise Fee)[4, 5]

---

[1] Please note that if Franchisee is able to wholly or partially finance the construction of the entire package above or only the leasehold improvements, the initial cash requirements will be reduced by the amount financed, but the monthly interest and principal debt service must be calculated in its place by the Franchisee according to its terms of the lender. Additionally, upon negotiation of lease, on occasion, some or all of tenant improvements may be paid by lessor of the property.

[2] If fixtures, furniture and/or equipment is leased, the amount of the minimum and maximum initial cash requirement may be decreased depending on local terms.

[3] This estimates your initial start-up expenses. These figures are estimates and we cannot guarantee that you will not have additional expenses starting the business. Your costs will depend on factors such as how much you follow our methods and procedures, your management skills, experience and business acumen, local economic conditions, market or your product, prevailing wage rate, competition and sales line reached during the initial start-up period.

[4] You should review our estimated figures carefully with a business advisor before making any decision to purchase the franchise.

[5] We do not offer direct or indirect financing to franchisees for any items.

(NOTE: If a specific amount is not ascertainable, use a low/high range based on your current experience. If a building is involved, describe the probable location of the building, such as a strip shopping mall, downtown, or rural, when filling out the chart pertaining to real estate and improvement. If you or an affiliate finance a part of the initial investment, state the expenditures that you will finance, the required down payment, annual percentage interest rate, rate factors, and the estimated loan repayments. Please make descriptions brief, and remember to answer this question again when referring to Item 10 of the offering circular regarding financing.)

25. Disclose any obligations you wish to impose on the franchisee to purchase or lease from you or your designee or from suppliers approved by you as franchisor or under your franchisor specifications:

_____

_____

_____

_____

_____

_____

_____

For each obligation, disclose:

(a) The required goods, services, supplies, fixtures, equipment, inventory, computer hardware or software or real estate relating to establishing or operating the franchise business: _____

_____

_____

_____

(b) The manner in which you issue and modify specifications or grants and revoke approval for suppliers: _____

_____

_____

(c) Whether and for what categories of goods and services you as franchisor or your affiliates are approved suppliers or the only approved suppliers: _____

_____

_____

(d) Whether, and if so, the precise basis by which you as the franchisor or your affiliates will or may derive revenue or other material consideration as a result of required purchases or leases from you or your designee or from your approved supplier: _____

_____

_____

_____

(e) Last but not least, if you require such purchases by the franchisee from you, your designee or from your approved supplier, estimate the proportion of these required purchases and leases to all purchases and leases by the franchisee of goods and services in establishing and operating a franchise business. In other words, if you require the franchisee to purchase $100 worth of equipment from you and the franchisee will purchase and lease other goods and services from other sources for $1,000, your estimated percentage proportion would be 10% (100 divided by 1,000). _____%

26. Is there or will there be a purchasing or distribution cooperative?   Yes ☐ No ☐

If yes, please describe. _____

_____

_____

(NOTE: do not include goods and services provided as part of the franchise without a separate charge. For example, a fee for initial training when the cost is included in the franchise fee. Do not include fees disclosed in your previous responses.)

27. Will you require the franchisee to follow specifications in standards?   Yes ☐ No ☐

If yes, please describe what the standards will apply to such items as procedures, construction, premises, software, hardware, or uniforms, and also how you would formulate and modify these specifications. _____

_____

_____

28. Disclose whether your specification standards are issued by you to franchisees, subfranchisors, or approved suppliers, and how and when they are updated. _____

_____

_____

29. Describe how your suppliers are evaluated, approved or disapproved by you. _____

_____

_____

30. Will your criteria for suppliers be available to the franchisees?   Yes ☐ No ☐

31. State the fees, if any, that a franchisee must pay you and the procedures they must follow to secure your approval of their suppliers as well as how your approval would be removed.

_____

_____

_____

_____

32. State the time period that it will take you to approve or disapprove a supplier. _____

_____

_____

33. Does a designated supplier make payments to you as franchisor because of transactions with your franchisees?   Yes ☐ No ☐

    If yes, disclose the basis for the payment and specify a percentage or flat amount that supplier will pay to you. _____

    _____

    _____

    (NOTE: when answering this question, please remember that purchases of similar goods or services by you at a lower price than available to your resale to the franchisee is a payment to you when you pass on the goods or services at a higher price to you franchisee.)

34. Do you negotiate purchase arrangements with suppliers including price terms for the benefit of franchisees?   Yes ☐ No ☐

35. Do you provide material benefits (for example, renew or granting additional franchises) to a franchisee based on a franchisee's use of designated or approved sources?   Yes ☐ No ☐

    If yes, please describe. _____

    _____

    _____

36. The following Items A–X include obligations that many franchisors impose upon franchisees. Please state after each obligation whether or not you desire at this time to impose such an obligation on your franchisees.

    a. Site Selection and Acquisition/Lease: Yes ☐ No ☐

    b. Pre-Opening Purchases/Lease: Yes ☐ No ☐

    c. Site Development and Other Pre-Opening Requirements: Yes ☐ No ☐

    d. Initial and Ongoing Training: Yes ☐ No ☐

    e. Opening Obligations: Yes ☐ No ☐

    f. Fees (these will include royalty, advertising, transfer, renewal):   Yes ☐ No ☐

    g. Compliance with Standards and Policies/Operating Manual: Yes ☐ No ☐

    h. Trademarks and Proprietary Information Obligations: Yes ☐ No ☐

    i. Restrictions on Products and Services Offered: Yes ☐ No ☐

    j. Warranty and Other Consumer Service Requirements: Yes ☐ No ☐

    k. Territorial Development and Sales Quota: Yes ☐ No ☐

    l. Ongoing Products and Service Purchases: Yes ☐ No ☐

m. Maintenance, Appearance and Remodeling Requirements: Yes ☐ No ☐

n. Insurance Requirements: Yes ☐ No ☐

o. Advertising Requirements: Yes ☐ No ☐

p. Indemnification: Yes ☐ No ☐

q. Owner's Participation/Management Staffing: Yes ☐ No ☐

r. Records and Reports: Yes ☐ No ☐

s. Inspections and Audits: Yes ☐ No ☐

t. Transfers: Yes ☐ No ☐

u. Renewals: Yes ☐ No ☐

v. Post-Termination Obligations: Yes ☐ No ☐

w. Non-Competition Covenants: Yes ☐ No ☐

x. Dispute Resolution such as Arbitration with FAM or the American Arbitration Association: Yes ☐ No ☐

y. Others: Yes ☐ No ☐

If yes, describe other obligations you will impose upon your franchisees:

_____

_____

_____

_____

NOTE: these obligations will be listed in the circular and cross referenced to the sections in the circular and franchise agreement.)

37. Financing: Do you intend to finance your franchisee including its initial franchise fee or its monetary requirements for equipment, etc. (remember, financing includes leasing and installment contracts. (Payments due you within 90 days on an open account need not be disclosed?)   Yes ☐ No ☐

If yes, describe the written arrangements between you, your affiliate, any lender for the lender to offer financing to the franchisee or an arrangement which you, as franchisor, or your affiliate receives a benefit from a lender for franchisee financing and "indirect offer of financing" since any benefit received from a lender is indirect financing. For example, you as franchisor guaranteeing a note, lease or obligation of a franchisee is an "indirect offer of financing" and must be disclosed:

_____

_____

_____

_____

_____

_____

If your answer is yes, that you finance, please complete the summary of financing hereinafter reproduced.

Item Financed (Source)	Amount Financed	Down Payment	Term (Yrs.)	Annual Percentage Rate	Monthly Payment	Prepay Penalty	Security Required	Liability upon Default	Loss of Legal Right on Default
INITIAL FEE (Name of Lender)	_____	_____	_____	_____	_____	_____	_____	_____	_____
	_____	_____	_____	_____	_____	_____	_____	_____	_____
LAND/ CONSTRUCT	_____	_____	_____	_____	_____	_____	_____	_____	_____
LEASED SPACE (Name of Lender)	_____	_____	_____	_____	_____	_____	_____	_____	_____
	_____	_____	_____	_____	_____	_____	_____	_____	_____
EQUIPMENT LEASE (Name of Lender)	_____	_____	_____	_____	_____	_____	_____	_____	_____
	_____	_____	_____	_____	_____	_____	_____	_____	_____
EQUIPMENT PURCH. (Name of Lender)	_____	_____	_____	_____	_____	_____	_____	_____	_____
	_____	_____	_____	_____	_____	_____	_____	_____	_____
OPENING INVENTORY	_____	_____	_____	_____	_____	_____	_____	_____	_____
OTHER FINANCING	_____	_____	_____	_____	_____	_____	_____	_____	_____

38. Franchisor's Obligations: Please describe your obligations you intend at this time to include in your agreement in assisting your client prior to opening:

PRIOR TO OPENING: The following is a list of some obligations you may impose on yourself requiring a brief description, if you choose to have same:

a) Will you locate a site for the franchised business and negotiate the purchase or lease of this site for the franchisee?   Yes ☐ No ☐

If yes, will you own the premises and lease it to the franchisee.   Yes ☐ No ☐

b) Will you conform the premises to local ordinances and building codes and obtain the required permits?   Yes ☐ No ☐

c) Will you construct, remodel, or decorate the premises for the franchised business? Yes ☐ No ☐

d) Will you purchase or lease equipment, signs, fixtures, opening inventory and supplies for the franchisee?   Yes ☐ No ☐

If yes, will you provide these items directly?   Yes ☐ No ☐

If no, will you merely provide the names of approved suppliers?   Yes ☐ No ☐

Do you have written specifications for these items? Yes ☐ No ☐

Do you deliver or install these items? Yes ☐ No ☐

e) Do you hire and train employees for the franchisee? Yes ☐ No ☐

f) List any other obligations you wish to impose on yourself prior to the franchisee's opening:

_____

_____

_____

AFTER OPENING: The following are a list of questions which seek out your obligations during the operation of the franchised business which you may feel should be in your agreement at this time:

a) Do you offer products or services to the franchisee to be offered to its customers during the term of the agreement? Yes ☐ No ☐

b) Do you hire and train employees of the franchisee during the term of the agreement? Yes ☐ No ☐

c) Do you make improvements and developments in the franchised business during the term of the agreement? Yes ☐ No ☐

d) Do you do pricing during the term of the agreement? Yes ☐ No ☐

e) Do you do administrative, bookkeeping, accounting and inventory control procedures during the term of the agreement? Yes ☐ No ☐

f) Do you handle or troubleshoot operating problems encountered by the franchisee during the term of the agreement? Yes ☐ No ☐

g) Do you desire an advertising program which will feature the product or service offered by your franchisee? Yes ☐ No ☐

If yes, answer the following questions:

1) Disclose the media in which you intend to disseminate the advertising (for example, print, radio, or television). _____

_____

_____

2) Disclose whether the coverage of the media is local, regional or national in scope:

_____

_____

3) Disclose the source of the advertising, e.g., in-house advertising department, a national or regional advertising agency). _____

_____

_____

4) Disclose the conditions when you will permit the franchisees to use their own advertising material. _____

_____

_____

5) If there is an advertising council composed of franchisees that advises you on advertising policies, disclose:

a) How members of the council are selected. _____

_____

_____

b) Whether the council serves in an advisory capacity only or has operational or decision-making power. _____

_____

_____

c) Whether you as franchisor has the power to form, change, or dissolve the advertising council. _____

_____

_____

6) If during the term of the agreement you feel the franchisee must participate in local or regional advertising cooperative, please answer the following:

a) How the area or membership of the cooperative is defined. _____

_____

_____

b) How the franchisee's contribution to the cooperative is calculated. _____

_____

_____

c) Who is responsible for administration of the cooperative, e.g., franchisor, franchisees, advertising agency)? _____

_____

_____

d) Whether cooperatives must operate from written governing documents and whether the documents are available for review by the franchisee. _____

_____

_____

e) Whether cooperatives must prepare annual or periodic financial statements and whether the statements are available for review by the franchisee. _____

_____

_____

f) Whether the franchisor has the power to require cooperatives to be formed, changed, dissolved or merged. _____

_____

_____

7) If applicable, for each advertising fund not described in above subpart (6), disclose:

a) Who contributes to each fund, e.g., franchisees, franchisor-owned units, outside vendors or suppliers). _____

_____

_____

b) Whether the franchisor-owned units must contribute to the fund and, if so, whether it is on the same basis as franchisees. _____

_____

_____

c) How much the franchisee must contribute to the advertising fund(s) and whether other franchisees are required to contribute at a different rate (it is not necessary to disclose the specific rates). _____

_____

_____

d) Who administers the fund(s)? _____

_____

_____

e) Whether the fund is audited and when, and whether financial statements of the fund are available for review by the franchisee. _____

_____

_____

f) If you already have a fund, please provide the following for the most recently concluded fiscal year: (a) the percentage spent on production: _____%; (b) the percentage spent on media: _____%; (c) the percentage spent on administrative expenses: _____%; and (d) the percentage spent on other (which should be defined _____ _____). Your total should equal 100%.

g) Whether you or an affiliate receives payment for providing goods or services to an advertising fund?   Yes ☐ No ☐

If yes, describe: _____

_____

_____

8) Will you as franchisor be obligated to spend any amount on advertising in the area or territory where the franchisee is located?   Yes ☐ No ☐

If yes, describe: _____

_____

_____

9) If all advertising fees are not spent in the fiscal year in which they accrue, please explain how the you will use the remaining amounts. _____

_____

_____

Will the franchisees receive a periodic accounting of how advertising fees are spent? Yes ☐ No ☐

If yes, how frequent is the accounting: _____

_____

_____

10) Disclose the percentage of advertising funds, if any, used for advertising that is principally a solicitation for the sale of franchises. _____

_____

_____

39. If your franchise agreement will require the franchisee to buy or use an electronic cash register or computer system, provide a general description of the systems in non-technical language. Include in your descriptive an identification of each hardware component and software program by brand, type and principal functions and whether or not it is your proprietary property or that of an affiliate or a third party.

_____

_____

_____

_____

_____

_____

40. Do you, an affiliate or third party have a contractual obligation to provide ongoing maintenance, repair, upgrades or updates to the hardware and software sold to your franchisee?   Yes ☐ No ☐

41. Disclose the current annual cost of any optional or required maintenance and support contracts, upgrades and updates. _____

_____

_____

42. Identify any third party by name, business address and telephone number in the event that the hardware component or software program is the proprietary property of a third party and no compatible equivalent is available. _____

_____

_____

43. If the hardware component or software program is not proprietary, identify compatible equivalent components or programs that perform the same functions and indicate whether they have been approved by you as franchisor. _____

_____

_____

44. State whether the franchisee has any contractual obligation to upgrade or update any hardware component or software program during the term of the franchise, and if so, whether there are any contractual limitations on the frequency and cost of the obligation. _____

_____

_____

_____

45. For each electronic cash register system or software program, describe how it will be used in the franchisee's business, and the types of business information or data that will be collected and generated. _____

_____

_____

_____

46. State whether you, as the franchisor, will have independent access to the information and data set forth above, and if so, whether there are any contractual limitations on the franchisor's right to access the information and data. _____

_____

_____

47. Attach a copy of the table of contents of your operating manual which will be provided to the franchisee as of the franchisor's last fiscal year end or a more recent date. Please indicate the number of pages devoted to each subject listed in the table of contents and the total number of pages in the manual as of this date.

    (NOTE: an alternative disclosure can be accomplished if the prospective franchisee is allowed to view the manual before the purchase of the franchise.)

Franchisor's Methods Used To Select The Location Of The Franchisee's Business:

48. Do you select the site or approve an area within which the franchisee selects a site?   Yes ☐ No ☐
    If yes, describe: _____

    _____

    _____

49. Disclose how and whether you must approve a franchisee's selected site. _____

    _____

    _____

    _____

50. Disclose the factors which you as franchisor consider in selecting or approving sites (for example, general location and neighborhood, traffic patterns, parking, size, physical characteristics of existing buildings and lease terms). _____

    _____

    _____

    _____

51. Disclose the time limit for you as franchisor to locate or to approve or disapprove the site. _____

    _____

    _____

    Disclose the consequences if the franchisor and franchisee cannot agree on a site. _____

    _____

    _____

52. Please disclose the typical length of time (a range is permissible) between the signing of the franchise agreement or the first payment of consideration for the franchise and the opening of the franchisee's business.

    _____

    _____

    _____

53. Describe any factors which may affect the time period of opening such as the ability to obtain a lease, financing or building permits, zoning and local ordinances, weather conditions, shortages, or delayed installation of equipment, fixtures and signs. _____

_____

_____

_____

Training Program of the Franchisor:

54. Describe the location, duration, and general outline of the training program. _____

_____

_____

_____

55. How often will the training program be conducted after the pre-opening training program and who is required to attend? _____

_____

_____

56. Please list the names and experience that your instructors will have in number of years and subjects.

_____

_____

_____

57. Please list charges to be made to the franchisee and who must pay travel and living expenses of the enrollees in the training program. _____

_____

_____

58. For all non-mandatory training programs, if available, state the percentage of new franchisees that enrolled in these non-mandatory training programs during the preceding 12 months. _____

_____

_____

59. Please state whether or not any additional training programs and/or refresher courses are required
Yes ☐ No ☐

If yes, please describe: _____

_____

_____

For your benefit, we are listing in chart form items to be completed by you regarding your training.

Subject	Time	Instructional Material	Hours of Classroom Training	Hours of On-the-Job Training	Instructor
_____	_____	_____	_____	_____	_____
_____	_____	_____	_____	_____	_____
_____	_____	_____	_____	_____	_____
_____	_____	_____	_____	_____	_____
_____	_____	_____	_____	_____	_____
_____	_____	_____	_____	_____	_____
_____	_____	_____	_____	_____	_____

Territory

60. Describe any exclusive territory granted the franchisee, and how its boundaries were determined — by population, zip code, or other method. _____

_____

_____

_____

61. Concerning the location, have you or will you establish another franchisee who may also use the franchisor's trademark in another franchisee's territory?   Yes ☐ No ☐

If yes, describe: _____

_____

_____

_____

62. Have you or may you establish a company-owned outlet or other channels of distribution using the your name in a franchisee's territory?   Yes ☐ No ☐

If yes, describe: _____

_____

_____

63. Describe the minimum area granted to the franchisee and how it is arrived at — by specific miles, specific population, or any other designation. _____

_____

_____

64. Will the franchise be granted for a specific location or a location to be approved by the franchisor? Yes ☐ No ☐

65. State the conditions under which you will approve the relocation of the franchised business or the establishment of additional franchised outlets. _____

_____

_____

_____

66. Describe restrictions on you as a franchisor regarding operating company-owned stores or granting franchised outlets for a similar or competitive business within the defined area. _____

_____

_____

_____

(NOTE: it is not a good policy to allow any company-owned stores or franchised outlets within a franchisee's territory for a similar or competitive business.)

67. Will you have restrictions on franchisees from soliciting or accepting orders outside of the defined territories? Yes ☐ No ☐

If yes, describe these restrictions: _____

_____

_____

_____

68. Describe any restrictions on you from soliciting or accepting orders inside the franchisee's defined territory: _____

_____

_____

69. State any compensation that you may pay to a franchisee as franchisor for soliciting or accepting orders inside your franchisee's defined territory, if any: _____

_____

_____

_____

70. Describe the franchisee's options, rights of first refusal or similar rights to acquire additional franchises within his territory or contiguous territories: _____

_____

_____

Trademarks

71. Describe your principal trademarks which means the primary trademarks, service marks, names, logos and symbols to be used by the franchisee to identify the franchised business: _____

_____

_____

_____

72. State the date and identification number of each trademark registration or registration application with the United States Patent and Trademark Office: _____

_____

_____

_____

73. State whether or not you have filed all required affidavits: Yes ☐ No ☐

74. State whether any registration has been renewed: Yes ☐ No ☐

75. State whether the principal marks are registered on the Principal or Supplemental Register of the U.S. Patent and Trademark Office: _____

_____

_____

76. State whether or not an Intent to Use application or an application or an application based on actual use has been filed with the U.S. Patent and Trademark Office listing the trademark in question and the serial number of the application: _____

_____

_____

77. Disclose any currently effective material determinations of the Patent and Trademark Office, Trademark Trial and Appeal Board, the Trademark Administrator or this State or any court; pending infringement, opposition or cancellation; and pending material litigation involving the principal trademarks including the name of the principal trademarks, a brief summary of such opposition and the current status. _____

_____

_____

_____

78. Describe any litigation affecting your trademarks if it could significantly affect the ownership or use of the trademarks. _____

_____

79. Disclose any agreements currently in effect which significantly limit the rights of you as franchisor to use or license other franchisees to use the trademark in a manner material to the franchise.

_____

_____

80. State whether you as franchisor will protect the franchisee's right to use the trademarks and protect the franchisee against claims or infringements or unfair competition arising out of the franchisor's use of them:　Yes ☐　No ☐

If no, indicate what, if any, protection will be given to the franchisee. _____

_____

_____

81. Do you wish to have the franchisee obligated to notify you in case of any claims?　Yes ☐　No ☐

82. Do you want the franchise agreement to require the franchisor to take affirmative action when notified of these uses or claims?　Yes ☐　No ☐

83. Do you want to have the right to control administrative proceedings or litigation?　Yes ☐　No ☐

84. Do you wish a clause which would require the franchisee to modify or discontinue use of the trademark as a result of a proceeding or settlement or any other obstacles which you are running across?　Yes ☐　No ☐

85. Do you actually know of either a superior prior right or infringing use that could materially affect the franchisee's use of the principal trademarks in this state or in the state in which the franchised business is to be located?　Yes ☐　No ☐

If yes, describe: _____

_____

_____

Patents, Copyrights, and Proprietary Information

86. If you as franchisor own any rights in patents or copyrights that are material to the franchise, describe these patents and copyrights and their relationship to the franchise. Include their duration and whether you as franchisor can and intend to renew the copyrights. If you are claiming proprietary rights in confidential information or trade secrets, disclose their general subject matter and the terms and conditions for use by the franchisee.

_____

_____

_____

_____

_____

87. If you have a patent, state the patent number, issue date and title for each patent as well as the serial number, filing date and title of each patent application. _____

_____

_____

88. If you know of any infringements or any actions affecting the patent or copyright, please describe:

_____

_____

_____

Obligation to Participate in the Actual Operation of the Franchise Business

89. Will you require personal on premises supervision?   Yes ☐ No ☐

    If the answer is no, will you recommend on-site supervision by the franchisee?   Yes ☐ No ☐

90. State any limitations on whom the franchisee can hire as an on-premises supervisor. _____

_____

_____

_____

91. State whether the on-premises supervisor be required to successfully complete your training program.   Yes ☐ No ☐

92. If the franchisee is a business entity, state the amount of equity interest that the on-premises supervisor must have in the franchise, if any: _____%

93. Do you wish restrictions placed on the franchisee in its manager including maintaining trade secrets, non-competition, etc.?   Yes ☐ No ☐

    If yes, describe: _____

_____

_____

Restrictions on What the Franchisee May Sell

94. Do you want the franchisee to be obligated to sell only goods and services approved by the you?
    Yes ☐ No ☐

95. Do you want the franchisee to sell only goods and services authorized by you?   Yes ☐ No ☐

96. Do you want to retain the right as franchisor to change the types of authorized goods and services?   Yes ☐ No ☐

    If yes, are there any limits on your right to make such changes?   Yes ☐ No ☐

If yes, what are they? _____

_____

_____

97. Do you wish your franchisee to be restricted regarding customers?   Yes ☐ No ☐
    If yes, describe the restrictions: _____

    _____

    _____

Renewal, Termination, Transfer, and Dispute Resolution

98. The following are areas that require answers if you can at this time:
    a) Desired length of term of the franchise agreement: _____
    b) Renewal or extension of the term: _____
    c) Do you wish requirements for franchisee to renew or extend?   Yes ☐ No ☐
    d) Will you allow the franchisee to terminate other than with good cause?   Yes ☐ No ☐
    e) Do you want provisions where you as franchisor can terminate without cause?   Yes ☐ No ☐
    f) Do you want provisions where you as franchisor can terminate the agreement with cause?
       Yes ☐ No ☐
    g) Do you want obligations on the franchisee on termination and renewal?   Yes ☐ No ☐
    h) Do you want the right to assignment of the agreement?   Yes ☐ No ☐
    i) Do you desire a transfer fee in the event the franchisee desires to transfer?   Yes ☐ No ☐
       If yes, what fee do you think is reasonable? $_____
    j) Do you want approval of any transfer of the franchisee?   Yes ☐ No ☐
    k) Do you want a right of first refusal to acquire the franchise business upon any transfer?
       Yes ☐ No ☐
    l) Do you want a general option to purchase franchisee's business at any time?   Yes ☐ No ☐
    m) Do you want a non-competition covenant during the term of the franchise?   Yes ☐ No ☐
    n) Do you want a noncompetition covenant after the franchise is terminated or expires?   Yes ☐ No ☐
       If yes, put the miles, restrictions and the years the non-compete would be in effect. _____

    _____

    o) Do you desire an arbitration clause?   Yes ☐ No ☐
    p) Do you desire a mediation clause?   Yes ☐ No ☐
    q) Do you want a particular state as the state where the action should be brought?   Yes ☐ No ☐
       If yes, name the state: _____
    r) Do you want the law of your state to apply?   Yes ☐ No ☐
       If yes, name the state: _____

    NOTE: your answers to the foregoing questions will be placed in table form, summarized, and cross-referenced to the franchise agreement.

Public Figures

99. Will there be a public figure, i.e., a person whose name or physical appearance is generally known to the public in a geographic area where the franchisor will be located?   Yes ☐ No ☐

    If yes, please disclose the name, compensation to be paid, the public figure's position and duties in your business structure and the amount of the public figure's investment, if any, in your franchise:

    _____

    _____

    _____

Earnings Claims

100. Do you intend to make earnings claims to your franchisees which must be revealed in your offering circular?   Yes ☐ No ☐

    If yes, please describe such claims and the reasonable basis in writing that can be presented to the authorities to substantiate the fact that these earnings claims have a reasonable basis.

    _____

    _____

    _____

List of Outlets

101. Do you have any franchises at this time?   Yes ☐ No ☐

    If yes, describe: _____

    _____

    _____

102. Do you have any number of your own outlets at this time?   Yes ☐ No ☐

    If yes, please describe including name, address, telephone number and years in business:

    _____

    _____

    _____

103. If you have any franchisees, we will need a complete list including names, addresses and telephone numbers. Please list on a separate sheet.

104. Please estimate the number of franchises to be sold during the one year period after the close of the franchisor's most recent fiscal year throughout the United States:

    _____

    _____

    _____

105. If you have any franchises that have closed, cancelled, not renewed, been reacquired, or otherwise ceased to do business, describe and list the name and last known address and telephone number of every franchisee on a separate sheet.

106. For your convenience, use the following columns to give a franchised center status summary for last three fiscal years.

Franchise Center Status Summary for the Last Three Fiscal Years (years: 20___, 20___, 20___)[1]

State	Transfers	Cancelled/ Terminated	Not Renewed	Reacquired by Franchisor	Left the System/ Other	Total From Left Columns[2]	Franchisees Operating At Year End
Alabama							
Alaska							
Arizona							
Arkansas							
California							
Colorado							
Connecticut							
Delaware							
Dist. of Col.							
Florida							
Georgia							
Hawaii							
Idaho							
Illinois							
Indiana							
Iowa							
Kansas							
Kentucky							
Louisiana							
Maine							
Maryland							
Massachusetts							
Michigan							
Minnesota							
Mississippi							
Missouri							
Montana							

Franchise Center Status Summary for the Last Three Fiscal Years (years: 20___, 20___, 20___)[1]

State	Transfers	Cancelled/ Terminated	Not Renewed	Reacquired by Franchisor	Left the System/ Other	Total From Left Columns[2]	Franchisees Operating At Year End
Nebraska							
Nevada							
New Hamp.							
New Jersey							
New Mexico							
New York							
North Carolina							
North Dakota							
Ohio							
Oklahoma							
Oregon							
Pennsylvania							
Rhode Island							
South Carolina							
South Dakota							
Tennessee							
Texas							
Utah							
Vermont							
Virginia							
Washington							
West Virginia							
Wisconsin							
Wyoming							
Totals							

---

[1] Note: All members are as of December 31 for each year.

[2] The numbers in the "Total" column may exceed the number of Centers affected because several events may have affected the same Center. For example, the same franchised center may have had multiple owners.

Status of Company-Owned Centers for the Last Three Fiscal Years (years: 20___, 20___, 20___)

State	Centers Closed During Year	Centers Opened During Year	Total Centers Operating At Year End
Alabama			
Alaska			
Arizona			
Arkansas			
California			
Colorado			
Connecticut			
Delaware			
Dist. of Col.			
Florida			
Georgia			
Hawaii			
Idaho			
Illinois			
Indiana			
Iowa			
Kansas			
Kentucky			
Louisiana			
Maine			
Maryland			
Massachusetts			
Michigan			
Minnesota			
Mississippi			
Missouri			
Montana			
Nebraska			
Nevada			
New Hamp.			
New Jersey			
New Mexico			
New York			

Status of Company-Owned Centers for the Last Three Fiscal Years (years: 20___, 20___, 20___)

State	Centers Closed During Year	Centers Opened During Year	Total Centers Operating At Year End
North Carolina			
North Dakota			
Ohio			
Oklahoma			
Oregon			
Pennsylvania			
Rhode Island			
South Carolina			
South Dakota			
Tennessee			
Texas			
Utah			
Vermont			
Virginia			
Washington			
West Virginia			
Wisconsin			
Wyoming			
Totals			

Projected Openings as of _____, 200_

State	Franchise Agreements Signed But Center Not Open	Projected Franchised New Centers in the Next Fiscal Year	Projected Company-Owned Center Openings in the Next Fiscal Year
Alabama			
Alaska			
Arizona			
Arkansas			
California			
Colorado			
Connecticut			
Delaware			
Dist. of Col.			
Florida			
Georgia			
Hawaii			
Idaho			
Illinois			
Indiana			
Iowa			
Kansas			
Kentucky			
Louisiana			
Maine			
Maryland			
Massachusetts			
Michigan			
Minnesota			
Mississippi			
Missouri			
Montana			
Nebraska			
Nevada			
New Hamp.			
New Jersey			
New Mexico			
New York			

Projected Openings as of _____, 200_

State	Franchise Agreements Signed But Center Not Open	Projected Franchised New Centers in the Next Fiscal Year	Projected Company-Owned Center Openings in the Next Fiscal Year
North Carolina	_____	_____	_____
North Dakota	_____	_____	_____
Ohio	_____	_____	_____
Oklahoma	_____	_____	_____
Oregon	_____	_____	_____
Pennsylvania	_____	_____	_____
Rhode Island	_____	_____	_____
South Carolina	_____	_____	_____
South Dakota	_____	_____	_____
Tennessee	_____	_____	_____
Texas	_____	_____	_____
Utah	_____	_____	_____
Vermont	_____	_____	_____
Virginia	_____	_____	_____
Washington	_____	_____	_____
West Virginia	_____	_____	_____
Wisconsin	_____	_____	_____
Wyoming	_____	_____	_____
Totals	_____	_____	_____

Financial Statements

107. You will be required to provide audited financials statements by an independent certified public accountant. If you will provide me with the name, address and telephone number of your accountant, I will provide him with the needed information. The audited financials should include the balance sheet of the franchise corporation for the last two fiscal years before the application date or, if less than two years, the actual that time that your franchise entity has been in business. In addition, you must include Statement of Operations of stockholders' equity and of cash flow for each of the franchisor's last three fiscal years or, if less than three fiscal years, the time it has been in business. If the most recent balance sheet and statement of operations are out of date for more than 90 days before the application date, then you must also submit an unaudited balance sheet and a statement of operations as of the date within 90 days of the application date.

Contracts

108. Please list all additional agreements in addition to the franchise agreement which we will prepare that will be used regarding the franchise agreement including any leases, options and purchase agreements that are separate from the franchise agreement but which you will require your franchisee to use.

_____

_____

_____

_____

_____

_____

_____

_____

_____

_____

_____

_____

_____

_____

_____

_____

_____

The undersigned has prepared the responses to this questionnaire and compiled the above material on behalf of the franchisor and declares that to the best of its knowledge, they are true and correct.

_____

Signature

_____

Title

_____

Date

Your offering circular cannot be drafted until your attorney knows the above information.

Please attach additional sheets as needed.

Notes

Appendix D

Background Information for Franchise Agreement

Introduction

As you franchise your business, keep in mind that the more carefully you choose your franchisees, the less your agreement will need onerous "weeding out" provisions, such as minimum annual sales quotas, nonexclusive sales territories, short-term franchise agreements, and new contractual provisions upon transfer or renewal.

This questionnaire was designed to help you, as a franchisor, retain just enough control to ensure quality and consistency in the way each franchisee offers your services or products while not economically strangling the franchisee's ability to make a reasonable profit.

Pay particular attention to establishing initial franchise and royalty fees that are fair and operable. Consider each franchised location as if it were a company-owned location with the franchisee paying the bills. Never sell a franchise to a person that you would not hire for life as a manager of your company-owned operation.

After considering these ideas, you can properly frame a franchise agreement that will be workable for both parties, allowing you to achieve greater success through your franchisees than if your agreement was heavily weighted in your favor.

Attach additional sheets if needed for each question.

Franchisor: Person to Contact about this Questionnaire:

Name: _____   Name: _____

Address: _____   Address: _____

City/State/Zip: _____   City/State/Zip: _____

Telephone: _____   Telephone: _____

Service Marks

Indicate the service marks or trademarks used, as well as their registration dates and registration numbers with the United States Patent and Trademark Office and/or state trademark authorities.

_____

_____

_____

Will you defend a franchise that is sued for using your service mark or trademark by a third party claiming your trademark or service mark is an infringement of its service mark or trademark?
☐ Yes ☐ No

Territory

Will each franchised territory be exclusive, meaning no other franchise or company units will be located in a territory?   ☐ Yes ☐ No

Describe how your territorial boundaries will be determined, for example, zip code, county, population, number of businesses.

_____

_____

_____

Definition of Franchise Business

Give a brief description of the type of business that will be franchised.

_____

_____

_____

_____

_____

_____

_____

_____

_____

Internal Franchisee Identification

Set forth any type of prefix or suffix you, as the franchisor, may require to identify each franchisee on your internal records. (Example: "McDonald's of Oakland" or "McDonald's #6.")

_____

_____

_____

_____

_____

_____

Franchisor Training

Initial Training Prior to Opening

Locations	Number of Trainers	Number of Working Days	Hours per Day

Training at Time of Franchise Opening (Grand Opening)

Locations	Number of Trainers	Number of Working Days	Hours per Day

What additional training will be available to the franchisee throughout the term of the agreement?

_____

_____

_____

Will such training will be mandatory?   ☐ Yes ☐ No

Other Franchisor Assistance

Describe any other assistance the franchisor will provide the franchisee.

Prior to the Opening

Site selection: _____

_____

Market-area survey: _____

_____

Inventory supplies: _____

_____

Equipment: _____

_____

Financial assistance: _____

_____

Hiring of personnel: _____

_____

Local business licenses: _____

_____

Public relations: _____

_____

Other: _____

_____

_____

After the Opening

Purchasing assistance: _____

_____

Accounting services: _____

_____

Product updates: _____

_____

Procedure improvements: _____

_____

Public relations: _____

_____

Inspections: _____

_____

Other: _____

_____

Franchisee Fee

Indicate the amount of the initial franchise fee you, as the franchisor, feel you can charge a franchisee.
$ _____.

How did you arrive at this fee? _____

_____

_____

_____

Terms of payment of the initial franchise fee:
Down-payment $ _____   Balance payment $ _____

Monthly Royalty

Percent of gross receipts you expect to receive as a royalty each month: _____%
List reasons for estimating this percentage: _____

_____

_____

_____

Would any minimums be desired? Amount of these minimums: $ _____

(Consideration can also be given to reducing a monthly royalty upon the attainment of a certain amount of gross receipts per month or deferring all or part of the royalty for an initial specified period of time.)

Promotion and Advertisements

Percent of gross receipts or other formula that you desire in establishing a general advertising fee fund: _____%

Your reasons in arriving at such a percentage:

_____

_____

_____

What amount must the franchisee spend on local advertising?

Percentage of gross sales: _____ %   or a minimum: $ _____

Must the franchisee enter into cooperative advertising with fellow franchisees?   ☐ Yes ☐ No

Explain any limits upon such advertising expenditures:

_____

_____

_____

Yellow Pages

Describe the minimum Yellow Page advertisement desired, if any: _____ inches by _____ columns

Operations Manual

Will a confidential operations manual be provided to the franchisee?   ☐ Yes ☐ No

Describe the areas covered.

Day-to-day operations: _____

_____

Marketing: _____

_____

Purchasing: _____

_____

Advertising: _____

_____

Accounting procedures: _____

_____

Hiring of employees: _____

_____

Training of staff: _____

_____

Public relations: _____

_____

Other: _____

_____

_____

_____

Franchise Operation

Is the franchisee allowed to sell products or render services other than those designated by the franchisor?   ☐ Yes ☐ No

If so, what are the restrictions on the products or services that can be rendered or sold by the franchisee?

_____

_____

_____

_____

Amount of supervisory time that a franchisee or approved manager must render for actual on-premises operation of the franchise: _____ hours per week _____ weeks per year

Insurance

Most franchisors desire public liability insurance in amounts of $1,000,000 combined single limits for bodily injury and property damage.

Is this satisfactory to your insurance agent for the type of franchise business in question?   ☐ Yes ☐ No

Is a fidelity bond insurance requirement of $50,000 necessary and satisfactory?   ☐ Yes ☐ No

If not, list the desired policy limits: _____

_____

_____

_____

Noncompetition Provisions

What noncompetition restrictions do you desire, if any, including distance from existing franchisees and number of years in which competition is prohibited?

_____

_____

_____

_____

Office Management Personnel

Are you agreeable to absentee management?   ☐ Yes ☐ No

Do you wish to require that all franchisees' managers and personnel be trained by your personnel?
☐ Yes ☐ No

Do you wish to require that any assignee of the franchise who purchases the business also be trained by you?   ☐ Yes ☐ No

Term and Transfers

Do you desire to have the franchise agreement last for an infinite amount of time with the only contingency being that any transfer either to third parties, heirs, or relatives be made with the approval of the franchisor as to financial ability and suitability?   ☐ Yes ☐ No

If not, do you desire a length of franchise term in number of years such as 10, 20, or 30? State your suggested term and renewal terms, if any: _____

Do you want a transfer fee payable to the franchisor when a franchisee sells his or her business and transfers it to another party with your approval?   ☐ Yes ☐ No

If yes, what transfer fee amount would you like? $ _____   What renewal fee amount? $ _____

Franchisee's Initial Investment

As best you can, provide the projected amount a franchisee would have to pay to start up a franchise of yours, in each of the following categories:

Category	Amount
Leasehold improvements	$ _____
Equipment	$ _____
Decor	$ _____
Furnishings	$ _____
Signs	$ _____
Rent* (first and last months)	$ _____
Cash registers	$ _____
Uniforms	$ _____
Opening inventory for three months	$ _____
Working capital necessary to commence or continue operation for one month	$ _____

Deposits

Rental	$ _____
Telephone	$ _____
Electricity	$ _____

Insurance

Auto	$ _____
Errors and omissions	$ _____
Fidelity bond	$ _____
Liability	$ _____

Other

_____	$ _____
_____	$ _____
Total	$ _____

*Average square footage of your franchise premises building is _____ sq. ft.

Obligation of Franchisee to Purchase from Franchisor or from Franchisor's Designated Supplier

Describe any obligations of the franchisee to purchase goods or services from you or from your designated supplier. (If the franchisee is required to purchase from a designated supplier, also give the name and address of the supplier, the reason for requiring the purchase from a designated supplier, and a brief description of what must be purchased.)

_____

_____

_____

_____

If the franchisee is obligated to purchase goods or services from you or from your designated supplier, will you receive any profit or revenue from such sales?   ☐ Yes ☐ No

If such purchases are required, what percent of the franchisee's total requirements of that service or product will constitute purchases from you or your designated supplier? _____ %

Financing Arrangement

Will you take back promissory notes or carry some paper from the franchisee?   ☐ Yes ☐ No
If so, please describe: _____

_____

_____

_____

Will you assist the franchisee in securing financing from independent third parties?   ☐ Yes ☐ No

If yes, please explain: _____

_____

_____

_____

Services the Franchisor May Provide

Describe any services you may provide although not legally obligated to do so under the franchise agreement.

Periodic visits by representatives: _____

_____

_____

Telephone consultation (describe limits on hours of such): _____

_____

_____

Suggested advertising: _____

_____

_____

Other advisory services: _____

_____

_____

Patents and Copyrights

Describe any patents or copyrights you may offer to the franchisee.

_____

_____

_____

_____

_____

_____

_____

Public Figures

Will you provide public figures in promotion of the franchise?   ☐ Yes ☐ No

If yes, please explain, providing the names of the public figures, basic arrangement with the public figures including compensation, duration of the agreement, and general description of the services of the public figure to the franchisee.

Public Figure	Compensation	Duration	Services
_____	_____	_____	_____
_____	_____	_____	_____
_____	_____	_____	_____
_____	_____	_____	_____
_____	_____	_____	_____
_____	_____	_____	_____

Actual Average, Projected, or Forecasted Franchise Sales, Profits, or Earnings

Do you wish to provide average, projected, or forecasted franchise sales to potential franchisees?
☐ Yes ☐ No

(In the event you do, your projections must be based on figures, data, and information that is documented and submitted to the Department of Corporations so that it can determine the feasibility of your forecast.)

If yes, provide a written substantiation showing that such projections will be valid for your franchisees operating in other locations. _____

_____

_____

_____

Provision for Legal Fees

Reasonable Attorney Fee to Prevailing Party

In some states, it is permissible to insert a clause to the effect that if there is a dispute and the matter is brought to arbitration or trial, the prevailing party would be entitled to reasonable attorney fees. This clause on its face seems desirable. However, the downside of the clause is that it may encourage franchisees to bring action since they feel that they will win and that the franchisor will have to pay their attorney fees. In some cases, an attorney may take the franchisee's lawsuit on a contingency basis figuring that he can always collect his fees if he wins from the franchisor. In addition, the courts do not always award all of the attorney fees to the prevailing party. In some cases, the court will order payment of an amount less than the actual amount billed on the grounds that this is what the courts feel is reasonable, not what the attorney actually charged.

As a franchisor, do you wish to have a clause inserted which would provide that the prevailing party in any law action or arbitration would have a right to an award for reasonable attorney fees? ☐ Yes ☐ No

Arbitration

More and more franchisors are utilizing arbitration as a means of solving problems between franchisees and franchisors. Arbitration allows the parties to pick knowledgeable arbitrators, and this is far less costly and takes considerably less time. An arbitration award is, for all practical purposes, unappealable but can eliminate many of the costly preliminary procedures such as depositions, interrogatories, motions, etc. Some franchisors prefer not to include arbitration clauses because they feel that if the franchisee were to go to court, he would eventually run out of money because of high court costs and attorney fees for court appearances. However, by the same token, if the franchisor were to have any appreciable amount of lawsuits, the franchisor would also run out of money.

The disadvantage of an arbitration clause is that it is not appealable. However, as a practical matter, appeals are extremely expensive and time consuming, and only the more financially endowed franchisee can avail himself of this procedure. In addition, the majority of appeals are cases in which the original decision is upheld.

Do you want to have an arbitration clause in your agreement with your franchisees? ☐ Yes ☐ No

Maximum Multiple Franchise Locations for One Franchisee

If a franchisee has the right to purchase more than one franchise, what total number of franchise locations will you allow a franchisee to open in one area? _____

(Some businesses such as fine restaurants require almost all of the time and attention of the franchisee and, therefore, allowing additional locations could cause the franchisee to fail. Take this into consideration when answering this question.)

Considerations: _____

_____

_____

_____

Other Desired Clauses

List your thoughts regarding additional clauses which are of particular importance to you and the business you are franchising.

_____

_____

_____

_____

_____

_____

_____

_____

_____

_____

_____

_____

_____

_____

_____

_____

The undersigned has prepared the responses to this questionnaire and compiled the above material on behalf of the franchisor.

_____
Date

_____
Signature of party answering questionnaire

_____
Printed or typed name and title of party answering questionnaire

Appendix E

State Franchise Information Guidelines

Introduction

Although all franchises are subject to the FTC regulations, many states have additional laws governing franchises and similar business opportunities. The information contained in this appendix is a compilation of the available data from those states which have franchise registration laws or business opportunity statutes, or both. Included under each state heading, where applicable, is information on:

- State franchise and business opportunity statutes;
- Laws affecting franchise transfers, renewals and terminations;
- State franchise law enforcement offices; and
- State advertising filings and review procedures.

The last two pages of this appendix consist of charts containing the most recent information on fees charged by states with franchise registration and business opportunity statutes.

Use these guidelines only as an initial reference resource. As a prospective franchisor or franchisee, you should consult your own state regarding its laws, especially to request updated instructions and forms for filing a uniform franchise offering circular. Registration states have personnel, usually attorneys, who examine each submitted offering circular.

Remember, any failure, on the part of the franchisor, in using, preparing, or filing the required circular could result in censure or penalties. Use this section of the book so you are knowledgeable when you talk to your attorney.

State Guidelines and Offices (as of March 1995)

Alabama

Alabama has enacted a Deceptive Trade Practices Act which makes it unlawful to make certain misrepresentations in any franchises, distributorships, and seller-assisted marketing plans. ALA. CODE Section 8-19-1.

Arkansas

Arkansas has a Franchise Practice Act which doesn't require registration or disclosure, but does prohibit termination or nonrenewal of franchisees without good cause. ARK. STAT. ANN. Section 4-72-201 through 4-72-210.

California

California has a Franchise Investment Act, which requires full disclosure and registration by the franchisor. CAL. CORP. CODE Section 31000 to 31516. It should be noted that California has what is called a "Seller Assisted Marketing Plan Act," which covers certain types of marketing that are akin to franchising. CAL. CIVIL CODE Section 1812-200 to 1812-221.

California's "Franchise Relations Act" became effective January 1, 1981, and pertains to termination with good cause and prior 180-day notification if the franchisor does not intend to renew a contract. The Act further provides for compensation for franchises that have not been renewed but are intended for reconversion to company-owned outlets. CAL. BUS. & PROF. CODE Section 20000.

Brochures and ads must be submitted in duplicate and avoid any statements regarding success, safe investments, unlikelihood of default, or earnings not supported by Item 19. The ad must be filed with the Department of Corporations at least three business days prior to publishing the ad.

California Corporations Commissioner
Department of Corporations
320 West 4th Street, Suite 750
Los Angeles, CA 90013
(213) 576-7500

Connecticut

Connecticut has a Business Opportunity investment Act which requires registration and disclosure by any person who is engaged in the business of selling or offering for sale a business opportunity. CONN. GEN. STAT. Title 36, sh. 662a, Section 36b-60 through 36b-80. Connecticut also has a Franchise Termination Act that requires good cause for nonrenewal or termination of franchises. CONN. GEN. STAT. Section 42-133e through 42-133g.

Delaware

Delaware has a Franchise Security Law requiring good cause for terminations and nonrenewals of franchises. DEL. CODE ANN. Title 6, Section 2551 through 2556.

Florida

Florida's Business Opportunity Act provides for filing, full disclosure, and the securing of an advertising number. Under certain conditions, an exception from filing can be secured. Certain misrepresentations are prohibited. FLA. STAT. 1995, Ch. 817, Section 559.8 to 559.815, effective Oct. 1, 1998. The Florida Deceptive and Unfair Practice Act pertains to misrepresentation by franchisors. FLA. STAT. Section 817.416.

Georgia

Georgia has a Business Opportunity Statute pertaining to fraudulent and deceptive practices in the sale of business opportunities. A disclosure must be provided in multilevel distributions. GA. CODE ANN. Section 10-1-410 through 10-1-417.

Hawaii

Hawaii has a Franchise Investment Law pertaining to filing an application and disclosure. HAW. REV. STAT. Section 482E.1 through 482E.5. Hawaii also has a Franchise Rights and Prohibitions Act regarding prohibited actions, and good cause requirements for nonrenewals and terminations. HAW. REV. STAT. Section 482E. Hawaii does not review advertising.

Hawaii Securities Examiner
1010 Richards Street
Honolulu, Hawaii 96813
(808) 586-2727

Illinois

Illinois has a Franchise Disclosure Act which regulates full disclosure, registration, good cause termination, and nonrenewal provisions. ILL. COMP. STATS 1992, Ch. 815, Section 705/1 through 705/44. Illinois has a Business Opportunity Sales Law of 1995. Illinois Laws of 1995, Public Act 89-209; ILL. COMP. STATS 1996, Ch. 815, Section 60215-1 to 60215-135.

Indiana

Indiana has a Registration Disclosure Statute in addition to a Deceptive Franchise Practice Act affecting good cause on nonrenewals and 90-day termination notices. 23 IND. CODE, Art. 2, Ch. 2.5, Section 1-51, Ch. 2.7, Section 1 through 7. See Business Opportunity Transaction, IND. CODE, Title 24, Art. 5, Ch. 8, Section 1-21.

Indiana Chief Deputy Commissioner
Secretary of State
Franchise Section
Securities Division
302 W Washington Street, Room E-111
Indianapolis, Indiana 46204
(317) 232-6681

Iowa

Iowa has passed a business opportunity law (1995) requiring registration of nonexempt offerings and a stringent new franchise act (1995) covering transfers, encroachments, good cause terminations, good cause nonrenewals and a duty of good faith performance. IOWA CODE (1995), d Title XX, Section 523B and 523B 13 and 523H, Section 523H.1 through 523 H.17.

Kentucky

Kentucky has a Business Opportunity Disclosure Act calling for registration of nonexempt offerings. KY. REV. STAT. Section 367.801, *et seq.* and 367.990.

Louisiana

Louisiana has a Business Opportunity Law that does not provide for filing, but a Surety Bond is required in certain instances. LA. REV. STAT. Section 51:1801 through 51:1804.

Maine

Maine has a Business Opportunity Act which includes registration of nonexempt offerings and disclosure requirements pertaining to the sale of any business opportunity. ME. REV. STAT. ANN. Chapter 69-B, Section 4691 and Chs. 542 and 597.

Maryland

Maryland has a Franchise Registration and Disclosure Law regulating franchises. MD. CODE ANN., Art. 56, Section 345. Maryland also has an Equity Participation Investment Program Act passed for the purpose of encouraging and developing franchises in Maryland, and the Maryland Fair Distributorship Act (1993) regarding cancellation or nonrenewal notices, repurchases, arbitration between a grantor and a distributor. ANN. CODE of Maryland, Title 14, Section 14-101 through 14-129. Section 14-201 through 14-233, Article of Commercial Law, Title 11, Section 11-1301 through 11-1306.

Maryland Franchise Examiner
Office of the Attorney General
Maryland Division of Securities
200 St. Paul Place, 20th Floor
Baltimore, Maryland 21202
(410) 576-7042

Michigan

Michigan has an annual notice filing Disclosure Act and Pyramid Statute which includes good cause for termination and renewal provision laws and repurchase requirements for nonrenewals. MICH. COMP. LAWS Section 445.1501 and 445.1545. It also has a Business Opportunity Act requiring a notice filing. MICH. COMP. LAWS Section 445.901 through 445.922, and a Void and Unenforceable Provisions Law, Section 445.1527. See Section MICH. COMP. LAWS Section 445.1525.

Michigan Franchise Administrator
Consumer Protection Division
Attention: Franchise Administrator
670 Law Building
Lansing, Michigan 48913
(517) 373-7117

Minnesota

Minnesota has a Franchise Registration and Full Disclosure Act which also covers Business Opportunities in addition to Pyramid and Unfair Practice Act and requires good cause for terminations and 90 days prior written notice with a 60-day cure period for nonrenewals. MINN. STAT. Section 80C-01 *et seq.* to 80-C-14.

Minnesota Franchising Examiner
Minnesota Department of Commerce
133 East Seventh Street
St. Paul, Minnesota 55101
(612) 296-6328

Mississippi

Mississippi's Franchise Termination Statute also includes provisions regarding profit projections and misrepresenting earnings. Take special notice of the Repurchase of Inventory from Retailers upon Termination of Contract Statute and required 90-day written nonrenewal and termination notices. MISS. CODE ANN. Section 75-24-51 to 75-24-61.

Missouri

Missouri's statute prohibits termination without notice, requires a nonrenewal written 90-day notice, and includes a Pyramid Sales Statute. MO. REV. STAT. Section 407.400 through 407.410, 407.420.

Nebraska

Nebraska's Franchise Practice Act has provisions regarding 60 days prior written notice and good cause for nonrenewals and terminations. NEB. REV. STAT. Section 87-404 through 87-410. In addition, it has a Business Practice Act which, in essence, is a Seller Assisted Marketing Plans Act. NEB. REV. STAT. Section 59-1701 through 59-1761.

New Hampshire

New Hampshire has a Distributor Disclosure Act. N.H. REV. STAT. ANN. Section 339-C:1 through 339-C:9 and Section 358-E1 through 358-E6.

New Jersey

New Jersey has a Franchise Practice Act, requiring 60 days prior written notice and good cause for terminations, cancellations, and nonrenewals. N.J. REV. STAT. Section 56:10-1 through 56:10-12.

New York

New York's Franchise Registration and Disclosure Statute became effective January 1, 1981. N.Y. GEN. BUS. LAW Section 680 through 695. Laws of 1989 Ch. 61 approved effective April 1, 1989.

Special Deputy Attorney General
Bureau of Investigation
New York State Department of Law
120 Broadway, 23rd Floor
New York, New York 10271
(212) 416-8211
FAX (212) 416-8816

North Carolina

North Carolina's Business Opportunities Disclosure Law requires filing 2 copies of the disclosure statement that are nonexempt offerings with the secretary of state. N.C. GEN. STAT. Section 66.94 to 66-100.

North Dakota

North Dakota's Franchise Investment Law governs registration, full disclosure, termination, and renewal of provisions. N.D. CENT. CODE ANN. Section 51.19.01 through Section 51-19-17. Ads must be submitted at least five business days prior to first publication.

North Dakota Franchise Examiner
Office of Securities Commission
600 East Boulevard, 5th Floor
Bismarck, North Dakota 58505
(701) 328-4712

Ohio

Ohio has a nonfiling Business Opportunity Act requiring a disclosure be provided to prospective purchasers. OHIO REV. CODE Section 13340.01 through 1334.15 and 1334.99.

Oklahoma

Oklahoma's Business Opportunity Sales Act requires registration of nonexempt offerings. OKLA. STAT. Section 71-4-801 through 828.

Oregon

Oregon's Franchise Transactions Statute requires full disclosure but does not require registration. OR. REV. STAT. Section 650.005 through 650.085. It also has a little FTC Act prohibiting certain misrepresentation actions. OR. REV. STAT. Section 646.605. No advertising filing is required.

Oregon Department of Insurance and Finance
Corporate Securities Section
Labor and Industries Building
Salem, Oregon 97310
(503) 378-4140

Rhode Island

Rhode Island's Franchise Distributor Investment Regulation Act requires the franchisor to fully disclose and register. R.I. GEN. LAWS Section 19-28-1 through 19-28.1-34.

Rhode Island Securities Examiner
Division of Securities
233 Richmond Street, #232
Providence, Rhode Island 02903
(401) 222-3048

South Carolina

South Carolina's Business Opportunities Sales Act requires filing a disclosure with the secretary of state. S.C. CODE Section 39-57-10 to 39-57-80.

South Dakota

South Dakota's Franchise for Brand-Name Goods and Services Law requires registration and full disclosure. S.D. CODIFIED LAWS ANN. Section 37-5A-1 through 37-5A-87. Its Business Opportunity Statute requires filing of business opportunities. S.D. CODIFIED LAWS ANN. Section 37-25A-1 through 37-25A-54.

South Dakota Franchise Administrator
Division of Securities
c/o 118 West Capitol
Pierre, South Dakota 57501
(605) 773-4013

Texas

Texas has a Business Opportunity Act requiring registration unless the offering is exempt as a franchise offering and a notice of exemption is filed with the secretary of state. TEX. BUS. & COM. CODE, Title 4, Ch. 41, Section 41.001 thru 41.303.

Statutory Document Section
Secretary of State
P.O. Box 12887
Austin, TX 78711
(512) 475-1769

Utah

Utah has a Business Opportunity Disclosure Act in which it refers to "assisted marketing plans" and requires filing of nonexempt offerings. A notice of claim for exception can be filed together with a fee. UTAH CODE ANN. Section 13-15-1 through 13-15-6.

Virginia

Virginia has a Retail Franchise Act which requires disclosure and registration. VA. CODE Section 13.1-557 through 13.1-1-574. Virginia also has a Business Opportunity Law that does not require registration. VA. CODE Section 59.1-262 through 59.1-269. It also has a statute requiring good cause for cancellation. VA. CODE Section 13.1-564.

Virginia Chief Examiner
State Corporation Commission
Division of Securities and
Retail Franchising
1300 E. Main Street
Richmond, Virginia 23219
(804) 371-9051

Washington

Washington has a Franchise Investment Protection Act which requires full disclosure and registration (REV. CODE 19.100 Section 19.100.10 through 19.100.940), as well as provisions regarding renewal with buyout compensation and good cause termination. WASH. REV. CODE Section 19.100.180 and 19.100.190. It also has a Business Opportunity Fraud Act requiring registration. WASH. REV. CODE Section 19.110.010 through 19.100.930.

Washington Securities Administrator
Department of Financial Institutions
P.O. Box 9033
Olympia, Washington 98507-9033
(360) 902-8760

Washington D.C.

D.C. Franchising Act, D.C. CODE ANN. Section 29-1201 requires good cause for terminations, cancellations, failure to renew, or failing to consent to a transfer with a required 60-day cure period.

Wisconsin

Wisconsin's Franchise Investment Law requires annual registration by notification on a notice form prescribed and full disclosure. WIS. STAT. Section 553.01 through 553.78. Its Fair Dealership Law requires "good cause" in order to terminate or fail to renew. WIS. STAT. Section 135.01 to 135.07.

Wisconsin Commissioner of Securities
Registration Division
P.O. Box 1768
Madison, Wisconsin 53701
(608) 266-8559

United States

The Federal Trade Commission (FTC) has a general disclosure act covering franchises and business opportunities. (Rule 436.1, entitled Disclosure Requirements and Prohibitions Concerning Franchising and Business Opportunity Ventures.) No registration is required. 16 C.F.R. Part 436. Legislation is pending regarding franchisor-franchisee relations, including good cause renewals and terminations and earnings claims, etc.

Note: All states are subject to the FTC Act whether or not they have Franchise or Business Opportunity statutes. The Federal Trade Commission (FTC) will recognize the Uniform Offering Disclosure of Franchise Registration States but Business Opportunity Disclosures must also include the requirements of the Federal Trade Commission disclosure. The Federal Trade Commission does not require registration of the FTC Disclosure.

Franchise Rule Coordinator
Federal Trade Commission (FTC)
Division of Enforcement
Bureau of Consumer Protection
Pennsylvania Avenue at 6th Street N.W.
Washington, DC 20580
(202) 326-3128

[Note: The FTC is the enforcement agency and does not require registration.

Filing Fees of Franchise Registration States (as of March 1995)

State	Initial Filing	Renewal	Pre-effective Amendment	Post-effective Amendment	Exemption Notice	Exemption Notice Renewal
California	$675	$450	$-0-	$50	$450	$150
Hawaii	250	250	N/A	250	N/A	N/A
Illinois	500	100	-0-	100	N/A	N/A
Indiana	500	250	-0-	50	250	N/A
Maryland	500	250	-0-	100	250	-0-
Michigan	250	-0-				
Minnesota	400	200	-0-	100	N/A	N/A
New York	750	N/A	-0-	150	-0-	-0-
North Dakota	250	100	-0-	50	100	50
Oregon	(no registration but statute dictates type of circular and contracts that must be used)					
Rhode Island	500	250	-0-	100	300	-0-
South Dakota	250	100	-0-	50	N/A	N/A
Virginia	500	250 + $50 if changes made	-0-	100	100	N/A
Washington	600	100	-0-	100	100	N/A
Wisconsin	400	400	-0-	200	200	-0-

Business Opportunity Registration Fees (as of March 1995)

State	Reg. Fee	Renewal Fee	Amendment Fee	Exemption
Alabama	(no registration)			
California	$100	$100	$30	
Connecticut	$400	$100	-0-	
Florida	$300	$300	$50	$100
Georgia	(no registration)			
Indiana	$ 50	$ 10	$10	
Iowa	$500	$250	-0-	$100
Kentucky	-0-	-0-	-0-	
Louisiana	-0-	-0-	-0-	
Maine	$ 25	$ 10	-0-	
Maryland	$250	$100	$50	
Michigan	-0-	-0-	-0-	
Minnesota	See General Franchise Law Fee			
Nebraska	$100	$ 50	$50	$100
New Hampshire	-0-	-0-	-0-	
North Carolina	$ 10			
Ohio	-0-	-0-	-0-	
Oklahoma	$250	$150	-0-	
South Carolina	$100	-0-	-0-	
South Dakota	$100	$ 50	-0-	
Texas	$195	$ 25	$25	$ 25
Utah	-0-	-0-	-0-	
Virginia	-0-	-0-	-0-	
Washington	$200	$125	$30	

Appendix F

Uniform Franchise Offering Circular (UFOC) Guidelines

Introduction

The guidelines reprinted here outline the new requirements for the Uniform Franchise Offering Circular (UFOC) as prepared and adopted by the North American Securities Administrators Association (NASAA) on April 25, 1993, and put into effect on January 1, 1995. These guidelines assist the franchisor by listing the requirements, instructions, and sample answers to the questions raised.

The numbered items under general instructions refer to numbered rules published by the FTC. Following the general instructions, the guidelines cover every item of the UFOC, from the cover page and table of contents, to Item 23, receipt of the offering circular by the franchisee.

This reproduction of the UFOC guidelines is designed to work together with Appendix A, the sample offering circular, and Appendix C, the background questionnaire for preparing the offering circular.

THE UNIFORM FRANCHISE OFFERING CIRCULAR GUIDELINES

GENERAL INSTRUCTIONS

90. Introduction: The Uniform Franchise Offering Circular (UFOC) Guidelines consist of the Requirements, the Instructions and the Sample Answers. The UFOC Guidelines were prepared and adopted by the North American Securities Administrators Association (NASAA) and its predecessor, the Midwest Securities Commissioners Association. The members of NASAA cannot create statutes since that is the constitutional province of state legislatures, but NASAA intends for the UFOC Guidelines to facilitate compliance with disclosure requirements under state franchise investment laws. Where possible, NASAA has developed uniform disclosure requirements, but differences in state laws bearing on the franchise relationship may necessitate changes. In addition, state administrators will continue to review the application for deficient disclosure and additional disclosure necessitated by special problems or risks in the proposed offering.

100. Follow these General Instructions and the Requirement and Instruction for each Item in franchise registration applications and disclosures in the Uniform Franchise Offering Circular.

110. Original Registration Application – Documents to File:

    (a) Uniform Franchise Registration Application Page (also known as Facing Page);

    (b) Supplemental Information page(s);

    (c) Certification page;

    (d) Uniform Consent to Service of Process;

    (e) Sales Agent Disclosure Form;

    (f) If the applicant is a corporation or partnership, an authorizing resolution if the application is verified by a person other than applicant's officer or general partner;

    (g) Uniform Franchise Offering Circular;

    (h) Application Fee;

    (i) Auditor's consent (or a photocopy of the consent) to the use of the latest audited financial statements in the offering circular; and

    (j) Advertising or promotional materials.

Examples of forms (a) through (f) are printed at the end of these Guidelines.

120. Renewal Application: When state law requires renewal, mark "renewal" on the application page. Submit all documents required for an initial application with additions to the previously filed documents underlined. Changes must be clearly marked so that the change is noticed easily. File a renewal application before the prior registration has expired. If the prior registration has expired, mark "Registration of an Offer or Sale of Franchises" on the facing page and pay the fee charged for initial registrations. Redlining and bracketing changes from the last filing will speed a re-registration. Do not mark the amendment boxes on the application page on the first renewal filing even if documents are revised.

150. "Disclose" means to state all material facts in an accurate and unambiguous manner. Disclose clearly, concisely, and in a narrative form that is understandable by a person unfamiliar with the franchise business. For clear and concise disclosure, avoid legal antiques[1] and repetitive phrases.[2] When possible, use active, not passive voice.[3] Limit the length and complexity of disclosure through careful organization of information in the disclosure. Avoid technical language and unnecessary detail. Make the format and chronological order consistent within each Item.

160. Since prospective franchisees must have sufficient disclosure to understand economic commitments and to develop a business plan, Items 5, 6, 7, and 8 must disclose the minimum and maximum franchisee cost. The franchisor should provide reasonably available information to allow franchisees to forecast future charges listed in these Items and to be paid to persons who are independent of the franchisor. Future payments to the franchisor should be specific as is required by individual Items.

170. The disclosure for each UFOC Item should be separately titled and in the required order. Do not repeat the UFOC question in the offering circular. Respond to each question fully. If the disclosure is not applicable, respond in the negative, but if an answer is required "if applicable," respond only if the requested information applies. Do not qualify a response with a reference to another document unless permitted by the instructions to that Item.

180. For each Item in the UFOC, type the Requirement's Item title and number. Sub-items may be designated by descriptive headings, but do not use sub-item letters and numbers.

---

[1] Avoid these legal antiques. Preferred substitutes are in parentheses: aforesaid; arising from (from); as between; as an inducement for; as part of the consideration; as set forth in (in); as the case may be; at a later point in time; binding upon and inure; commence (begin); condition precedent (before); condition subsequent (after); consist of (are); engaged in the business of offering (offers); for and in consideration of the grant of the franchise; for a period of (for); foregoing; forthwith; from time to time; further; hereby; herein; hereinafter; hereto; heretofore; if necessary; in the event (if); including but not limited to (including); in any manner whatsoever; including without limitation (including); in conjunction with; in connection with; in no event; in the event of (if); in whole or in part; it will be specifically understood that; manner in which; not later than (within, by); not less than (at least); notwithstanding; offers to an individual, corporation or partnership (offer); on behalf of (for); precedent (before); prescribed (required); prior to (before); provided however (but, unless); provided that (if, unless); purporting to; relating to (under); subsequent (after); such (this); so as to (to); so long as (while); thereafter; therefrom; thereof; thereunder; without limiting the foregoing; whatsoever; with respect to.

[2] Avoid repetitive phrases. Preferred substitutes are in parentheses: agrees, acknowledges and recognizes; any and all; are and remain; based upon, related to, or growing out of (because); certified as true and correct (certified); consultation, assistance and guidance (guidance); each and every; equipment, furniture, supplies and inventory set forth on the equipment list attached as Exhibit_____ (items on Exhibit_____); necessary and appropriate; sample, test and review (test); and twenty-three (23) (write as 23).

[3] The preferred phrase is in parentheses: As the franchisor prescribes (you must); being offered (offers); consist of (is); engaged in the business of offering (offer); giving rise to; if it becomes necessary for (if); inure to the benefit of (benefits) is granted the right to (can); is given an opportunity to (can); is required to (must); shall be no less than (a minimum of); shall continue in effect (continues); with the exception of (except).

190. Separate documents (for example, a confidential Operations Manual) must not make representations or impose terms that contradict or are materially different from the disclosure in the offering circular.

200. Use 8 ½ by 11 inch paper for the entire application.

210. When the applicant is a master franchisor seeking to sell subfranchisor, references in these requirements and instructions to "franchisee" include the subfranchisor unless the language context requires a different meaning.

220. The offer of subfranchises is an offer separate from the offer of franchises and usually requires a separate registration or exemption. A single application may register the sale of single unit and multi-unit franchises if the offering circular is not confusing.

230. When the applicant is a subfranchisor, disclose to the extent applicable the same information concerning the subfranchisor that is required about the franchisor.

240. In offerings by a subfranchisor, "franchisor" means both the franchisor and subfranchisor.

250. When state requirements conflict with these Guidelines, the state requirements control. The State Administrator may modify or waive these Guidelines or may require additional documentation or information.

260. Grossly deficient applications may be rejected summarily by the administrator as incomplete for filing. It is not the function of an administrator to prepare, in effect, an applicant's application. The additional examiner time reviewing the grossly deficient product delays the processing of diligently prepared and pursued applications.

265. These Guidelines are effective six months after the Federal Trade Commission and each NASAA member whose jurisdiction requires presale registration of a franchise adopts them. In any event, these Guidelines will be effective no earlier than January 1, 1994 and no later than January 1, 1995. After the effective date of these Guidelines, all initial franchise applications, renewals and re-registrations must comply with these Guidelines.

270. The Guidelines that continue after these instructions use the following format:

   (a) The title of the Item follows the Item number. It is capitalized and centered on the page.
   (b) The "Item" is a restatement of the Uniform Franchise Offering Circular ("UFOC") Item Requirement. It is capitalized and follows the title of the Item.
   (c) The "Instruction" appears beneath the Item. It explains portions of the Item Requirements.
   (d) The "Sample Answer" at the end of each Item provides sample disclosures. Double horizontal lines divide the Sample Answer from the Instructions.

REQUIREMENTS FOR PREPARATION OF A UNIFORM FRANCHISE OFFERING CIRCULAR COVER PAGE

The state cover page of the offering circular must state:

1. The title in boldface type: FRANCHISE OFFERING CIRCULAR.

2. The franchisor's name, type of business organization, principal business address and telephone number.

3. A sample of the primary business trademark, logotype, trade name, or commercial label or symbol under which the franchisee will conduct its business. (Place in upper left-hand corner of the cover page.)

4. A brief description of the franchised business.

5. The total amounts in Items 5 and 7 of the offering circular: Franchisee's Initial Franchisee Fee or Other Payment and Franchisee's Initial Investment.

6. The following statements:

Information comparing franchisors is available. Call the state administrators listed in Exhibit _____ or your public library for sources of information.

Registration of this franchise by a state does not mean that the state recommends it or has verified the information in this offering circular. If you learn that anything in the offering circular is untrue, contact the Federal Trade Commission and (State or Provincial authority).

7. Effective Date: (Leave blank until notified of effectiveness by state regulatory authority.)

<u>Cover Page Instructions:</u>

   i. Present information in the required order. Except for risk factors or when instructed by the examiner, do not capitalize or underline.

  ii. The estimated cash investment should agree with the Item 7 total. This total should represent the franchisees entire initial investment minus only exclusions allowed by Item 7. Do not state what the total includes.

 iii. Limit the cover page disclosure to one page unless risk factors require additional space. Disclosure on the cover page should be brief. Limit the description of the business to the product or service offered by the franchisor. Unless required by a state regulator, do not disclose financing arrangements or the franchisee's right to use the trademark. Exclude non-required information unless necessary as a risk factor or required by a state regulator.

  iv. If applicable, disclose the following risk factors using the following language on the cover:

   1. THE FRANCHISE AGREEMENT PERMITS THE FRANCHISEE (TO SUE) (TO ARBITRATE WITH) _____ ONLY IN _____. OUT OF STATE (ARBITRATION) (LITIGATION) MAY FORCE YOU TO ACCEPT A LESS FAVORABLE SETTLEMENT FOR DISPUTES. IT MAY ALSO COST MORE (TO SUE) (TO ARBITRATE WITH) _____ IN _____ THAN IN YOUR HOME STATE.

2. THE FRANCHISE AGREEMENT STATES THAT _____ LAW GOVERNS THE AGREEMENT, AND THIS LAW MAY NOT PROVIDE THE SAME PROTECTION AND BENEFITS AS LOCAL LAW. YOU MAY WANT TO COMPARE THESE LAWS.

3. THERE MAY BE OTHER RISKS CONCERNING THIS FRANCHISE.

v. In addition to the above language, disclose other risk factors required by a state regulator.

vi. Use capital letters for risk factor disclosure.

vii. In multi-state offerings in which the franchisor uses a single offering circular, refer to an exhibit to the offering circular for a list of State or Provincial authority.

SAMPLE COVER PAGE

(Logo)
FRANCHISE OFFERING CIRCULAR

Belmont Mufflers, Inc.
A Minnesota Corporation
First Street
Jackson, Minnesota 55000
(612) 266-3430

The franchisee will repair and install motor vehicle exhaust systems.

The initial franchise fee is $10,000. The estimated initial investment required ranges from $132,700 to $160,200. This sum does not include rent for the business location.

Risk Factors:

THE FRANCHISE AGREEMENT REQUIRES THAT ALL DISAGREEMENTS BE SETTLED BY ARBITRATION IN MINNESOTA. OUT OF STATE ARBITRATION MAY FORCE YOU TO ACCEPT A LESS FAVORABLE SETTLEMENT FOR DISPUTES. IT MAY ALSO COST YOU MORE TO ARBITRATE WITH US IN MINNESOTA THAN IN YOUR HOME STATE.

Information about comparisons of franchisors is available. Call the state administrators listed in Exhibit _____ or your public library for sources of information.

Registration of this franchise with the state does not mean that the state recommends it or has verified the information in this offering circular. If you learn that anything in this offering circular is untrue, contact the Federal Trade Commission and (State or Provincial authority).

Effective Date:

TABLE OF CONTENTS

INCLUDE A TABLE OF CONTENTS BASED ON THE REQUIREMENTS OF THIS OFFERING CIRCULAR.

Table of Contents Instruction

  i. Refer to UFOC Items and state the page where each UFOC Item disclosure begins. List exhibits by letter. Use the following format:

TABLE OF CONTENTS

Item   Title   Page

SAMPLE TABLE OF CONTENTS

TABLE OF CONTENTS

Item	Title	Page*
1.	The Franchisor, its Predecessors and Affiliates	
2.	Business Experience	
3.	Litigation	
4.	Bankruptcy	
5.	Initial Franchise Fee	
6.	Other Fees	
7.	Initial Investment	
8.	Restrictions on Sources of Products and Services	
9.	Franchisees Obligations	
10.	Financing	
11.	Franchisor's Obligations	
12.	Territory	
13.	Trademarks	
14.	Patents, Copyrights and Proprietary Information	
15.	Obligation to Participate in the Actual Operation of the Franchise Business	
16.	Restrictions on What the Franchisee May Sell	
17.	Renewal, Termination, Transfer and Dispute Resolution	
18.	Public Figures	
19.	Earnings Claims	
20.	List of Outlets	

* Note: **In** your actual document, page numbers must be filled in, but they have been omitted in this publication to avoid confusion with the book's page numbers.

Item 1. THE FRANCHISOR, ITS PREDECESSORS AND AFFILIATES

Item 1 Instructions:

i.   Use the word "we," initials, or one or two words to refer to the franchisor. Use different initials or a different one or two words to refer to other persons contracting with the franchisee under the franchise agreement. Except in the 23 Item titles, use these initials or the word(s) to describe these persons or entities throughout the offering circular.

ii.   Define the franchisee as "you" and use this description throughout the offering circular. If the franchisee could be a corporation, partnership or other entity, disclose whether "you" includes the franchisee's owners.

iii.   "Predecessor" in Item 1 means a person from whom the franchisor acquired directly or indirectly the major portion of the franchisor's assets.

iv.   The disclosure regarding Predecessors need only cover the 10 year period immediately before the close of the franchisor's most recent fiscal year.

v.   "Affiliate" in Item 1 means a person (other than a natural person) controlled by, controlling or under common control with the franchisor, which is offering franchises in any line of business or is providing products or services to the franchisees of the franchisor.

DISCLOSE IN SUMMARY FORM:

A. THE NAME OF THE FRANCHISOR, ITS PREDECESSORS AND AFFILIATES.

B. THE NAME UNDER WHICH THE FRANCHISOR DOES OR INTENDS TO DO BUSINESS.

Item 1B Instruction:

If the franchisor does business under a name different from the name disclosed in Item A, state that other name. If not, state that the franchisor does not do business under another name.

C. THE PRINCIPAL BUSINESS ADDRESS OF THE FRANCHISOR, ITS PREDECESSORS AND AFFILIATES, AND THE FRANCHISOR'S AGENT FOR SERVICE OF PROCESS.

Item 1C Instructions:

i. Principal business address means "home office" in the United States, not in the state for which the offering circular was prepared. If appropriate, also disclose the location of an international "home office." The business address can not be a post office box.

ii. In a multi-state offering in which the agent for service of process is required, the franchisor may use an exhibit or the acknowledgement of receipt to disclose this agent.

D. THE BUSINESS FORM OF THE FRANCHISOR

Item 1D Instructions:

i. Disclose the state of incorporation or business organization and the type of business organization.

E. THE FRANCHISOR'S BUSINESS AND THE FRANCHISES TO BE OFFERED IN THIS STATE.

Item 1E Instructions:

Disclose the following:

i. That the franchisor sells or grants franchises;

ii. Whether the franchisor operates businesses of the type being franchised;

iii. The franchisors other business activities;

iv. The business to be conducted by the franchisees;

v. The general market for the product or service to be offered by the franchisee. (For example, is the market developed or developing? Will the goods be sold primarily to a certain group? Are sales seasonal?)

vi. In general terms any regulations specific to the industry in which the franchise business operates. It is not necessary to include laws or regulations that apply to businesses generally.

vii. A general description of the competition.

F. THE PRIOR BUSINESS EXPERIENCE OF THE FRANCHISOR, ITS PREDECESSORS AND AFFILIATES INCLUDING:

(1) THE LENGTH OF TIME THE FRANCHISOR HAS CONDUCTED A BUSINESS OF THE TYPE TO BE OPERATED BY THE FRANCHISEE.

(2) THE LENGTH OF TIME EACH PREDECESSOR AND AFFILIATE HAS CONDUCTED A BUSINESS OF THE TYPE TO BE OPERATED BY THE FRANCHISEE.

(3) THE LENGTH OF TIME THE FRANCHISOR HAS OFFERED FRANCHISES FOR THE SAME TYPE OF BUSINESS AS THAT TO BE OPERATED BY THE FRANCHISEE.

(4) THE LENGTH OF TIME EACH PREDECESSOR AND AFFILIATE OFFERED FRAN-CHISES FOR THE SAME TYPE OF BUSINESS AS THAT TO BE OPERATED BY THE FRANCHISEE.

(5) WHETHER THE FRANCHISOR HAS OFFERED FRANCHISES IN OTHER LINES OF BUSINESS, INCLUDING:

  (A) A DESCRIPTION OF EACH OTHER LINE OF BUSINESS;

  (B) THE NUMBER OF FRANCHISES SOLD IN EACH OTHER LINE OF BUSINESS; AND

  (C) THE LENGTH OF TIME THE FRANCHISOR HAS OFFERED EACH OTHER FRAN-CHISE.

(6) WHETHER EACH PREDECESSOR AND AFFILIATE OFFERED FRANCHISES IN OTHER LINES OF BUSINESS, INCLUDING:

  (A) A DESCRIPTION OF EACH OTHER LIKE OF BUSINESS;

  (B) THE NUMBER OF FRANCHISES SOLD IN EACH OTHER LINE OF BUSINESS; AND

  (C) THE LENGTH OF TIME EACH PREDECESSOR AND AFFILIATE OFFERED EACH OTHER FRANCHISE.

<u>Item 1F Instruction:</u>

Limit disclosure about predecessors to the time before the franchisor acquired the predecessor's assets. Thus, under the 10 year limitation, if a franchisor acquired the assets of a predecessor 8 years ago, the disclosure about the predecessor should cover only the 2 year period before the acquisition.

SAMPLE ANSWER 1

To simplify the language in this offering circular "Belmont" means Belmont Mufflers Inc., the franchisor. "You" means the person who buys the franchise. Belmont is a Minnesota corporation that was incorporated on September 3, 1963. Belmont does business as Belmont Muffler Shops. Our principal business address is 111 First Street, Jackson, Minnesota 55555.

Belmont's agent for service of process is disclosed in Exhibit _____.

Belmont currently operates 12 Belmont Muffler Shops and sells pipe bending machines and mufflers to various muffler shops.

Belmont franchises the right to sell and install mufflers for the public. You must honor our guarantee to replace mufflers or exhaust pipes that wear out if the vehicle ownership has not changed. Belmont's franchisees often operate their muffler shop franchise with their service stations or tire center. Your competitors include department store service departments, service stations and other national chains of muffler shops. Exhibit _____ is attached to this offering circular and contains a summary of the special regulations for muffler installation in your state.

During the past 5 years Belmont has operated 7 muffler shops that are similar to the franchised shops being offered. All these shops are located in urban areas, have approximately _____ square feet of floor space and are located on busy streets. An additional 3 muffler shops were opened in 1990. From 1968 to 1973, Belmont offered franchises for "Repair-All Transmission Shops." "Repair-All" franchisees repaired and replaced motor vehicle transmissions under a marketing plan similar to the franchise in this offering circular. Belmont sold 40 of these franchises primarily in the states of Minnesota, Michigan, Wisconsin and Illinois. In 1973, Belmont sold this transmission repair company to CTF Inc.

Item 2. BUSINESS EXPERIENCE

LIST BY NAME AND POSITION THE DIRECTORS, TRUSTEES AND/OR GENERAL PARTNERS, THE PRINCIPAL OFFICERS AND OTHER EXECUTIVES OR SUBFRANCHISORS WHO WILL HAVE MANAGEMENT RESPONSIBILITY RELATING TO THE FRANCHISES OFFERED BY THIS OFFERING CIRCULAR. LIST ALL FRANCHISE BROKERS. STATE EACH PERSONS PRINCIPAL OCCUPATIONS AND EMPLOYERS DURING THE PAST FIVE YEARS.

Item 2 Instructions:

i. Principal officers include the chief executive and chief operating officer, the president, financial, franchise marketing, training and franchise operations officers.

ii. First disclose the position and the name of the person holding it. Underline this information; then skip one line.

iii. Disclose the beginning date and departure date for each job held in the five year period whether or not this date is within the past five years. Disclose the location of the job.

iv. Do not disclose home addresses, home telephones, social security numbers or birth dates in this Item.

v. Disclose the required information concerning the franchise broker's directors, principal officers and executives with management responsibility to market or service the franchises.

vi. In a multi-state offering in which the franchisor uses a single offering circular and franchise brokers and executives with direct management responsibility to the franchisees differs from state to state, use an exhibit to refer to these personnel.

SAMPLE ANSWER 2

President: Jane J. Doe

From June, 1978, until April, 1986, Ms. Doe was Vice-President of Atlas Inc., a Houston, Texas based manufacturer of automobile wheels. In April, 1986, she joined Belmont as a Director and Vice President. She was promoted to president in June, 1987.

Item 3. LITIGATION

DISCLOSE WHETHER THE FRANCHISOR, ITS PREDECESSOR, A PERSON IDENTIFIED IN ITEM 2 OR AN AFFILIATE OFFERING FRANCHISES UNDER THE FRANCHISOR'S PRINCIPAL TRADEMARK:

A. HAS AN ADMINISTRATIVE, CRIMINAL OR MATERIAL CIVIL ACTION PENDING AGAINST THAT PERSON ALLEGING A VIOLATION OF A FRANCHISE, ANTITRUST OR SECURITIES LAW, FRAUD, UNFAIR OR DECEPTIVE PRACTICES, OR COMPARABLE ALLEGATIONS. IN ADDITION, INCLUDE ACTIONS OTHER THAN ORDINARY ROUTINE LITIGATION INCIDENTAL TO THE BUSINESS WHICH ARE SIGNIFICANT IN THE CONTEXT OF THE NUMBER OF FRANCHISEES AND THE SIZE, NATURE OR FINANCIAL CONDITION OF THE FRANCHISE SYSTEM OR ITS BUSINESS OPERATIONS. IF SO, DISCLOSE THE NAMES OF THE PARTIES, THE FORUM, NATURE, AND CURRENT STATUS OF THE PENDING ACTION. FRANCHISOR MAY INCLUDE A SUMMARY OPINION OF COUNSEL CONCERNING THE ACTION IF A CONSENT TO USE OF THE SUMMARY OPINION IS INCLUDED AS PART OF THIS OFFERING CIRCULAR.

B. HAS DURING THE 10 YEAR PERIOD IMMEDIATELY BEFORE THE DATE OF THE OFFERING CIRCULAR BEEN CONVICTED OF A FELONY OR PLEADED NOLO CONTENDERE TO A FELONY CHARGE; OR BEEN HELD LIABLE IN A CIVIL ACTION BY FINAL JUDGMENT OR BEEN THE SUBJECT OF A MATERIAL ACTION INVOLVING VIOLATION OF A FRANCHISE, ANTITRUST OR SECURITIES LAW, FRAUD, UNFAIR OR DECEPTIVE PRACTICES, OR COMPARABLE ALLEGATIONS. IF SO, DISCLOSE THE NAMES OF THE PARTIES THE FORUM AND DATE OF CONVICTION OR DATE JUDGMENT WAS ENTERED, PENALTY OR DAMAGES ASSESSED AND/OR TERMS OF SETTLEMENTS.

C. IS SUBJECT TO A CURRENTLY EFFECTIVE INJUNCTIVE OR RESTRICTIVE ORDER OR DECREE RELATING TO THE FRANCHISE OR UNDER A FEDERAL, STATE OR CANADIAN FRANCHISER SECURITIES, ANTITRUST, TRADE REGULATION OR TRADE PRACTICE LAW RESULTING FROM A CONCLUDED OR PENDING ACTION OR PROCEEDING BROUGHT BY A PUBLIC AGENCY. IF SO, DISCLOSE THE NAME OF THE PERSON THE PUBLIC AGENCY AND COURT, A SUMMARY OF THE ALLEGATIONS OR FACTS FOUND BY THE AGENCY OR COURT AND THE DATE NATURE, TERMS AND CONDITIONS OF THE ORDER OR DECREE.

Item 3 Definitions:

  i. For purposes of these instructions to Item 3, "franchisor" includes the franchisor, its predecessors, persons identified in Item 2 and affiliates offering franchises under the franchisor's principal trademarks.

 ii. "Action" includes complaints, cross claims, counterclaims, and third party complaints in a judicial proceeding, and their equivalents in an administrative action or arbitration proceeding. The franchisor may disclose its counterclaims. Omit actions that were dismissed by final judgment without liability of or entry of an adverse order against the franchisor.

iii. Included in the definition of material is an action or an aggregate of actions if a reasonable prospective franchisee would consider it important in making a decision about the franchised business.

iv. In this Item, settlement of an action does not diminish its materiality if the franchisor agrees to pay material consideration or agrees to be bound by obligations which are materially adverse to its interests.

v. "Ordinary routine litigation" means actions which ordinarily result from the business and which do not depart from the normal kinds of actions in the business.

vi. "Held liable" includes a finding by final judgment in a judicial, binding arbitration or administrative proceeding that the franchisor, as a result of claims or counterclaims must pay money or other consideration, must reduce an indebtedness by the amount of an award, cannot enforce its rights, or must take action adverse to its interests.

vii. "Currently Effective": An injunctive or restrictive order, or decree is "currently effective" unless it has been vacated or rescinded by a court or by the issuing public agency. An order that has expired by its own terms is not "currently effective." If the named party(s) have fully complied with an order (for example, through registration of its franchise offer), the order is not "currently effective." A party has not fully complied with an order to act or to refrain from an act (for example to comply with the franchise law or to refrain from violating the franchise law) until the order expires by its own terms.

Item 3 Instructions:

Civil litigation, or Injunctive or Restrictive Order:

viii. Use sample answer 3-1 for a negative response to Item 3 if the franchisor has never been named in litigation or if the only litigation naming the franchisor is outside the scope of Item 3.

ix. Disclose in the same order as the instructions below appear.

x. Title each action and state its case number or citation in parentheses. Underline the title of the action.

xi. For each action state the action's initial filing date and the opposing party's name and relationship with the franchisor. Relationships include competitor, supplier, lessor, franchisee, former franchisee, or class of franchisees.

xii. Summarize the legal and factual nature of each claim in the action.

xiii. Summarize the relief sought or obtained. Summarize conclusions of law or fact.

xiv. State that other than these (list number of actions) no litigation is required to be disclosed in this offering circular.

Criminal convictions or Pleas:

xv. Disclose in the same order as the following instructions appear.

xvi. Title each action and state its citation in parentheses. Underline the title of the action.

xvii. Name the person convicted or who pleaded.

xviii. Next, state the crime or violation and the date of conviction.

xix. Next, disclose the sentence or penalty imposed.

xx. Lastly, state that other than these (list the number of actions) actions, no litigation is required to be disclosed in this offering circular.

SAMPLE ANSWER 3-1

No litigation is required to be disclosed in this offering circular.

SAMPLE ANSWER 3-2

Doe v. Belmont Muffler Service, Inc. (cite) On March 1, 1985, our franchisee, Donald Doe, sought to enjoin us from terminating him for nonpayment of royalty fees. Doe alleged _____. On April 3, 1986, Doe withdrew the case when we repurchased his franchise for $90,000 and agreed not to enforce non-compete clauses against him.

Indiana v. Belmont Muffler Service, Inc. (cite) On April 1, 1985, the Attorney General of Indiana sought to enjoin us from offering unregistered franchises and from using false income representations. The Attorney General alleged that the earnings claims were false because.... The court found that we had offered franchises, that the offers were not registered and that we had made the alleged false representations in our earnings claims. The court enjoined us from repeating those acts.

Other than these 2 actions, no litigation is required to be disclosed in this offering circular.

Item 4. BANKRUPTCY

STATE WHETHER THE FRANCHISOR, ITS AFFILIATE, ITS PREDECESSOR, OFFICERS OR GENERAL PARTNER DURING THE 10 YEAR PERIOD IMMEDIATELY BEFORE THE DATE OF THE OFFERING CIRCULAR (A) FILED AS DEBTOR (OR HAD FILED AGAINST IT) A PETITION TO START AN ACTION UNDER THE U.S. BANKRUPTCY CODE; (B) OBTAINED A DISCHARGE OF ITS DEBTS UNDER THE BANKRUPTCY CODE; OR (C) WAS A PRINCIPAL OFFICER OF A COMPANY OR A GENERAL PARTNER IN A PARTNERSHIP THAT EITHER FILED AS A DEBTOR (OR HAD FILED AGAINST IT) A PETITION TO START AN ACTION UNDER THE U.S. BANKRUPTCY CODE OR THAT OBTAINED A DISCHARGE OF ITS DEBTS UNDER THE BANKRUPTCY CODE DURING OR WITHIN 1 YEAR AFTER THE OFFICER OR GENERAL PARTNER OF THE FRANCHISOR HELD THIS POSITION IN THE COMPANY OR PARTNERSHIP. IF SO, DISCLOSE THE NAME OF THE PERSON OR COMPANY THAT WAS THE DEBTOR UNDER THE BANKRUPTCY CODE, THE DATE OF THE ACTION AND THE MATERIAL FACTS.

Item 4 Instructions:

   i. First, name the party that filed (or had filed against it) the petition in bankruptcy and the party's relationship to the franchisor. If the debtor in a bankruptcy proceeding was or is affiliated with the franchisor, state the relationship. If the debtor in a bankruptcy proceeding is unaffiliated with the franchisor, state the name, address and principal business of the bankrupt company.

  ii. Disclose that the entity filed bankruptcy or reorganization under the bankruptcy law and the date of the original filing.

 iii. Identify the bankruptcy court, and the case name and number. Put this information in parentheses.

 iv. State the date on which the debtor obtained a discharge in bankruptcy (including discharges under Chapter 7 and confirmation of any plans of reorganization under Chapters 11 and 13 of the U.S. Bankruptcy Code).

  v. Disclose other material facts.

 vi. Cases, actions and other proceedings under the laws of foreign nations relating to bankruptcy proceedings should be included in answers, where responses are required, as if those cases, actions and proceedings took place under the U.S. Bankruptcy Code.

 vii. If information is disclosed in this Item, at the end of the disclosure add sample answer 4-1 with the qualification "other than these actions."

viii. Use Sample Answer 4-1 if no person listed in Items 1 or 2 has been involved as a debtor in bankruptcy proceedings or any person listed in Items 1 or 2 has been involved as a debtor in bankruptcy proceedings but the bankruptcy proceedings (under the U.S. Bankruptcy Code or its predecessor, the National Bankruptcy Act of 1898) were discharged more than 10 years ago. "Person" includes natural persons and legal entities listed in Items 1 and 2. Person does not include anyone acting solely as the franchisors agent for service of process.

SAMPLE ANSWER 4-1

No person previously identified in Items 1 or 2 of this offering circular has been involved as a debtor in proceedings under the U.S. Bankruptcy Code required to be disclosed in this Item.

SAMPLE ANSWER 4-2

On March 2, 1984, Belmont filed a petition to reorganize under Chapter 11 of the U.S. Bankruptcy Code. We were allowed to continue to operate under bankruptcy court supervision. On October 2, 1985, the bankruptcy court approved our plan of reorganization and discharged the proceedings. (U.S. Bankruptcy Court for the District of _____ Case B 84-301).

Belmont's present president, Roger Rowe, was president of Acme Muffler Service, Inc., a Houston, Texas based manufacturer of exhaust systems, from July 1, 1978, through June 14, 1983. On June 6, 1983, an involuntary petition under the U.S. Bankruptcy Code was filed against Acme by its creditors. On July 14, 1983, the court entered an order of relief. Acme sold its assets and was dissolved.

Other than these 2 actions, no person previously identified in Items 1 or 2 of this offering circular has been involved as a debtor in proceedings under the U.S. Bankruptcy Code required to be disclosed in this Item.

Item 5. INITIAL FRANCHISE FEE

DISCLOSE THE INITIAL FRANCHISE FEE AND STATE THE CONDITIONS WHEN THIS FEE IS REFUNDABLE.

<u>Item 5 Instructions:</u>

  i. "Initial fee" includes all fees and payments for services or goods received from the franchisor before the franchisees business opens. "Initial fee" includes all fees and payments whether payable in lump sum or installments.

  ii. If the initial fee is not uniform, disclose the formula or the range of initial fees paid in the fiscal year before the application date and the factors that determined the amount.

  iii. Disclose installment payment terms in this Item or in Item 10.

SAMPLE ANSWER 5-1

All franchisees pay a $10,000 lump sum franchise fee when they sign the franchise agreement. Belmont will refund the entire amount if we do not approve your application within 45 days. Belmont will refund $9,000 of this fee if you do not satisfactorily complete your 2-week training. There are no refunds under other circumstances.

SAMPLE ANSWER 5-2

You must pay a franchise license fee of $____ per thousand licensed drivers who reside within your exclusive area when the franchise agreement is signed. The number of licensed drivers is determined by the latest abstract of the state agency which issues driver's licenses. The minimum fee is $20,000. When you send your application, you must pay a non-refundable $500 application fee. You must pay an additional $10,000 when you receive your equipment. The balance of your fee is payable in 12 equal monthly installments of $____. The first installment payment is due 1 year after your shop opens. Belmont charges 10% annual interest on the unpaid balance. Interest compounds daily and accrues from the date that you receive your equipment. All buyers pay this uniform fee and receive the same financing terms on the fee. If your application is not accepted, Belmont retains the $500 for investigative costs, but you are not liable for the $19,500 remainder. Belmont does not give refunds under other circumstances.

Item 6. OTHER FEES

DISCLOSE OTHER RECURRING OR ISOLATED FEES OR PAYMENTS THAT THE FRAN-
CHISEE MUST PAY TO THE FRANCHISOR OR ITS AFFILIATES OR THAT THE FRAN-
CHISOR OR ITS AFFILIATES IMPOSE OR COLLECT IN WHOLE OR IN PART ON BEHALF
OF A THIRD PARTY. INCLUDE THE FORMULA USED TO COMPUTE THESE OTHER FEES
AND PAYMENTS. IF ANY FEE IS REFUNDABLE, STATE THE CONDITIONS WHEN EACH
FEE OR PAYMENT IS REFUNDABLE.

Item 6 Instructions:

i. First disclose fees in tabular form. Use footnotes or a "remarks" column to elaborate on the information in the table or to disclose caveats. If elaborations are lengthy, use footnotes instead of a remarks column.

ii. Disclose the amount of each fee. A dollar amount or a percentage of gross sales is acceptable if the term gross sales is defined. If dollar amounts may increase, disclose the formula which determines the increase or the maximum amount of the increase.

iii. Disclose the due date for recurring payments.

iv. If all fees are payable to only the franchisor, disclose this in a footnote.

v. If all fees are imposed and collected by the franchisor, disclose this in a footnote.

vi. If all fees are non-refundable, state this in a footnote.

vii. Disclose the voting power of franchisor owned outlets on any fees imposed by cooperatives. If franchisor outlets have controlling voting power, disclose a range for the fee. Disclose this information in a footnote or a "remarks" column.

viii. The franchisor need not repeat information contained in Items 8 & 9, but the table should direct the franchisees to those Items.

ix. Examples of fees are royalty, lease negotiation, construction, remodeling, additional training, advertising, group advertising, additional assistance, audit, accounting/ inventory, and transfer and renewal fee.

SAMPLE ANSWER 6-1

Name of fee	Amount	Due Date	Remarks
Royalty[1]	4% of total gross sales	Payable monthly on the 10th day of the next month	Gross sales includes all revenue from the franchise location. Gross sales does not include sales tax or use tax.
Advertising[1]	2% of total gross sales	Same as Royalty fee	

Name of fee	Amount	Due Date	Remarks
Cooperative Advertising[1]	Maximum — 2% of total gross sales	Established by franchisees	Franchisees may form an advertising cooperative and establish local advertising fees. Company owned stores have no vote in these cooperatives.
Additional Training[1]	$1,000 per person	2 weeks prior to beginning of training	Belmont trains 2 persons free — See Item 11.
Additional Assistance[1]	$500 per day	30 days after billing	Belmont provides opening assistance free — See Item 11.
Transfer[1]	$1,000	Prior to consummation of transfer	Payable when you sell your franchise. No charge if franchise transferred to a corporation which you control.
Audit[1]	Cost of audit plus 10% interest on underpayment[2]	30 days after billing	Payable only if audit shows an understatement of at least 2% of gross sales for any month.
Renewal Fee[1]	$1,000	30 days before renewal	

---

[1] All fees are imposed by and are payable to Belmont. All fees are non-refundable.

[2] Interest begins from the date of the underpayment.

Item 7. INITIAL INVESTMENT

DISCLOSE THE FOLLOWING EXPENDITURES STATING TO WHOM THE PAYMENTS ARE MADE, WHEN PAYMENTS ARE DUE, WHETHER EACH PAYMENT IS REFUNDABLE, THE CONDITIONS WHEN EACH PAYMENTS IS REFUNDABLE, AND, IF PART OF THE FRANCHISEE'S INITIAL INVESTMENT IN THE FRANCHISE MAY BE FINANCED, AN ESTIMATE OF THE LOAN REPAYMENTS, INCLUDING INTEREST:

A. REAL PROPERTY, WHETHER PURCHASED OR LEASED. IF NEITHER ESTIMABLE NOR DESCRIBABLE BY A LOW-HIGH RANGE, DESCRIBE REQUIREMENTS, SUCH AS PROPERTY TYPE, LOCATION, AND BUILDING SIZE.

B. EQUIPMENT, FIXTURES, OTHER FIXED ASSETS, CONSTRUCTION, REMODELING, LEASEHOLD IMPROVEMENTS AND DECORATING COSTS, WHETHER PURCHASED OR LEASED.

C. INVENTORY REQUIRED TO BEGIN OPERATION.

D. SECURITY DEPOSITS, UTILITY DEPOSITS, BUSINESS LICENSES, OTHER PREPAID EXPENSES.

E. ADDITIONAL FUNDS REQUIRED BY THE FRANCHISEE BEFORE OPERATIONS BEGIN AND DURING THE INITIAL PHASE OF THE FRANCHISE.

F. OTHER PAYMENTS THAT THE FRANCHISEE MUST MAKE TO BEGIN OPERATIONS.

<u>Item 7 Instructions:</u>

i. Begin disclosure by listing expenditures in tabular form. List pre-opening expenses first. Use footnotes to comment on expected expenditures.

ii. Disclose payments required by the franchise agreement and all costs necessary to begin operation of the franchise and operate the franchise during the initial phase of the business. A reasonable tune for the initial phase of the business is at least 3 months or a reasonable period for the industry. Include an entry titled "additional funds" and disclose the length of the initial phase in the entry.

iii. If a specific expenditure amount is not ascertainable, use a low-high range based on the franchisor's current experience. If real property costs can not be estimated in a low-high range, disclose the approximate size of the property and building involved. Describe the probable location of the building (for example, strip shopping center, mall, downtown, rural or highway).

iv. The franchisor may include additional expenditure tables to show expenditure variations caused by differences in site location, premise size, etc. Describe in general terms the factors, basis and experience that the franchisor considered or relied upon in formulating the amount required for additional funds.

v. If the franchisor or an affiliate finances part of the initial investment, state the expenditures that it will finance. State the required down payment, annual percentage rate of interest, rate factors, and the estimated loan repayments. Make the discussion brief, and refer to Item 10.

vi. Total the initial investment. This total should be the same as the total investment on the offering circular cover.

SAMPLE ANSWER 7

YOUR ESTIMATED INITIAL INVESTMENT

Payment	Amount	Method of Payment	When Due	To Whom Payment Is To Be Made
Initial Franchise Fee	$20,000[1]	Lump Sum	At Signing of Franchise Agreement	Belmont, Inc.
Travel and Living Expenses While Training	$2,500–5,000	As Incurred	During Training	Airlines, Hotels, and Restaurants
Real Estate and Improvements[2]				

Payment	Amount	Method of Payment	When Due	To Whom Payment Is To Be Made
Equipment	$40,000[3]	Lump Sum	Prior To Opening	Belmont or Vendors
Signs	$2,200	Lump Sum	Prior To Opening	Abbey Sign Company
Miscellaneous and Opening Costs	$8,000[4]	As Incurred	As Incurred	Suppliers and Utilities
Opening Inventory	$8,000[5]	Lump Sum	Prior To Opening	Belmont or Vendors
Advertising Fee 3 Months	$500		Monthly	Belmont
Additional Funds 3 Months	$50,000– $75,000[6]	As Incurred	As Incurred	Employees, Suppliers, Utilities
TOTAL	$132,700– 160,200[7]	(Does not include real estate costs)		

---

[1] See Item 5 for the conditions when this fee is partly refundable. Belmont does not finance any fee.

[2] If you do not own adequate shop space, you must lease the land and building for the Belmont Muffler Shop. Typical locations are light industrial and commercial areas. The typical Belmont Muffler Shop has 5,000-8,000 square feet. Former three or four bay gasoline service stations have been converted with relative ease into Belmont Muffler Shops. Rent is estimated to be between $12,000-20,000 per year depending on factors such as size, condition and location of the leased premises.

[3] This payment is fully refundable before equipment installation. After installation, Belmont deducts $3,000 installation costs from your refund.

[4] Includes security deposits, utility costs, incorporation fee.

[5] This payment is fully refundable before Belmont delivers your inventory. After delivery Belmont deducts a 10% restocking fee from your refund.

[6] This estimates your initial start up expenses. These expenses include payroll costs. These figures are estimates and Belmont cannot guarantee that you will not have additional expenses starting the business. Your costs will depend on factors such as: how much you follow Belmont's methods and procedures; your management skill, experience and business acumen; local economic conditions; the local market for our product; the prevailing wage rate; competition; and the sales level reached during the initial period.

[7] Belmont relied on its 30 years of experience in the muffler business to compile these estimates. You should review these figures carefully with a business advisor before making any decision to purchase the franchise.

[8] Belmont does not offer direct or indirect financing to franchisees for any items.

Item 8. RESTRICTIONS ON SOURCES OF PRODUCTS AND SERVICES

DISCLOSE FRANCHISEE OBLIGATIONS TO PURCHASE OR LEASE FROM THE FRAN-CHISOR ITS DESIGNEE OR FROM SUPPLIERS APPROVED BY THE FRANCHISOR OR UNDER THE FRANCHISOR'S SPECIFICATIONS. FOR EACH OBLIGATION DISCLOSE:

A. THE GOODS, SERVICES, SUPPLIES, FIXTURES, EQUIPMENT, INVENTORY, COMPUTER HARDWARE AND SOFTWARE OR REAL ESTATE RELATING TO ESTABLISHING OR OPERATING THE FRANCHISED BUSINESS.

B. THE MANNER IN WHICH THE FRANCHISOR ISSUES AND MODIFIES SPECIFICATIONS OR GRANTS AND REVOKES APPROVAL TO SUPPLIERS.

C. WHETHER, AND FOR WHAT CATEGORIES OF GOODS AND SERVICES, THE FRANCHISOR OR ITS AFFILIATES ARE APPROVED SUPPLIERS OR THE ONLY APPROVED SUPPLIERS.

D. WHETHER, AND IF SO, THE PRECISE BASIS BY WHICH THE FRANCHISOR OR ITS AFFILIATES WILL OR MAY DERIVE REVENUE OR OTHER MATERIAL CONSIDERATION AS A RESULT OF REQUIRED PURCHASES OR LEASES.

E. THE ESTIMATED PROPORTION OF THESE REQUIRED PURCHASES AND LEASES TO ALL PURCHASES AND LEASES BY THE FRANCHISEE OF GOODS AND SERVICES IN ESTABLISHING AND OPERATING THE FRANCHISED BUSINESS.

F. THE EXISTENCE OF PURCHASING OR DISTRIBUTION COOPERATIVES.

Item 8 Instructions:

i. An obligation includes those imposed by written agreement or by the franchisors practice. The franchisor may include the reason for the requirement.

ii. Do not include goods or services provided as part of the franchise and without a separate charge, (for example, a fee for initial training when the cost is included in the franchise fee). These fees should be described in Item S. Do not include fees disclosed in response to Item 6.

iii. For "precise basis," disclose the franchisor's total revenues and the franchisors revenues from all required purchases and leases of products and services. Also, disclose the percentage of the franchisors total revenues represented by the franchisors revenues from required purchases or leases. If the franchisors affiliates also sell or lease products or services to franchisees, disclose affiliate revenues from those sales or leases. These amounts should be taken from the franchisors statement of operations (or profit and loss statement) from the most recent annual audited financial statement attached to the offering circular. If the franchisors annual audited financial statement is not required to be attached to the offering circular or if the franchisors affiliate sells or leases required products or services to franchisees, disclose the sources of information used in computing revenues.

iv. State how the franchisor formulates and modifies specifications and standards imposed on franchisees.

v. Disclose whether specifications and standards are issued to franchisees, subfranchisors, or approved suppliers.

vi. Describe how suppliers are evaluated, approved or disapproved. Disclose whether the franchisors criteria for supplier approval are available to franchisees. State the fees and procedure to secure approval and how approvals are revoked. State the time period when the franchisee will receive notification of approval or disapproval.

vii. If the designated supplier will make payments to the franchisor because of transactions with franchisees, disclose the basis for the payment. Specify a percentage or a flat amount. Purchases of similar goods or services by the franchisor at a lower price than that available to franchisees is a payment.

viii. Disclose whether the franchisor negotiates purchase arrangements with suppliers (including price terms) for the benefit of franchisees.

ix. Disclose whether the franchisor provides material benefits (for example renewal or granting additional franchises) to a franchisee based on a franchisees use of designated or approved sources.

x. Use sample answer 8-1 if the response to Item 8 is negative.

SAMPLE ANSWER 8-1

Belmont has no required specifications, designated suppliers, or approved suppliers for goods, services or real estate relating to your franchise business. Belmont will not derive revenue from your purchases or leases.

SAMPLE ANSWER 8-2

You must purchase your pipe bending machine, hoist, cutting torch and supplies under specifications in the operations manual. These specifications include standards for delivery, performance, design and appearance. You may purchase this equipment from Belmont. In the year ending December 31, 1992, Belmont's revenues from the sale of this equipment to franchisees was $500,000, or 5% of Belmont's total revenues of $10,000,000. The cost of equipment purchased in accordance with specifications represents 10% of your total purchases in connection with establishment of your store.

Belmont's affiliate, Muffler Supply Co., is an approved supplier of mufflers to franchisees. In the year ending December 31, 1992, the affiliate's revenues from the sale of mufflers to franchisees was $2,000,000. The purchase of mufflers from approved sources will represent 15 to 20% of your overall purchases in operating the store. Belmont has approved other suppliers of mufflers and exhaust pipe. If you would like to purchase these items from another supplier, you may request our "Supplier Approval Criteria and Request Form." Based on the information and samples you supply to us and your payment of a $500 fee, we will test the item supplied and review the proposed supplier's financial records, business reputation, delivery performance, credit rating and other information. our review typically is completed in 30 days.

One of the approved suppliers of mufflers and exhaust pipes, Scotties Pipes, Inc., pays Belmont a rebate of 1% of all franchisee purchases, which is deposited in the Belmont Advertising Fund. Another approved supplier, Michael's CleanAir, Inc., pays Belmont 2% of all franchisee purchases of catalytic converters. This amount is used in Belmont's training center for classes in catalytic converter repair and replacement.

Item 9. FRANCHISEE'S OBLIGATIONS

DISCLOSE THE PRINCIPAL OBLIGATIONS OF THE FRANCHISEE UNDER THE FRANCHISE AND OTHER AGREEMENTS AFTER THE SIGNING OF THESE AGREEMENTS.

<u>Item 9 Instructions:</u>
i. Disclose obligations in tabular form. Refer to the section of the agreement that contains the obligation and any item of the Offering Circular that further describes the obligation.
ii. The table should contain a response to each category listed below. If the response to any category is that no obligation is imposed, the table should state that. Do not change the names of the categories. Fit all obligations within the listed categories. If other material obligations fall outside the scope of all of the prescribed categories, add additional categories as needed. The categories of franchisee obligations are:

a. Site selection and acquisition/lease
b. Pre-opening purchases/leases
c. Site development and other pre-opening requirements
d. Initial and ongoing training
e. Opening
f. Fees
g. Compliance with standards and policies/Operating Manual
h. Trademarks and proprietary information
i. Restrictions on products/services offered
j. Warranty and customer service requirements
k. Territorial development and sales quotas
l. Ongoing product/service purchases
m. Maintenance, appearance and remodeling requirements
n. Insurance
o. Advertising
p. Indemnification
q. Owner's participation/management/staffing
r. Records and reports
s. Inspections and audits
t. Transfer
u. Renewal
v. Post-termination obligations
w. Non-competition covenants
x. Dispute resolution
y. Other (describe)

iii. Before the table, state the following:

THIS TABLE LISTS YOUR PRINCIPAL OBLIGATIONS UNDER THE FRANCHISE AND OTHER AGREEMENTS. IT WILL HELP YOU FIND MORE DETAILED INFORMATION ABOUT YOUR OBLIGATIONS IN THESE AGREEMENTS AND IN OTHER ITEMS OF THIS OFFERING CIRCULAR.

SAMPLE ANSWER 9

THIS TABLE LISTS YOUR PRINCIPAL OBLIGATIONS UNDER THE FRANCHISE AND OTHER AGREEMENTS. IT WILL HELP YOU FIND MORE DETAILED INFORMATION ABOUT YOUR OBLIGATIONS IN THESE AGREEMENTS AND IN OTHER ITEMS OF THIS OFFERING CIRCULAR.

Obligation	Section in Agreement	Item in Offering Circular
a. Site selection and acquisition/lease	Section 2A of Franchise Agreement	Items 6 and 11
b. Pre-opening purchases/ leases	Section 3D of Franchise Agreement	Item 8
c. Site development and other pre-opening requirements	Sections 3A and 3B of Franchise Agreement	Items 6, 7 and 11
d. Initial and ongoing training	Section 5 of Franchise Agreement	Item 11
e. Opening	Section 4 of Franchise Agreement	Item 11
f. Fees	Section 6 of Franchise Agreement	Items 5 and 6
g. Compliance with standards and policies/ Operating Manual	Section 8A of Franchise Agreement	Item 11
h. Trademarks and proprietary information	Sections 7 and 11 of Franchise Agreement	Items 13 and 14
i. Restrictions on products/services offered	Section 12 of Franchise Agreement	Item 16
j. Warranty and customer service requirements	Section 8B of Franchise Agreement	Item 11
k. Territorial development and sales quotas	None	

Obligation	Section in Agreement	Item in Offering Circular
l. Ongoing product/service purchases	Section 9 of Franchise Agreement	Item 8
m. Maintenance, appearance, and remodeling requirements	Sections 8C and 10 of Franchise Agreement	Item 11
n. Insurance	Section 13A of Franchise Agreement	Items 6 and 8
o. Advertising	Section 15 of Franchise Agreement	Items 6 and 11
p. Indemnification	Section 13B of Franchise Agreement	Item 6
q. Owner's participation/ management/staffing	Sections 4, 5 and 14 of Franchise Agreement	Items 11 and 15
r. Records/reports	Section 17A of Franchise Agreement	Item 6
s. Inspections/audits	Section 17B of Franchise Agreement	Items 6 and 11
t. Transfer	Section 18 of Franchise Agreement	Item 17
u. Renewal	Section 20 of Franchise Agreement	Item 17
v. Post-termination obligations	Section 22 of Franchise Agreement	Item 17
w. Non-competition covenants	Sections 11, 18 and 22C of Franchise Agreement	Item 17
x. Dispute resolution	Section 24 of Franchise Agreement	Item 17

Item 10. FINANCING

DISCLOSE THE TERMS AND CONDITIONS OF EACH FINANCING ARRANGEMENT THAT THE FRANCHISOR, ITS AGENT OR AFFILIATES OFFERS DIRECTLY OR INDIRECTLY TO THE FRANCHISEE, INCLUDING:

Item 10 Instructions:

i. "Financing" includes leases and installment contracts.

ii. Payments due within 90 days on open account financing need not be disclosed under this Item.

iii. A written arrangement between a franchisor or its affiliate and a lender for the lender to offer financing to the franchisee or an arrangement in which a franchisor or its affiliate receives a benefit from a lender for franchisee financing is an "indirect offer of financing" and must be disclosed under this Item. The franchisors guarantee of a note, lease or obligation of the franchisee is an "indirect offer of financing" and must be disclosed under this Item.

iv. If financing of the initial fee is disclosed in the Item 7 disclosure, a cross reference to Item 7 is sufficient if all the disclosure which Item 10 requires is provided in Item 7.

v. If an affiliate offers financing, identify the affiliate and its relationship to the franchisor.

vi. The franchisor may summarize the terms of each financing arrangement in tabular form, using footnotes to entries in the chart to provide additional information required by these instructions that does not fit in the chart.

vii. If a financing arrangement is for the establishment of the franchised business, disclose what the financing covers, including:

   a) Initial franchise fee;

   b) Site acquisition;

   c) Construction or remodeling;

   d) Equipment or fixtures; and

   e) Opening inventory or supplies.

viii. If the franchisor generally offers financing for the operation of the franchised business, disclose what the financing arrangement covers, including:

   a) Inventory or supplies;

   b) Replacement equipment or fixtures; and

   c) Other continuing expenses.

ix. Disclose the terms of each financing arrangement, including:

   a) The identity of the lender(s) providing the financing and its relationship to the franchisor (for example, affiliate);

   b) The amount of financing offered or, if the amount depends on an actual cost that may vary, the percentage of the cost that will be financed;

   c) The annual percentage rate of interest ("APR") charged, computed as provided by Sections 106-107 of the Consumer Protection Credit Act, 15 U.S.C. §§ 106-107. If the APR may differ depending on when the financing is issued, disclose the APR on a specified recent date;

   d) The number of payments or the period of repayment;

   e) Nature of security interest required by the lender;

   f) Whether a person other than the franchisee (for example spouse, shareholder of the franchisee) must personally guarantee the debt;

g) Whether the debt can be prepaid and the nature of any prepayment penalty;

h) The franchisee's potential liabilities upon default, including any accelerated obligation to pay the entire amount due, court costs and attorney's fees for collection, and termination of the franchise, or other cross default clauses whether directly, as a result of non-payment, or indirectly, as a result of loss of necessary facilities; and

i) Other material financing terms.

x. Include specimen copies of the financing documents as an exhibit to Item 22. Cite the section and name of the document containing the financing terms. Put this information in parentheses at the end of the description of the term.

xi. Use Sample Answer 10-1 if the franchisor does not offer financing.

A. A WAIVER OF DEFENSES OR SIMILAR PROVISIONS IN A DOCUMENT.

Item 10A Instructions:

i. Disclose the terms of waivers of legal rights by the franchisee under the terms of the financing arrangement (for example confession of judgment).

ii. Describe provisions of the loan agreement that bar the franchisee from asserting a defense against the lender, the lender's assignee or the franchisor.

iii. If the loan agreement does not contain the provisions in (i) or (ii), disclose that fact.

iv. Cite the section and name of the document containing these terms. Put this information in parentheses at the end of the description of the term.

B. THE FRANCHISORS PRACTICE OR ITS INTENT TO SELL, ASSIGN, OR DISCOUNT TO A THIRD PARTY ALL OR PART OF THE FINANCING ARRANGEMENT.

Item 10B Instructions:

i. Practice includes past or present practice and future intent to sell or assign franchisee financing arrangements.

ii. Disclose the assignment terms including whether the franchisor will remain primarily obligated to provide the financed goods or services.

iii. If the franchisor may sell or assign its rights under the financing agreement, disclose that the franchisee may lose all its defenses against the lender as a result of the sale or assignment.

iv. Cite the section and name of the document containing these terms. Put this information in parentheses at the end of the description of the term.

v. If no disclosure is required by Instruction B, disclose that fact.

C. PAYMENTS TO THE FRANCHISOR OR AN AFFILIATE(S) FOR THE PLACEMENT OF FINANCING WITH THE LENDER.

Item 10C Instructions:

   i. Describe the payments.

  ii. If no disclosure is required by Instruction 1OC(i) for a financing arrangement, disclose that fact.

 iii. Identify the source of the payment and the relationship of the source to the franchisor or its affiliates.

 iv. Disclose the amount or the method of determining the payment.

  v. Cite the section and name of the document containing these arrangements. Put this information in parentheses at the end of the description of the term.

SAMPLE ANSWER 10-1

Belmont does not offer direct or indirect financing. Belmont does not guarantee your note, lease or obligation.

SAMPLE ANSWER 10-2

SUMMARY OF FINANCING OFFERED

See Table on page 269.

Notes to Table: SUMMARY OF FINANCING OFFERED

[1] If you meet Belmont's credit standards, Belmont will finance the $10,000 initial franchisee fee over a 10-year period at an APR of 18%, using the standard form note in Exhibit A. The only security Belmont requires is a personal guarantee of the note by you and your spouse or by all the shareholders of your corporation. (Loan Agreement Section ____) The note can be prepaid without penalty at any time during its 10-year term. (Loan Agreement Section ____) If you do not pay on time, Belmont can call the loan and demand immediate payment of the full outstanding balance and obtain court costs and attorney's fees if a collection action is necessary. (Loan Agreement Section ____) Belmont also has the right to terminate your franchise if you do not make your payments on time more than three times during the note term. (Loan Agreement Section ____) You waive your rights to notice of a collection action and to assert any defenses to collection against Belmont. (Loan Agreement Section ____) Belmont discounts these notes to a third party who may be immune under the law to any defenses to payment you may have against Belmont. (Loan Agreement Section ____)

[2] In most cases Belmont will sublease the franchised premises to you but will guarantee your lease with a third party if you have acceptable credit and that is the only way to obtain an exceptional location. (Lease Section ____) The precise terms of Belmont's standard lease in Exhibit B will vary depending on the size and location of the premises, but the chart reflects a typical range of payments for Belmont's standard 6-day franchise outlet, including payment of one month's rent as a security deposit. (Lease Section ____) The only other security Belmont requires is a personal guarantee of the lease by you and your spouse or by all the shareholder of your corporation. (Lease Section ____) The lease can be prepaid without penalty at any time during its term. (Lease Section ____) If you do not make a rent payment on time, Belmont has the right to collect the unpaid rent plus an additional two months rent, as liquidated damages. (Lease Section ____) Belmont can also obtain court costs and attorney's fees if a collection action is necessary. (Lease Section ____) If you are late with your rent more than three

SUMMARY OF FINANCING OFFERED

Item Financed (Source)	Amount Financed	Down Payment	Term (Years)	APR %	Monthly Payment	Prepay Penalty	Security Required	Liability Upon Default	Loss of Legal Right on Default
Initial fee[1]	$10,000		10	18	$	None	Personal Guarantee	Loss of Franchise	Waive Notice – Confess
Judgment (Belmont)								Unpaid Loan	
Land/Construct	None								
Leased Space[2] (Belmont)		$2,000 (Security)	7–10	N/A	$	None	Personal Guarantee	Loss of Franchise– Back Rent + 2 mos. – Franchise Rights – Atty's Fees	None
Equipment Lease[3] (USA Credit Corp.)	$5,000	None	5	15	$	None Personal	Equipment, Removal Guarantee	Cost of Defenses	Lose All
Equip. Purch.[4] (Belmont)	$3,750	$1,250 (25%)	2–7	15	$	$500	Equipment, Personal Guarantee	Loss of Franchise– Atty's Fees	None
Opening Invest.	None								
Other Financing	None								

See Notes on page 268.

times during the lease term, Belmont has the right to terminate the lease, take over the premises, and terminate your franchise. If Belmont guarantees your lease, Belmont will require you to sign the guarantee agreement in Exhibit F (Lease Section _____) This gives Belmont the same legal rights as the sublease but requires you to give Belmont the right to approve your lease and pay the rent for you if you fail to pay on time. (Lease Section _____)

[3] If you want to lease the pipe bending machine and other equipment you need, Belmont has arranged an equipment lease (see Exhibit C) from USA Credit Corporation of Las Vegas, Nevada. If you choose this option, you will pay $100 a month for 60 months (5 years) at an APR of 15% based on a cash price of $5,000, with no money down. (Equipment Lease Section _____) At the end of the lease term, you may purchase the equipment with a one-time payment of $2,500. (Equipment Lease Section _____) USA Credit requires a personal guarantee from you and your spouse or from all the shareholders of your corporation and retains a security interest in the equipment. (Equipment Lease Section _____) The equipment lease can be prepaid at any time, but the interest you might otherwise save will be reduced by application of the Rule of 78's for computing finance charges. (Equipment Lease Section _____) If you do not make a payment on time, USA Credit can demand payment of all past due payments, remove the equipment, and charge you $1,000 as liquidated damages. (Equipment Lease Section _____) USA Credit can also recover its costs of collection, including court costs and attorney's fees. (Equipment Lease Section _____) While Belmont does not know USA Credit's policies, USA Credit may discount the lease to a third party who may be immune under the law to claims or defenses you may have against USA Credit, the equipment manufacturer or Belmont. Belmont receives a referral fee of $500 from USA Credit for every franchisee who leases equipment from it.

[4] If you prefer, Belmont will sell you the pipe bending machine and other necessary equipment on time (Equipment Purchase Agreement Section _____). Belmont requires a 25% down payment of $1,250. (Equipment Purchase Agreement Section _____) Belmont will finance the remainder over a 2-7 year period at your option at an APR of 15%. (Equipment Purchase Agreement Section _____) Payments range from $228.11 a month over 7 years to $821.58 a month over 2 years. (Equipment Purchase Agreement Section _____) Belmont's standard equipment financing note in Exhibit D must be personally guaranteed by you and your spouse or by all the shareholders of your corporation, and Belmont will retain a security interest in the equipment. (Equipment Purchase Agreement Section _____) You may purchase the equipment at any time during the lease period by paying the remainder of the principal plus a $500 prepayment penalty. (Equipment Purchase Agreement Section _____) If you do not make a payment on time, Belmont can demand all overdue payments, repossess the equipment, and terminate your franchise. Belmont can also recover its costs of collection, including court costs and attorney's fees. (Equipment Purchase Agreement Section _____)

Except as disclosed in Note 1, Belmont does not offer financing that requires you to waive notice, confess judgment or waive a defense against Belmont or the lender, although you may lose your defenses against Belmont and others in a collection action on a note that is sold or discounted, as disclosed in Notes 2 and 3.

Except as disclosed in Note 3, Belmont does not arrange financing from other sources.

Except as disclosed in Notes 1 and 3, commercial paper from franchisees has not been and is not sold or assigned to anyone, and Belmont has no plans to do so.

Except as disclosed in Note 3, Belmont does not receive direct or indirect payments for placing financing.

Except as disclosed in Note 2, Belmont does not guarantee your obligations to third parties.

Item 11. FRANCHISOR'S OBLIGATIONS

DISCLOSE THE FOLLOWING:

A. THE OBLIGATIONS THAT THE FRANCHISOR WILL PERFORM BEFORE THE FRANCHISE BUSINESS OPENS. CITE BY SECTION THE PROVISIONS OF THE AGREEMENT REQUIRING PERFORMANCE.

<u>Item 11A Instructions:</u>

i. Begin the disclosure by stating: "Except as listed below, (the franchisor) need not provide any assistance to you."

ii. Pre-opening obligations include assistance to:

    a) Locate a site for the franchised business and negotiate the purchase or lease of this site. State whether the franchisor generally owns the premises and leases it to the franchisee;

    b) Conform the premises to local ordinances and building codes and obtain the required permits (i.e. health, sanitation, building, driveway, utility and sign permits);

    c) Construct, remodel or decorate the premises for the franchised business;

    d) Purchase or lease equipment, signs, fixtures, opening inventory and supplies. Disclose whether the franchisor provides these items directly or merely the names of approved suppliers. Disclose whether the franchisor provides written specifications for these items. Disclose whether the franchisor delivers or-installs these items (the franchisor may cross reference Item 8 for details); and

    e) Hire and train employees.

iii. After describing the obligation, cite the section number of the agreement imposing the obligation. Put the citation in parentheses. Use this format throughout this Item.

B. THE OBLIGATIONS TO BE MET BY THE FRANCHISOR DURING THE OPERATION OF THE FRANCHISE BUSINESS.

<u>Item 11B Instructions:</u>

i. Include assistance in:

    a) Products or services to be offered by the franchisee to its customers;

    b) Hiring and training of employees;

    c) Improvements and developments in the franchised business;

    d) Pricing;

    e) Administrative, bookkeeping, accounting and inventory control procedures; and

    f) Operating problems encountered by the franchisee.

ii. For the Franchisor's advertising program for the product or service offered by the franchisee:

    a) Disclose the media in which the advertising may be disseminated (for example, print, radio, or television).

    b) Disclose whether the coverage of the media is local, regional, or national in scope.

    c) Disclose the source of the advertising (for example, in-house advertising department, a national or regional advertising agency).

    d) Disclose the conditions when the franchisor permits franchisees to use their own advertising material.

e) If there is an advertising council composed of franchisees that advises the franchisor on advertising policies, disclose:

   (1) How members of the council are selected.

   (2) Whether the council serves in an advisory capacity only or has operational or decision-making power.

   (3) Whether the franchisor has the power to form, change, or dissolve the advertising council.

f) If the franchisee must participate in a local or regional advertising cooperative, disclose:

   (1) How the area or membership of the cooperative is defined.

   (2) How the franchisee's contribution to the cooperative is calculated (may reference Item 6).

   (3) Who is responsible for administration of the cooperative (for example, franchisor, franchisees, advertising agency).

   (4) Whether cooperatives must operate from written governing documents and whether the documents are available for review by the franchisee.

   (5) Whether cooperatives must prepare annual or periodic financial statements and whether the statements are available for review by the franchisee.

   (6) Whether the franchisor has the power to require cooperatives to be formed, changed, dissolved or merged.

g) If applicable, for each advertising fund not described in above sub-part (f), disclose:

   (1) Who contributes to each fund (for example, franchisees, franchisor, franchisor-owned units, outside vendors or suppliers);

   (2) Whether the franchisor-owned units must contribute to the fund and, if so, whether it is on the same basis as franchisees.

   (3) How much the franchisee must contribute to the advertising fund(s) (may reference Item 6) and whether other franchisees are required to contribute at a different rate (it is not necessary to disclose the specific rates).

   (4) Who administers the fund(s). Whether the fund is audited and when, and whether financial statements of the fund are available for review by the franchisee.

   (5) Use of the fund(s) in the most recently concluded fiscal year, the percentages spent on production, media placement, administrative expenses, and other (with a description of what constitutes "other"). Totals should equal 100%.

   (6) Whether the franchisor or an affiliate receives payment for providing goods or services to an advertising fund.

h) State whether the franchisor must spend any amount on advertising, in the area or territory where the franchisee is located.

i) If all advertising fees are not spent in the fiscal year in which they accrue, explain how the franchisor uses the remaining amounts. Indicate whether franchisees will receive a periodic accounting of how advertising fees are spent.

j) Disclose the percentage of advertising funds, if any, used for advertising that is principally a solicitation for the sale of franchises.

k) Cross reference Items 6, 8 and 9.

iii. If the franchisor requires that franchisees buy or use electronic cash register or computer systems, provide a general description of the systems in non-technical language:

a) Identify each hardware component and software program by brand, type and principal functions.

(1) If the hardware component or software program is the proprietary property of the franchisor, an affiliate or a third party, state whether the franchisor, an affiliate or a third party has the contractual right or obligation to provide ongoing maintenance, repairs, upgrades or updates. Disclose the current annual cost of any optional or required maintenance and support contracts, upgrades and updates.

(2) If the hardware component or software program is the proprietary property of a third party, and no compatible equivalent component or program has been approved by the franchisor for use with the system to perform the same functions, identify the third party by name, business address and telephone number, and state the length of time the component or program has been in continuous use by the franchisor and its franchisees.

(3) If the hardware component or software program is not proprietary, identify compatible equivalent components or programs that perform the same functions and indicate whether they have been approved by the franchisor.

b) State whether the franchisee has any contractual obligation to upgrade or update any hardware component or software program during the term of the franchise, and if so, whether there are any contractual limitations on the frequency and cost of the obligation.

c) For each electronic cash register system or software program, describe how it will be used in the franchisees business, and the types of business information or data that will be collected and generated. State whether the franchisor will have independent access to the information and data, and if so, whether there are any contractual limitations on the franchisors right to access the information and data.

iv. After describing the obligation, cite the section number of the agreement imposing the obligation. Put the citation in, parentheses.

v. Disclose if the franchisor is not obligated to provide or to assist the franchisee to obtain the above items or services.

vi. Do not repeat, but do cross reference disclosure made in Item 6.

vii. Disclose the table of contents of the operating manual(s) provided to the franchisee as of the franchisors last fiscal year end or a more recent date. State the number of pages devoted to each subject and the total number of pages in the manual as of this date. Alternatively, this disclosure may be omitted if the prospective franchisee views the manual before purchase of the franchise.

C. THE METHODS USED BY THE FRANCHISOR TO SELECT THE LOCATION OF THE FRANCHISEE'S BUSINESS.

Item 11C Instructions:

i. Disclose whether the franchisor selects the site or approves an area within which the franchisee selects a site. Disclose how and whether the franchisor must approve a franchisee selected site.

ii. Disclose the factors which the franchisor considers in selecting or approving sites (for example general location and neighborhood, traffic patterns, parking, size, physical characteristics of existing buildings and lease terms).

iii. Disclose the time limit for the franchisor to locate or to approve or disapprove the site. Disclose the consequences if the franchisor and franchisee cannot agree on a site.

iv. Disclosures made in response to Item 11A need not be repeated or cross-referenced in the response to Item 11C.

D. THE TYPICAL LENGTH OF TIME BETWEEN THE SIGNING OF THE FRANCHISE AGREEMENT OR THE FIRST PAYMENT OF CONSIDERATION FOR THE FRANCHISE AND THE OPENING OF THE FRANCHISEES BUSINESS.

Item 11D Instructions:

i. Disclosure may be a range of times if the range is specific.

ii. Describe the factors which may affect the time period such as ability to obtain a lease, financing or building permits, zoning and local ordinances, weather conditions, shortages, or delayed installation of equipment, fixtures and signs.

E. THE TRAINING PROGRAM OF THE FRANCHISOR AS OF THE FRANCHISORS LAST FISCAL YEAR END OR A MORE RECENT DATE INCLUDING:

(1) THE LOCATION, DURATION AND GENERAL OUTLINE OF THE TRAINING PROGRAM;

(2) HOW OFTEN THE TRAINING PROGRAM WILL BE CONDUCTED;

(3) THE EXPERIENCE THAT THE INSTRUCTORS HAVE WITH THE FRANCHISOR;

(4) CHARGES TO BE MADE TO THE FRANCHISEE AND WHO MUST PAY TRAVEL AND LIVING EXPENSES OF THE ENROLLEES IN THE TRAINING PROGRAM;

(5) IF THE TRAINING PROGRAM IS NOT MANDATORY, THE PERCENTAGE OF NEW FRANCHISEES THAT ENROLLED IN THE TRAINING PROGRAM DURING THE PRECEDING 12 MONTHS; AND

(6) WHETHER ANY ADDITIONAL TRAINING PROGRAMS AND/OR REFRESHER COURSES ARE REQUIRED,

Item 11E Instructions:

i. Use a table to state the subjects taught and the number of hours of classroom and "on the job training" devoted to each subject in the franchisors training program. Use footnotes to explain.

ii. For each subject disclose the training location and how often training classes are held.

iii. Describe the location or facility where the training is held (for example, company, home, office, company owned store.)

iv. State how long after the signing of the agreement or before the opening date of the business the franchisee must complete the required training.

v. Describe the nature of instructional material. Disclose the minimum experience of the instructors. Disclose only experience that is relevant to the subject taught and the franchisors operations.

vi. State who may and who is required to attend the training. State whether the franchisee or other persons must complete the program to the franchisors satisfaction.

vii. Charges for training or training materials should be disclosed in Item 5 if the obligation to pay arises before the franchise location opens.

viii. Disclose who pays the travel and living expenses of the persons receiving the training.

SAMPLE ANSWER 11

Except as disclosed below, Belmont need not provide any assistance to you.

Before you open your business, Belmont will:

1) Designate your exclusive territory (Franchise Agreement – Paragraph 2).

2) Assist you in selecting a business site. Your site must be at least _____ square feet in area, have parking spaces, and an average of cars per hour driving by. We must approve or disapprove your site within 20 days after we receive notice of the location.

3) Within 30 days of your signing the Franchise Agreement, assist you to find and negotiate the lease or purchase of a location for your muffler shop (Franchise Agreement – Paragraph ___). Your store location will be purchased or leased by you from independent third parties.

4) Within 60 days of your signing the Franchise Agreement, provide written specifications for store construction or remodeling and for all required and replacement equipment,

inventory and supplies (Franchise Agreement – Paragraph _____). See Item 8 of this offering circular.

5) Within 60 days of your signing the Franchise Agreement, provide blueprints for your store construction or remodeling and obtain health, sanitation, building, utility and sign permits for your premises. You pay for the construction or remodeling. (Franchise Agreement – Paragraph _____).

6) Within 60 days of your signing the Franchise Agreement, train you and one other person as follows:

Subject	Instructional Material	Time Begun	Hours of Classroom Training	Hours of On-the-Job Training	Instructor & Years of Experience

Belmont does not charge for this training or service, but you must pay the travel and living expenses for you and your employees. All training occurs at Belmont's Jackson, Minnesota headquarters.

During the operation of the franchised business, Belmont will:

1) Develop new products and methods and provide you with information about developments. (Franchise Agreement – Paragraph _____).

2) Loan you a copy of our operations manual which contains mandatory and suggested specifications, standards and procedures. This manual is confidential and remains our property. Belmont will modify this manual, but the modification will not alter your status and rights under the Franchise Agreement. (Franchise Agreement – Paragraph _____). The table of contents is as follows:

Each week for the first 90 days after you open your shop, Belmont will telephone to discuss your operational problems.

Belmont will hold annual conferences to discuss sales techniques, personnel training, bookkeeping, accounting, inventory control, performance standards, advertising programs and merchandising procedures. There is no conference fee, but you must pay all your travel and living expenses. These elective conferences are held at our Jackson, Minnesota headquarters or at a location chosen by a majority vote of all franchisees.

Belmont provides advertising materials and services to you through a national advertising fund (the "National Fund"). Materials provided by the National Fund to all franchisees include video and audio tapes, mats, posters, banners and miscellaneous point-of-sale items. You will receive one sample of each at no charge. If you want additional copies you must pay duplication costs.

You may develop advertising materials for your own use, at your own cost. Belmont must approve the advertising materials in advance and in writing.

Belmont occasionally provides for placement of advertising on behalf of the entire Belmont system, including franchisees. However, most placement is done on a local basis, typically by local advertising agencies hired by individual franchisees or advertising cooperatives. Belmont reserves the right to use advertising fees from the Belmont system to place advertising in national media (including broadcast, print or other media) in the future. In the past Belmont has used an outside advertising agency to create and place advertising. Neither Belmont nor its affiliate receives payment from the National Fund. Advertising funds are used to promote the product sold by the franchisee and are not used to sell additional franchises.

The National Fund is a nonprofit corporation which collects advertising fees from all franchisees. Each franchisor owned store of Belmont contributes to the National Fund on the same basis as franchisees. All payments to the National Fund must be spent on advertising, promotion and marketing of goods and services provided by Belmont Muffler Shops. You must contribute the amounts described in Item 6, under the heading "Advertising, Fees and Expenses."

The National Fund is administered by Belmont's accounting and marketing personnel under the direction of the Advertising Council. An annual audited financial statement of the National Fund is available to any franchisee upon request. During the last fiscal year of the National Fund (ending on December 31, 1990), the National Fund spent 39% of its income on the production of advertisements and other promotional materials, 36% for media placement, 18% for general and administrative expenses, and 7% for other expenses (the purchase of glassware given to customers of Belmont shops as part of a promotional campaign).

The Advertising Council acts as the board of directors of the National Fund. The Advertising Council has 8 members: the President, Treasurer, Vice President-Marketing, and Vice President-Operations of Belmont; and 4 franchisee representatives who are elected by the governing board of the Belmont Franchisee Association.

Once your shop opens, you must participate in the local advertising cooperative established in the Area of Dominant Influence (ADI) where your store is located. The amount of your contribution to the local advertising cooperative is described in Item 6 under the heading "Advertising Fees and Expenses."

Each local advertising cooperative must adopt written governing documents. A copy of the governing documents of the cooperative (if one has been established) for your ADI is available upon request. Each cooperative may determine its own voting procedures; however, each company-owned Belmont Shop will be entitled to one vote in any local advertising cooperative. The members and their elected officers are responsible for administration of the cooperative. Advertising cooperatives must prepare quarterly and annual financial statements. The annual financial statement must be prepared by an independent CPA and be made available to all franchisees in that advertising cooperative.

You select your business site within your exclusive area subject to our approval. Belmont assists in site selection by telling you the number of new car registrations, population density, traffic patterns and proximity of the proposed site to other Belmont Muffler Shops.

Franchisees typically open their shops 4 to 7 months after they sign a franchise agreement. The factors that affect this time are the ability to obtain a lease, financing or building permits, zoning and local ordinances, weather conditions, shortages, and delayed installation of equipment fixtures and signs.

Item 12. TERRITORY

DESCRIBE ANY EXCLUSIVE TERRITORY GRANTED THE FRANCHISEE. CONCERNING THE FRANCHISEES LOCATION (WITH OR WITHOUT EXCLUSIVE TERRITORY), DISCLOSE WHETHER:

A. THE FRANCHISOR HAS ESTABLISHED OR MAY ESTABLISH ANOTHER FRANCHISEE WHO MAY ALSO USE THE FRANCHISOR'S TRADEMARK.

B. THE FRANCHISOR HAS ESTABLISHED OR MAY ESTABLISH A COMPANY-OWNED OUTLET OR OTHER CHANNELS OF DISTRIBUTION USING THE FRANCHISOR'S TRADEMARK.

Item 12 Instructions:

  i. As used in Item 12, trademark includes names, trademarks, logos and other commercial symbols.

  ii. If appropriate, describe the minimum area granted to the franchisee. The franchisor may use an area encompassed within a specific radius, a distance sufficient to encompass a specified population or another specific designation.

  iii. State whether the franchise is granted for a specific location or a location to be approved by the franchisor.

  iv. If appropriate, state the conditions under which the franchisor will approve the relocation of the franchised business or the establishment of additional franchised outlets.

  v. Describe restrictions on the franchisor regarding operating company owned stores or on granting franchised outlets for a similar or competitive business within the defined area.

  vi. Describe restrictions on franchisees from soliciting or accepting orders outside of their defined territories.

  vii. Describe restrictions on the franchisor from soliciting or accepting orders inside the franchisees defined territory. State compensation that the franchisor must pay for soliciting or accepting orders inside the franchisees defined territories.

  viii. Describe franchisee options, rights of first refusal or similar rights to acquire additional franchises within the territory or contiguous territories.

  ix. If the franchisor does not grant territorial rights, use Sample Answer 12-1.

C. THE FRANCHISOR OR ITS AFFILIATE HAS ESTABLISHED OR MAY ESTABLISH OTHER FRANCHISES OR COMPANY-OWNED OUTLETS OR ANOTHER CHANNEL OF DISTRIBUTION SELLING OR LEASING SIMILAR PRODUCTS OR SERVICES UNDER A DIFFERENT TRADEMARK.

Item 12C Instructions:

i. "Similar products and services" includes competing, interchangeable or substitute products but not products or services which are not part of the same product or service market.

ii. If the franchisor or an affiliate operates, franchises or has present plans to operate or franchise a business under a different trademark and that business sells goods or services similar to those to be offered by the franchisee, describe:

   a) The similar goods and services;

   b) The trade names and trademarks;

   c) Whether outlets will be franchisor owned or operated;

   d) Whether the franchisor or its franchisees who use the different trademark will solicit or accept orders within the franchisees territory;

   e) A timetable for the plan;

   f) How the franchisor will resolve conflicts between the franchisor and the franchisees and between the franchisees of each system regarding territory, customers or franchisor support; and

   g) If appropriate, disclose the principal business address of the franchisors similar operating business. If it is the same as the franchisors principal business address disclosed in Item 1, disclose whether the franchisor maintains (or plans to maintain) physically separate offices and training facilities for the similar competing business.

D. CONTINUATION OF THE FRANCHISEES TERRITORIAL EXCLUSIVITY DEPENDS ON ACHIEVEMENT OF A CERTAIN SALES VOLUME, MARKET PENETRATION OR OTHER CONTINGENCY AND UNDER WHAT CIRCUMSTANCES THE FRANCHISEES TERRITORY MAY BE ALTERED.

Item 12D Instructions:

i. Disclose conditions for the franchisees keeping its territorial rights (for example, sales quotas or the opening of additional business outlets). Specify the quotas or conditions and the franchisors rights if the franchisee fails to meet the requirements.

ii. Disclose other circumstances that permit the franchisor to modify the franchisees territorial rights (for example, a population increase in the territory giving the franchisor the right to grant an additional franchise within the area). Disclose the effect on the franchisees rights.

SAMPLE ANSWER 12-1

You will not receive an exclusive territory. Belmont may establish other franchised or company owned outlets that may compete with your location.

SAMPLE ANSWER 12-2

You will receive an exclusive territory with a minimum population of 50,000 people. You will operate from one location and must receive Belmont's permission before relocating. Belmont will not operate stores or grant franchises for a similar or competitive business within your area. Except when advertising cooperatively with appropriate franchisees, neither Belmont nor you can advertise or solicit orders within another franchisees territory. You and Belmont can accept orders from outside your territory without special payment.

You do not receive the right to acquire additional franchises within your area.

There is no minimum sales quota. You maintain rights to your area even though the population increases.

Item 13. TRADEMARKS

DISCLOSE THE PRINCIPAL TRADEMARKS TO BE LICENSED TO THE FRANCHISEE INCLUDING:

Item 13 Instructions:
  i. As used in Item 13, "Principal trademarks" means the primary trademarks, service marks, names, logos and symbols to be used by the franchisee to identify the franchised business. It does not include every trademark owned by the franchisor.

  ii. The franchisor may limit Item 13 disclosure to information that is relevant to the state where the franchised business will be located. The franchisor may include all states to eliminate the need for multiple disclosure in Item 13 but must amend its offering circular to reflect any material change in the list.

A. WHETHER THE PRINCIPAL TRADEMARKS ARE REGISTERED WITH THE UNITED STATES PATENT AND TRADEMARK OFFICE. FOR EACH REGISTRATION STATE THE REGISTRATION DATE AND NUMBER AND WHETHER THE REGISTRATION IS ON THE PRINCIPAL OR SUPPLEMENTAL REGISTER.

Item 13A Instructions:
  i. Identify each principal trademark which the franchisee may use. The franchisor may reproduce these trademarks in this Item.

  ii. State the date and identification number of each trademark registration or registration application listed. State whether the franchisor has filed all required affidavits. State whether any registration has been renewed.

  iii. State whether the principal trademarks are registered on the principal or supplemental register of the U.S. Patent and Trademark Office, and if not, whether an "intent to use" application or an application based on actual use has been filed with the U.S. Patent and Trademark Office. If the principal trademark to be used by the franchisee is not registered on the Principal Register of the U.S. Patent and Trademark Office, state:

By not having a Principal Register federal registration for (name or description of symbol), (Name of Franchisor) does not have certain presumptive legal rights granted by a registration.

B. DISCLOSE CURRENTLY EFFECTIVE MATERIAL DETERMINATIONS OF THE PATENT AND TRADEMARK OFFICE, TRADEMARK TRIAL AND APPEAL BOARD, THE TRADEMARK ADMINISTRATOR OF THIS STATE OR ANY COURT; PENDING INFRINGEMENT, OPPOSITION OR CANCELLATION; AND PENDING MATERIAL LITIGATION INVOLVING THE PRINCIPAL TRADEMARKS.

Item 13B Instructions:
   i. Litigation or an action is material if it could significantly affect the ownership or use of a trademark listed under Item 13. Describe how the determination affects the ownership, use or licensing. Describe any decided infringement, cancellation or opposition proceedings. Include infringement, opposition or cancellation proceedings in which the franchisor unsuccessfully sought to prevent registration of a trademark in order to protect a trademark licensed by the franchisor.

   ii. For pending material federal or state litigation regarding the franchisors use or ownership rights in a trademark disclose:
      a) The forum and case number;
      b) The nature of claims made opposing the franchisors use or by the franchisor opposing another person's use; and
      c) Any effective court or administrative agency ruling concerning the matter.

   iii. Do not repeat disclosure made in response to Item 13A.

   iv. The franchisor need not disclose historical challenges to registrations of trademarks listed in Item 13 that were resolved in the franchisors favor.

   v. The franchisor may include an attorney's opinion relative to the merits of litigation or of an action if the attorney issuing the opinion consents to its use. The text of the disclosure may include a summary of the opinion if the full opinion is attached and the attorney issuing the opinion consents to the use of the summary.

C. DISCLOSE AGREEMENTS CURRENTLY IN EFFECT WHICH SIGNIFICANTLY LIMIT THE RIGHTS OF THE FRANCHISOR TO USE OR LICENSE THE USE OF TRADEMARKS LISTED IN ITEM 13 IN A MANNER MATERIAL TO THE FRANCHISE.

Item 13C Instructions:
For each agreement disclose:
   i. The manner and extent of the limitation or grant;
   ii. The agreement's duration;
   iii. The parties to the agreement;

iv. The circumstances under which the agreement may be cancelled or modified; and

v. All other material terms.

D. THE FRANCHISOR MUST PROTECT THE FRANCHISEES' RIGHT TO USE THE PRINCIPAL TRADEMARKS LISTED IN ITEM 13, AND MUST PROTECT THE FRANCHISEE AGAINST CLAIMS OF INFRINGEMENT OR UNFAIR COMPETITION ARISING OUT OF THE FRANCHISEE'S USE OF THEM.

Item 13D Instructions:

i. Disclose the franchisees obligation to notify the franchisor of the use of or claims of rights to a trademark identical to or confusingly similar to a trademark licensed to the franchisee.

ii. State whether the franchise agreement requires the franchisor to take affirmative action when notified of these uses or claims. Identify who has the right to control administrative, proceedings or litigation.

iii. State whether the franchise agreement requires the franchisor to participate in the franchisees defense and/or indemnify the franchisee for expenses or damages if the franchisee is a party to an administrative or judicial proceeding involving a trademark licensed by the franchisor to the franchisee, or if the proceeding is resolved unfavorably to the franchisee.

iv. Disclose the franchisees rights under the franchise if the franchisor requires the franchisee to modify or discontinue the use of a trademark as a result of a proceeding or settlement.

E. WHETHER THE FRANCHISOR ACTUALLY KNOWS OF EITHER SUPERIOR PRIOR RIGHTS OR INFRINGING USES THAT COULD MATERIALLY AFFECT THE FRANCHISEES USE OF THE PRINCIPAL TRADEMARKS IN THIS STATE OR THE STATE IN WHICH THE FRANCHISED BUSINESS IS TO BE LOCATED.

Item 13E Instructions:

For each use of a principal trademark that the franchisor believes constitutes an infringement that could materially affect the franchisee's use of a trademark, state:

i. The location(s) where the infringement is occurring;

ii. To the extent known, the length of time of the infringement; and

iii. Action taken by the franchisor.

If the franchisor knows of a use of a trademark by another in a geographic area relevant to the franchisee which is or is likely to be based on a claim of superior prior rights to the franchisors, state the nature of the use by the other person and the place or area where it is occurring.

SAMPLE ANSWER 13

Belmont grants you the right to operate a shop under the name Belmont Muffler Shop. You may also use our other current or future trademarks to operate your shop. By trademark

Belmont means trade names, trademarks, service marks and logos used to identify your shop. Belmont registered the below trademark on the United State Patent and Trademark Office principal register:

You must follow our rules when you use these marks. You can not use a name or mark as part of a corporate name or with modifying words, designs or symbols except for those which Belmont licenses to you. You may not use Belmont's registered name in connection with the sale of an unauthorized product or service or in a manner not authorized in writing by Belmont.

On June 4, 1973, the United States Patent and Trademark Office rejected Belmont's application to register the mark "Super Mufflers" because the mark was found to be confusingly similar to a registered mark. Belmont's-inability to register this mark on a federal level permits others to establish rights to use the mark. This use will not be in areas where our franchisees are operating, or advertising under the mark, or in the natural zone of expansion for Belmont's shops. In addition, these users must act in good faith and without actual knowledge of Belmont's prior use of the mark. However, if others establish rights to use Belmont's mark, Belmont may not be able to expand into these areas using the mark.

No agreements limit Belmont's right to use or license the use of Belmont's trademarks.

You must notify Belmont immediately when you learn about an infringement of or challenge to your use of our trademark. Belmont will take the action we think appropriate. while Belmont is not required to defend you against a claim against your use of our trademark, Belmont will reimburse you for your liability and reasonable costs in connection with defending Belmont's trademark. To receive reimbursement you must have notified Belmont immediately when you learned about the infringement or challenge.

You must modify or discontinue the use of a trademark if Belmont modifies or discontinues it. If this happens, Belmont will reimburse you for your tangible costs of compliance (for example, changing signs). You must not directly or indirectly contest our right to our trademarks, trade secrets or business techniques that are part of our business.

Belmont does not know of any infringing uses that could materially affect your use of Belmont's trademark.

or

John E. Jones, 4231 Main Street, Reno, Nevada is currently doing business as Belmont Muffler Shoppe at 4231 Main Street, Reno, Nevada. We believe that this is an infringing use of our federally registered trademark "Belmont Muffler Shop," and we have filed an action to enjoin Mr. Jones and to recover damages If the court holds that Mr. Jones' use is not infringing, Belmont may not be able to use Belmont's trademark in Mr. Jones, immediate area. (Belmont Muffler Shop v. Belmont Muffler Shoppecite)

Item 14. PATENTS, COPYRIGHTS AND PROPRIETARY INFORMATION

IF THE FRANCHISOR OWNS RIGHTS IN PATENTS OR COPYRIGHTS THAT ARE MATERIAL TO THE FRANCHISE, DESCRIBE THESE PATENTS AND COPYRIGHTS AND THEIR

RELATIONSHIP TO THE FRANCHISE. INCLUDE THEIR DURATION AND WHETHER THE FRANCHISOR CAN AND INTENDS TO RENEW THE COPYRIGHTS. TO THE EXTENT RELEVANT, DISCLOSE THE INFORMATION REQUIRED BY ITEM 13 CONCERNING THESE PATENTS AND COPYRIGHTS. IF THE FRANCHISOR CLAIMS PROPRIETARY RIGHTS IN CONFIDENTIAL INFORMATION OR TRADE SECRETS, DISCLOSE THEIR GENERAL SUBJECT MATTER AND THE TERMS AND CONDITIONS FOR USE BY THE FRANCHISEE.

<u>Item 14 Instructions:</u>

  i. State the patent number, issue date and title for each patent. State the serial number, filing date and title of each patent application. Describe the type of patent or patent application (for example mechanical, process, or design). State the registration number and date of each copyright.

  ii. Describe the relationship of the patent, patent application or copyright to the franchised business.

  iii. Describe any current determination of the Patent and Trademark Office, Copyright Office (Library of Congress) or court regarding the patent or copyright. Include the forum, case number and effect on the franchised business.

  iv. State the forum, case number, claims asserted, issues involved and effective determinations for any proceedings pending in the Patent and Trademark Office or the Court of Appeals for the Federal Circuit.

  v. If counsel consents, the franchisor may include a counsel's opinion or a summary of the opinion about patent or copyright issues discussed in this Item.

  vi. If an agreement limits the use of the patent, patent application or copyright, state the parties to and duration of the agreement, the extent to which the franchisee may be affected by the agreement, and other material terms of the agreement.

  vii. Disclose the franchisors obligation to protect the patent, patent application or copyright. State:

    a) Whether franchisee must notify the franchisor of claims or infringements or if the action is discretionary.

    b) Whether the franchisor must take affirmative action when notified of infringement or if the action is discretionary.

    c) Who has the right to control litigation.

    d) Whether the franchisor must participate in the defense of a franchisee or indemnify the franchisee for expenses or damages in a proceeding involving a patent, patent application or copyright licensed to the franchisee.

    e) Requirements that the franchises modify or discontinue use of the subject matter covered by the patent or copyright.

    f) Franchisee's rights if the franchisor requires the franchisee to modify or discontinue the use of the subject matter covered by the patent or copyright.

viii. If the franchisor actually knows of an infringement that could materially affect the franchisee state:

   a) The nature of the infringement.

   b) The locations where the infringement is occurring.

   c) The length of time of the infringement.

   d) Action taken or anticipated by the franchisor.

ix. State whether the franchisor intends to renew the copyright when the registration expires.

x. Discuss in general terms other proprietary information communicated to the franchisee (for example, whether there is a formula or recipe considered to be a trade secret).

xi. Use Sample Answer 14-1 if no patents or copyrights are material to the franchise.

SAMPLE ANSWER 14-1

No patents or copyrights are material to the franchise.

SAMPLE ANSWER 14-2

You do not receive the right to use an item covered by a patent or copyright, but you can use the proprietary information in Belmont's Operations Manual. The Operations Manual is described in Item 11. Although Belmont has not filed an application for a copyright registration for the operations Manual, it claims a copyright and the information is proprietary. Item 11 describes limitations on the use of this manual by you and your employees. You must also promptly tell us when you learn about unauthorized use of this proprietary information. Belmont is not obligated to take any action but will respond to this information as we think appropriate. Belmont will indemnify you for losses brought by a third party concerning your use of this information.

SAMPLE ANSWER 14-3

U.S. Patent 3999442 was issued on December 14, 1980. It describes a process for exhaust system installation. The process describes the steps in making a straight length of exhaust pipe, bending this pipe, coating the inside and outside of this pipe with our Pipe Protector and installing the exhaust pipe on a motor vehicle. You will use equipment utilizing this process.

On December 15, 1970, Belmont obtained a copyright registration for its Operations Manual under Registration A41139. Amendments to the manual were registered on January 7, 1983 (Reg. A521,371) and June 6, 1974 (Reg. A 541,333). Belmont intends to renew these copyrights. Item 11 of this Offering Circular describes the Operations Manual and the manner in which you are permitted to use it.

Belmont's right to use or license these patents and copyrighted items is not materially limited by any-agreement or known infringing use.

You must tell us immediately if you learn about an infringement or challenge to our use of these patents or copyrights. Belmont will take the action that Belmont thinks appropriate. You must also agree not to contest Belmont's interest in these or our other trade secrets.

If Belmont decides to add, modify or discontinue the use of an item or process covered by a patent or copyright, you must also do so. Belmont's sole obligation is to reimburse you for the tangible cost of complying with this obligation.

Although Belmont is not obligated to defend your use of these items or processes, Belmont will reimburse you for damages and reasonable costs incurred in litigation about them.

Item 15. OBLIGATION TO PARTICIPATE IN THE ACTUAL OPERATION OF THE FRANCHISE BUSINESS

DISCLOSE THE FRANCHISEE'S OBLIGATION TO PARTICIPATE PERSONALLY IN THE DIRECT OPERATION OF THE FRANCHISE BUSINESS AND WHETHER THE FRANCHISOR RECOMMENDS PARTICIPATION.

Item 15 Instructions:

i. Include obligations arising from written agreement (including personal guaranty, confidentiality agreement or non-competition agreement) or from the franchisors practice.

ii. If personal "on premises" supervision is not required:

   a) If the franchisee is an individual, state whether the franchisor recommends "on-premises" supervision by the franchisee;

   b) State limitations on whom the franchisee can hire as an on-premises supervisor;

   c) Whether this "on-premise" supervisor must successfully complete the franchisor's training program; and

   d) If the franchisee is a business entity, state the amount of equity interest that the "on premises" supervisor must have in the franchise.

iii. Disclose the restrictions which the franchisee must place on its manager (for example, maintain trade secrets, non-competition).

iv. The franchisor may reference Items 14 and 17 in its answer.

SAMPLE ANSWER 15-1

If you are an individual, you must directly supervise the franchised business on its premises. If you are a corporation the direct, on-site supervision must be done by a person who owns at least 1/3 of the corporate equity.

SAMPLE ANSWER 15-2

Belmont does not require that you personally supervise the franchised business. The business must be directly supervised "on-premises" by a manager who has successfully completed Belmont's training program. The on-premises manager can not have an interest or business relationship with any of Belmont's business competitors. The manager need not have an ownership interest in a corporate or partnership franchisee. The manager must sign a written agreement to maintain confidentiality of the trade secrets described in Item 14 and to conform with the covenants not to compete described in Item 17.

Each individual who owns a 5% or greater interest in the franchisee entity must sign an agreement (Exhibit _____) assuming and agreeing to discharge all obligations of the "Franchisee" under the Franchise Agreement.

Item 16. RESTRICTIONS ON WHAT THE FRANCHISEE MAY SELL

DISCLOSE RESTRICTIONS OR CONDITIONS IMPOSED BY THE FRANCHISOR ON THE GOODS OR SERVICES THAT THE FRANCHISEE MAY SELL OR THAT LIMIT THE CUSTOMERS TO WHOM THE FRANCHISEE MAY SELL GOODS OR SERVICES.

Item 16 Instructions:
  i. Describe the franchisee's obligation to sell only goods and services approved by the franchisor.
  ii. Disclose any franchisee obligation to sell all goods and services authorized by the franchisor. Disclose whether the franchisor has the right to change the types of authorized goods and services and whether there are limits on the franchisors right to make changes.
  iii. If the franchisee is restricted regarding customers, disclose the restrictions.
  iv. The applicant may cross reference disclosures made in Items 8, 9, and 12.
  v. Use Sample Answer 16-1 for a negative response.

SAMPLE ANSWER 16-1

Belmont does not restrict the type of goods or services that you may offer.

SAMPLE ANSWER 16-2

Belmont requires you to offer and sell only those goods and services that Belmont has approved (see Item 9).

You must offer all goods and services that Belmont designates as required for all franchisees. These required services are muffler inspection, repair and replacement. Parts, supplies, and equipment used in your Belmont Muffler business must be approved by Belmont (see Item 8).

Belmont has the right to add additional authorized services that the franchisee is required to offer. There are no limits on Belmont's right to do so except that the investment required of a franchisee (for equipment, supplies and initial inventory) will not exceed $5,000 per year.

Belmont also designates some services as optional for qualified franchisees. Current optional services are brake inspection, repair and replacement, tire rotation, wheel balancing, and alignment and rust-proofing. To offer optional goods or services, you must be in substantial compliance with all material obligations under your Franchise Agreement. In addition, Belmont may require you to comply with other requirements (such as training, marketing, insurance) before Belmont will allow you to offer certain optional services.

As long as you meet your annual agreed sales quotas (see Item 12), Belmont will not restrict you from soliciting any customers, no matter who they are or where they are located. If you do not meet your annual sales quota, Belmont may deny you the right to receive any further fleet business referrals from Belmont and may either keep the fleet business referrals for itself or give them to another franchisee. Failure to meet your annual sales quota is a default under your Franchise Agreement and grounds for termination of your franchise (see Item 17).

Item 17. RENEWAL, TERMINATION, TRANSFER AND DISPUTE RESOLUTION

SUMMARIZE THE PROVISIONS OF THE FRANCHISE AND OTHER AGREEMENTS DEALING WITH TERMINATION, RENEWAL, TRANSFER, DISPUTE RESOLUTION AND OTHER IMPORTANT ASPECTS OF THE FRANCHISE RELATIONSHIP.

Item 17 Instructions:

i.   Begin Item 17 disclosure with the following statement:

This table lists certain important provisions of the franchise and related agreements. You should read these provisions in the agreements attached to this offering circular.

ii. Respond in tabular form. Refer to the section of the agreement which covers each subject.

iii. Use a separate table for any other significant franchise-related agreements. If a provision in any other agreement affects the provisions of the franchise or franchise-related agreements disclosed in this Item (for example, the term of the franchise will be equal to the term of the lease), disclose that provision in the applicable category in the table.

iv. The table should contain a "summary" column to summarize briefly the disclosed provision. The summary is intended to provide a concise overview of the provision in no more than a few words or a sentence. Do not specify in detail all matters covered by a provision.

v.   The table should respond to each category listed below. Do not change the names of the categories. List all contractual provisions relevant to each category in the table. If the response to any category is that the agreement does not contain the relevant provision, the table should so state. If the agreement is silent concerning a category but the franchisor unilaterally offers to provide certain benefits or protection to franchisees as a matter of policy, a footnote should describe this policy and state whether the policy is subject to change. The categories are:

a. Length of the term of the franchise

b. Renewal or extension of the term

c. Requirements for franchisee to renew or extend

d. Termination by franchisee

e. Termination by franchisor without cause

f. Termination by franchisor with "cause"

g. "Cause" defined – curable defaults

h. "Cause" defined – defaults which cannot be cured

i. Franchisee's obligations on termination/non-renewal

j. Assignment of contract by franchisor

k. "Transfer" by franchisee – defined

l. Franchisor approval of transfer by franchisee

m. Conditions for franchisor approval of transfer

n. Franchisor's right of first refusal to acquire franchisee's business

o. Franchisor's option to purchase franchisee's business

p. Death or disability of franchisee

q. Non-competition covenants during the term of the franchise

r. Non-competition covenants after the franchise is terminated or expires

s. Modification of the agreement

t. Integration/merger clause

u. Dispute resolution by arbitration or mediation

v. Choice of forum

w. Choice of law

SAMPLE ANSWER 17

This table lists important provisions of the franchise and related agreements. You should read these provisions in the agreements attached to this offering circular.

Provision	Section in Franchise Agreement	Summary
a. Term of the franchise	Section 1, (also) Section 1 of Lease, Exhibit F)	Term is equal to lease term — 10 years

Provision	Section in Franchise Agreement	Summary
b. Renewal or exten-sion of the term	Section 20	If you are in good standing you can add additional term equal to renewal term of lease (10 years maximum)
c. Requirements for you to renew or extend	Section 20	Sign new agreement, pay fee, remodel and sign release
d. Termination by you	None	
e. Termination by Belmont without cause	None	
f. Termination by Belmont with cause	Section 21	Belmont can terminate only if franchisee defaults
g. "Cause" defined – defaults which can be cured	Section 21B	You have 30 days to cure: non-payment of fees, sanitation problems, non-submission of reports and any other default not listed in Sec. 21A
h. "Cause" defined – defaults which cannot be cured	Section 22	Non-curable defaults: conviction of felony, repeated defaults even if cured, abandonment trademark misuse and unapproved transfers
i. Your obligations on termination/nonrenewal	Section 22	Obligations include complete de-identification and payment of amounts due (also see "r" below)
j. Assignment of contract by Belmont	Section 18	No restriction on Belmont's right to assign
k. "Transfer" by you – definition	Section 19A	Includes transfer of contract or assets or ownership change
l. Belmont's approval of transfer by franchisee	Section 19B	Belmont has the right to approve all transfers but will not unreasonably withhold approval
m. Conditions for Belmont approval of transfer	Section 19C	New Franchisee qualifies, transfer fee paid, purchase agreement approved, training arranged, release signed by you and current agreement signed by new franchisee (also see "r" below)
n. Belmont's right of first refusal to acquire your business	Section 19F	Belmont can match any offer for the franchisee's business

Provision	Section in Franchise Agreement	Summary
o. Belmont's option to purchase your business	None, but see policy described in Note 1	
p. Your death or disability	Section 19D	Franchise must be assigned by estate to approved buyer in 6 months
q. Non-competition covenants during the term of the franchise	Section 11	No involvement in competing business anywhere is U.S.
r. Non-competition covenants after the franchise is terminated or expires	Sections 19C and 22C	No competing business for 2 years within 20 miles of another Belmont franchise (including after assignment)
s. Modification of the agreement	Section 8A	No modifications generally but Operating Manual subject to change
t. Integration/merger clause	Section 29	Only the terms of the franchise agreement are binding (subject to state law); any other promises may not be enforceable
u. Dispute resolution by arbitration or mediation	Section 24	Except for certain claims, all disputes but be arbitrated in _____, _____
v. Choice of forum	Section 27	Litigation must be in _____
w. Choice of law	Section 28	_____ law applies

---

1 Franchisor is not obligated by the Agreement to do so, but, if the franchise is terminated, franchisor's policy is to buy back inventory at fair market value. This policy is subject to change at any time.

These states have statutes which may supersede the franchise agreement in your relationship with the franchisor including the areas of termination and renewal of your franchise: ARKANSAS [Stat. Section 70-807], CALIFORNIA [Bus. & Prof. Code Sections 20000-20043], CONNECTICUT [Gen Stat. Section 42-133e et seq.], DELAWARE [Code, tit.], HAWAII [Rev. Stat. Section 482E-1], ILLINOIS [Rev. Stat. Chapter 121_ par 1719-1720], INDIANA [Stat. Section 23-2-2.7], IOWA [Code Sections 523H.1-523H.17], MICHIGAN [Stat. Section 19.854(27)], MINNESOTA [Stat. Section 80C.14], MISSISSIPPI [Code Section 75-24-51], MISSOURI [Stat. Section 407.400], NEBRASKA [Rev. Stat. Section 87-401], NEW JERSEY [Stat. Section 56:10-1], SOUTH DAKOTA [Codified Laws Section 37-5A-51], VIRGINIA [Code 13.1-557-574-13.1-564], WASHINGTON [Code Section 19.100.180], WISCONSIN [Stat. Section 135.03]. These and other states may have court decisions which may supersede the franchise agreement in your relationship with the franchisor including the areas of termination and renewal of your franchise.

Item 18. PUBLIC FIGURES

DISCLOSE THE FOLLOWING:

A. COMPENSATION OR OTHER BENEFIT GIVEN OR PROMISED TO A PUBLIC FIGURE ARISING FROM:

> (1) THE USE OF THE PUBLIC FIGURE IN THE FRANCHISE NAME OR SYMBOL OR

> (2) THE ENDORSEMENT OR RECOMMENDATION OF THE FRANCHISE TO PROSPECTIVE FRANCHISEES.

B. THE EXTENT TO WHICH THE PUBLIC FIGURE IS INVOLVED IN THE ACTUAL MANAGEMENT OR CONTROL OF THE FRANCHISOR.

C. THE TOTAL INVESTMENT OF THE PUBLIC FIGURE IN THE FRANCHISOR.

<u>Item 18 Instructions:</u>

i. A "public figure" is a person whose name or physical appearance is generally known to the public in the geographic area where the franchise will be located.

ii. Disclose the compensation paid or promised for the endorsement or use of the name of the public figure.

iii. Describe the public figures position and duties in the franchisors business structure.

iv. State the amount of the public figure's investment. Describe the extent of the amount contributed in services performed or to be performed. State the type of investment (for example, common stock, promissory note).

v. Use sample answer 18-1 for a negative response.

SAMPLE ANSWER 18-1

Belmont does not use any public figure to promote its franchise.

SAMPLE ANSWER 18-2

Belmont has paid Ralph Doister $50,000 for the use of his name in promoting the sale of our franchise. The right expires December 31, 1992. Belmont has produced newspaper ads, a brochure and a video which feature Mr. Doister. Mr. Doister does not manage or own an interest in Belmont.

Item 19. EARNINGS CLAIMS

A. AN EARNINGS CLAIM MADE IN CONNECTION WITH AN OFFER OF A FRANCHISE MUST BE INCLUDED IN FULL IN THE OFFERING CIRCULAR AND MUST HAVE A REASONABLE BASIS AT THE TIME IT IS MADE. IF NO EARNINGS CLAIM IS MADE, ITEM 19 OF THE OFFERING CIRCULAR MUST CONTAIN THE NEGATIVE DISCLOSURE PRESCRIBED IN THE INSTRUCTION.

Item 19 Instructions:

i. Definition: "Earnings claim" means information given to a prospective franchisee by, on behalf of, or at the direction of the franchisor or its agent, from which a specific level or range of actual or potential sales, costs, income or profit from franchised or non-franchised units may be easily ascertained.

A chart, table or mathematical calculation presented to demonstrate possible results based upon a combination of variables (such as multiples of price and quantity to reflect gross sales) is an earnings claim subject to this item.

An earnings claim limited solely to the actual operating results of a specific unit being offered for sale need not comply with this item if it is given only to potential purchasers of that unit and is accompanied by the name and last known address of each owner of the unit during the prior three years.

ii. Supplemental earnings claim: If a franchisor has made an earnings claim in accordance with this Item 19, the franchisor may deliver to a prospective franchisee a supplemental earnings claim directed to a particular location or circumstance, apart from the offering circular. The supplemental earnings claim must be in writing, explain the departure from the earnings claim in the offering circular, be prepared in accordance with this item 19, and be left with the prospective franchisee.

iii. Scope of requirement: An earnings claim is not required in connection with the offer of franchises; if made, however, its presentation must conform with this Item 19. If an earnings claim is not made, then Negative Disclosure 19 (below) must be used.

iv. Claims regarding future performance: A statement or prediction of future performance that is prepared as a forecast or projection in accordance with the statement on standards for accountants' services on prospective financial information (or its successor) issued by the American Institute of Certified Public Accountants, Inc., is presumed to have a reasonable basis.

v. Burden of proof: The burden is upon the franchisor to show that it had a reasonable basis for its earnings claim.

[NEGATIVE DISCLOSURE 19]

REPRESENTATIONS REGARDING EARNINGS CAPABILITY

Belmont does not furnish or authorize its salespersons to furnish any oral or written information concerning the actual or potential sales, costs, income or profits of [a Belmont muffler shop]. Actual results vary from unit to unit and Belmont cannot estimate the results of any particular franchise.

B. AN EARNINGS CLAIMS SHALL INCLUDE A DESCRIPTION OF ITS FACTUAL BASIS AND THE MATERIAL ASSUMPTIONS UNDERLYING ITS PREPARATION AND PRESENTATION.

Item 19B Instructions:

  i. FACTUAL BASIS: The factual basis of an earnings claim includes significant matters upon which a franchisees future results are expected to depend. This includes for example, economic or market conditions which are basic to a franchisees operation and encompass matters affecting, among other things, franchisees sales, the cost of goods or services sold and operating expenses.

  In the absence of an adequate operating experience of its own, a franchisor may base an earnings claim upon the results of operations of a substantially similar business of a person affiliated with the franchisor or franchisees of that person; provided that disclosure is made of any material differences in the economic or market conditions known to, or reasonably ascertainable by, the franchisor.

  ii. Basic Disclosures: The earnings claim must state:

  (a) Material assumptions, other than matters of common knowledge, underlying the claim (see Definition iii under Item 3 for the definition of material);

  (b) A concise summary of the basis for the claim including a statement of whether the claim is based upon actual experience of franchised units and, if so, the percentage of franchised outlets in operation for the period covered by the earnings claim that have actually attained or surpassed the stated results;

  (c) A conspicuous admonition that a new franchisees individual financial results are likely to differ from the result stated in the earnings claim; and

  (d) A statement that substantiation of the data used in preparing the earnings claim will be made available to the prospective franchisee on reasonable request.

Item 20. LIST OF OUTLETS

DISCLOSE THE FOLLOWING:

A. THE NUMBER OF FRANCHISES OF A TYPE SUBSTANTIALLY SIMILAR TO THOSE OFFERED AND THE NUMBER OF FRANCHISOR OWNED OR OPERATED OUTLETS AS OF THE CLOSE OF EACH OF THE FRANCHISORS LAST 3 FISCAL YEARS. SEGREGATE FRANCHISES THAT ARE OPERATIONAL FROM FRANCHISES NOT YET OPERATIONAL. SEGREGATE DISCLOSURE BY STATE. TOTAL EACH CATEGORY.

B. THE NAMES OF ALL FRANCHISEES AND THE ADDRESSES AND TELEPHONE NUMBERS OF ALL OF THEIR OUTLETS. THE FRANCHISOR MAY LIMIT ITS DISCLOSURE TO ALL FRANCHISEE OUTLETS IN THE STATE,.BUT IF THESE FRANCHISEE OUTLETS TOTAL FEWER THAN 100,, DISCLOSE FRANCHISEE OUTLETS FROM ALL CONTIGUOUS STATES AND THEN THE NEXT CLOSEST STATE(S) UNTIL AT LEAST 100 FRANCHISEE OUTLETS ARE LISTED.

C. THE ESTIMATED NUMBER OF FRANCHISES TO BE SOLD DURING THE 1 YEAR PERIOD AFTER THE CLOSE OF THE FRANCHISOR'S MOST RECENT FISCAL YEAR.

D. THE NUMBER OF FRANCHISEE OUTLETS IN THE FOLLOWING CATEGORIES THAT, FOR THE 3-YEAR PERIOD IMMEDIATELY BEFORE THE CLOSE OF FRANCHISORS' MOST RECENT FISCAL YEAR HAVE:

    (1) TRANSFERRED CONTROLLING OWNERSHIP;

    (2) BEEN CANCELLED OR TERMINATED BY THE FRANCHISOR;

    (3) NOT BEEN RENEWED BY THE FRANCHISOR;

    (4) BEEN REACQUIRED BY THE FRANCHISOR; OR

    (5) BEEN REASONABLY KNOWN BY THE FRANCHISOR TO HAVE OTHERWISE CEASED TO DO BUSINESS IN THE SYSTEM.

E. THE NAME AND LAST KNOWN HOME ADDRESS AND TELEPHONE NUMBER OF EVERY FRANCHISEE WHO HAS HAD AN OUTLET TERMINATED, CANCELLED, NOT RENEWED, OR OTHERWISE VOLUNTARILY OR INVOLUNTARILY CEASED TO DO BUSINESS UNDER THE FRANCHISE AGREEMENT DURING THE MOST RECENTLY COMPLETED FISCAL YEAR OR WHO HAS NOT COMMUNICATED WITH THE FRANCHISOR WITHIN 10 WEEKS OF THE APPLICATION DATE.

<u>Item 20 Instructions:</u>

    i. Do not include a transfer when beneficial ownership of the franchise does not change.

    ii. List an outlet that is reacquired by the franchisor in that column whether or not it also fits another category.

    iii. Other than the franchisee names addresses, and telephone numbers, disclose Item 20 information in tabular form. Use footnotes or a "remarks" column to elaborate on information in the table or to disclose caveats. Disclose the number of franchised and franchisor owned outlets sold, opened and closed. Disclose the total number of franchised and franchisor owned outlets open at the end of each year. Disclose information for each of the last 3 fiscal years.

    iv. If an outlet has been operated by more than one franchisee, disclose each transfer in the transfer column.

    v. Disclose information about franchisor owned outlets that are substantially similar to the franchised outlets. In this Item "franchisor owned" outlets include outlets owned by the franchisor and by its affiliates. Use a separate table with a format similar to the format for franchised outlets. The same table may be used if the franchisor owned outlets are separated from franchised outlets.

    vi. For franchisees operating within the system disclose franchisee business addresses and telephone numbers. List outlets owned by the persons listed in Item 2 and their immediate families or by business entities owned by then as franchisor owned outlets. These outlets can be identified in the table by an asterisk.

    vii. Separate information by state. List all states for which franchisor has information responsive to this Item.

viii. When the requirement states "most recent fiscal year," the franchisor may use a more recent date if it discloses that date and uses that date for all disclosures in this Item.

ix. When the requirement states "most recent fiscal year," the state may require a more recent date.

SAMPLE ANSWER 20

FRANCHISED STORE STATUS SUMMARY FOR YEARS 1992/1991/1990[1]

State	Transfers	Cancelled/ Terminated	Not Renewed	Reacquired by Franchisor	Left the System Other	Total from Left Columns[2]	Franchises Operating at Year End
Alaska							2/0/0
Arizona	2/1/0					2/1/0	8/6/2
Arkansas							6/4/2
California					1/1/0	1/1/0	4/0/0
Colorado							3/3/3
Connecticut							5/3/1
Delaware		1/0/0				1/0/0	6/4/0
Florida							2/0/0
Georgia							2/0/0
Idaho							2/0/0
TOTALS	2/1/0	1/0/0	0/0/0	0/0/0	1/1/0	4/2/0	40/20/8

[1] All numbers are as of December 31 for each year.

[2] The numbers in the "Total" column may exceed the number of stores affected because several events may have affected the same store. For example, the same store may have had multiple owners.

STATUS OF COMPANY OWNED STORES FOR YEARS 1992/1991/1990

State	Stores Closed During Year	Stores Opened During Year	Total Stores Operating at Year End
Alaska			
Arizona			
Arkansas			
California			
Colorado			
Connecticut			
Delaware			
Florida			
Georgia			
Idaho			
TOTALS	0/0/0	0/0/0	0/0/0

Note: Belmont no longer operates company owned stores.

PROJECTED OPENINGS AS OF DECEMBER 31, 1992

State	Franchise Agreements Signed but Store Not Open	Projected Franchised New Stores in the Next Fiscal Year	Projected Company-Owned Openings In the Next Fiscal Year
Alaska	1	1	0
Arizona			
Arkansas			
California			
Colorado			
Connecticut		2	
Delaware			
Florida			
Georgia			
Idaho	1		
TOTALS	2	3	0

Note: As of December 31, 1992

Item 21. FINANCIAL STATEMENTS

PREPARE FINANCIAL STATEMENTS IN ACCORDANCE WITH GENERALLY ACCEPTED ACCOUNTING PRINCIPLES. THESE FINANCIAL STATEMENTS MUST BE AUDITED BY AN INDEPENDENT CERTIFIED PUBLIC ACCOUNTANT. UNAUDITED STATEMENTS MAY BE USED FOR INTERIM PERIODS. INCLUDE THE FOLLOWING FINANCIAL STATEMENTS.

A. THE FRANCHISOR'S BALANCE SHEETS FOR THE LAST TWO FISCAL YEAR ENDS BEFORE THE APPLICATION DATE. IN ADDITION INCLUDE STATEMENTS OF OPERATIONS, OF STOCKHOLDERS EQUITY AND OF CASH FLOWS FOR EACH OF THE FRANCHISORS LAST THREE FISCAL YEARS. IF THE MOST RECENT BALANCE SHEET AND STATEMENT OF OPERATIONS ARE AS OF A DATE MORE THAN 90 DAYS BEFORE THE APPLICATION DATE, THEN ALSO SUBMIT AN UNAUDITED BALANCE SHEET AND STATEMENT OF OPERATIONS AS OF A DATE WITHIN 90 DAYS OF THE APPLICATION DATE.

B. AFFILIATED COMPANY STATEMENTS. INSTEAD OF THE DISCLOSURE REQUIRED BY ITEM 21A, THE FRANCHISOR MAY INCLUDE FINANCIAL STATEMENTS OF ITS AFFILIATED COMPANY IF THE AFFILIATED COMPANY'S FINANCIAL STATEMENTS SATISFY ITEM 21A AND THE AFFILIATED COMPANY ABSOLUTELY AND UNCONDITIONALLY GUARANTEES TO ASSUME THE DUTIES AND OBLIGATIONS OF THE FRANCHISOR UNDER THE FRANCHISE AGREEMENT.

C. CONSOLIDATED AND SEPARATE STATEMENTS:

(1) WHEN A FRANCHISOR OWNS A DIRECT OR BENEFICIAL, CONTROLLING FINANCIAL INTEREST IN ANOTHER CORPORATION, ITS FINANCIAL STATEMENTS SHOULD REFLECT THE FINANCIAL CONDITION OF THE FRANCHISOR AND ITS SUBSIDIARIES.

(2) IF THE APPLICANT IS A SUBFRANCHISOR INCLUDE SEPARATE FINANCIAL STATEMENTS FOR THE FRANCHISOR AND SUBFRANCHISOR RELATED ENTITY.

(3) PREPARE CONSOLIDATED AND SEPARATE FINANCIAL STATEMENTS IN ACCORDANCE WITH GENERALLY ACCEPTED ACCOUNTING PRINCIPLES.

Item 21 Instructions:

i. States may require financial statements additional to those listed in this Item.

ii. A company controlling 80% or more of a franchisor may be required to include its financial statements.

iii. Present required financial in a format of columns which compare at least 2 fiscal years.

iv. In Item 21A, the required financial statements for a franchisor with a calendar fiscal year end and a July 15, 1989 application filing date are:

  a) Unaudited balance sheet as of either April 30, May 31 or June 30, 1989 with an unaudited income statement for the period from January 1. 1989 to the date of the balance sheet;

  b) Balance sheets, statements of operations, of stockholders equity and of cash flow. The balance sheets should be audited and as of December 31, 1987 and 1988. The remaining statements should be audited and should be for periods ending December 31, 1986, 1987 and 1988; and

  c) If the franchisor has never had an audit, it need not supply the financial statement required by (b) if it supplies either an audit as of its last fiscal year end or the statements required by (a) in an audited form.

v. In the Item 21B response, the affiliate's guarantee need cover only the franchisors obligations to the franchisee. The guarantee need not extend to third parties. A sample guarantee is on page in Exhibit _____.

vi. In the Item 21B Response the filing state may permit a surety bond instead of the parent company's guarantee.

vii. Disclose the existence of a guarantee.

Item 22. CONTRACTS

ATTACH A COPY OF ALL AGREEMENTS PROPOSED FOR USE OR IN USE IN THIS STATE REGARDING THE OFFERING OF A FRANCHISE, INCLUDING, THE FRANCHISE AGREEMENT, LEASES, OPTIONS AND PURCHASE AGREEMENTS.

Item 22 Instructions:

i. Copies of agreements attached to the offering circular under Item 22 are part of the offering circular. Each offering circular delivered to a prospective franchisee must include copies of all agreements to be offered.

ii. The franchisor may cross reference Item 10 for financing agreements.

Item 23. RECEIPT

THE LAST PAGE OF THE OFFERING CIRCULAR IS A DETACHABLE DOCUMENT ACKNOWLEDGING RECEIPT OF THE OFFERING CIRCULAR BY THE PROSPECTIVE FRANCHISEE. IT MUST CONTAIN THE FOLLOWING STATEMENT IN BOLDFACE TYPE:

THIS OFFERING CIRCULAR SUMMARIZES CERTAIN PROVISIONS OF THE FRANCHISE AGREEMENT AND OTHER INFORMATION IN PLAIN LANGUAGE. READ THIS OFFERING CIRCULAR AND ALL AGREEMENTS CAREFULLY.

IF _____ OFFERS YOU A FRANCHISE, _____ MUST PROVIDE THIS OFFERING CIRCULAR TO YOU BY THE EARLIEST OF:

 (1) THE FIRST PERSONAL MEETING TO DISCUSS OUR FRANCHISE; OR

 (2) TEN BUSINESS DAYS BEFORE THE SIGNING OF A BINDING AGREEMENT; OR

 (3) TEN BUSINESS DAYS BEFORE A PAYMENT TO _____.

YOU MUST ALSO RECEIVE A FRANCHISE AGREEMENT CONTAINING ALL MATERIAL TERMS AT LEAST FIVE BUSINESS DAYS BEFORE YOU SIGN A FRANCHISE AGREEMENT.

IF _____ DOES NOT DELIVER THIS OFFERING CIRCULAR ON TIME OR IF IT CONTAINS A FALSE OR MISLEADING STATEMENT, OR A MATERIAL OMISSION, A VIOLATION OF FED AND STATE LAW MAY HAVE OCCURRED AND SHOULD BE REPORTED TO THE FEDERAL TRADE COMMISSION, WASHINGTON, D.C. 20580 AND (STATE AGENCY). (ANY ADDITIONAL STATE DISCLOSURE TIME OR REQUIRED STATUTORY LANGUAGE.)

Item 23 Instructions:

 i. Place the name of the franchisor in the blank.

 ii. Make two copies of the Receipt: one for retention by the franchisee and one by the franchisor.

 iii. Disclose the name, principal business address and telephone number of the subfranchisor or franchise broker offering the franchise in this state.

 iv. List the title of all attached exhibits.

 v. Effective Date: (Leave blank until notified of effectiveness by state regulatory authority.)

 vi. The name and address of the franchisors registered agent authorized to receive service of process if not disclosed in Item 1.

SAMPLE ANSWER 23

RECEIPT

THIS OFFERING CIRCULAR SUMMARIZES PROVISIONS OF THE FRANCHISE AGREEMENT AND OTHER INFORMATION IN PLAIN LANGUAGE. READ THIS OFFERING CIRCULAR AND ALL AGREEMENTS CAREFULLY.

IF BELMONT OFFERS YOU A FRANCHISE, BELMONT MUST PROVIDE THIS OFFERING CIRCULAR TO YOU BY THE EARLIEST OF:

(1) THE FIRST PERSONAL MEETING TO DISCUSS OUR FRANCHISE; OR

(2) TEN BUSINESS DAYS BEFORE SIGNING OF A BINDING AGREEMENT; OR

(3) TEN BUSINESS DAYS BEFORE ANY PAYMENT TO BELMONT.

YOU MUST ALSO RECEIVE A FRANCHISE AGREEMENT CONTAINING ALL MATERIAL TERMS AT LEAST FIVE BUSINESS DAYS BEFORE YOU SIGN ANY FRANCHISE AGREEMENT.

IF BELMONT DOES NOT DELIVER THIS OFFERING CIRCULAR ON TIME OR IF IT CONTAINS A FALSE OR MISLEADING STATEMENT, OR A MATERIAL OMISSION, A VIOLATION OF FEDERAL AND STATE LAW MAY HAVE OCCURRED AND SHOULD BE REPORTED TO THE FEDERAL TRADE COMMISSION, WASHINGTON, D.C. 20580 AND (STATE AGENCY).

Belmont authorizes Legal Process Corp at 448 West Washington Avenue, City, State to receive service of process for Belmont.

I have received a Uniform Franchise Offering Circular dated _____. This offering circular included the following Exhibits:

A. License Agreement

B. Equipment Lease

C. Lease for Premises

D. Loan Agreement

_____   _____

Date   **Franchisee**

JRH:ufoc

FORM A – UNIFORM FRANCHISE REGISTRATION APPLICATION

(Insert file number
of previous filings
of Applicant)

FEE: _____

(Enclosed when
application is initially
filed)

APPLICATION FOR (Check only one):

_____ REGISTRATION OF AN OFFER AND SALE OF FRANCHISES

_____ REGISTRATION RENEWAL STATEMENT OR ANNUAL REPORT

AMENDMENT NUMBER _____ TO APPLICATION

_____ POST-EFFECTIVE   FILED UNDER SECTION _____

_____ PRE-EFFECTIVE   DATED _____

1. Name of Franchisor. (If applicant is subfranchisor, the name of the subfranchisor.)
   Name under which the Franchisor is doing or intends to do business.

2. Franchisor's principal business address.
   Name and address of Franchisor's agent in the State of (Name of State) authorized to receive process.

3. Name, address and telephone number of subfranchisors, if any, for this state.

4. Name, address and telephone number of person to whom communications regarding this application should be directed.

FORM B – SUPPLEMENTAL INFORMATION

1. Disclose:

    A. The states in which this proposed registration application is effective.

    B. The states in which this proposed registration application is or will be shortly on file.

    C. The states that have refused to register this franchise offering.

    D. The states that have revoked or suspended the right to offer franchises.

    E. The states in which this proposed registration of these franchises has been withdrawn within the last five years, and the reasons for revocation or suspension.

2. Source of Funds for Establishing New Franchises

    Disclose franchisors total costs for performing its pre-opening obligations to provide goods or services in connection with establishing each franchise, including real estate, improvements, equipment, inventory, training and other items stated in the offering. State separately the sources of all required funds.

FORM C – CERTIFICATION

I certify under penalty of law that I have read and know the contents of this application and the documents attached as exhibits and incorporated by reference and that the statements in all these documents are true and correct.

Executed at _____, _____, 20_____

_____
(Signature(s) of Franchisor and/or Subfranchisor)

By _____

Title _____

(Seal)

STATE OF _____)

) ss.

COUNTY OF _____)

Personally appeared before me this _____ day of _____, 20_____ the above-named _____ _____ and _____ _____ to me known to be the person(s) who executed the foregoing application (as _____ and _____ respectively, of the above-named applicant) and (each), being first duly sworn, stated upon oath that said application, and all exhibits submitted herewith, are true and correct.

_____

_____
(Notary)

CORPORATE ACKNOWLEDGMENT

STATE OF _____   )
) ss.
COUNTY OF _____   )

On this _____ day of _____, 20_____, before me
_____ (Name of Notary) the undersigned officer, personally
appeared _____ and _____, known personally
to me to be the _____ President and _____ Secretary,
respectively, of the above-named corporation, and that they, as such officers, being authorized to do so, executed the foregoing instrument for the purposes therein contained, by
signing the name of the corporation by themselves as such officers.

IN WITNESS WHEREOF I have hereunto set my hand and official seal.

_____
(Notary Public)

(NOTARIAL SEAL)   My commission expires: _____

INDIVIDUAL OR PARTNERSHIP ACKNOWLEDGMENT

STATE OF _____   )
) ss.
COUNTY OF _____   )

On this _____ day of _____, 20_____, before me
_____, the undersigned officer, personally appeared
_____ to me personally known and known to me to be the same
person(s) whose name(s) is (are) signed to the foregoing instrument, and acknowledged the
execution thereof for the uses and purposes therein set forth.

IN WITNESS WHEREOF I have hereunto set my hand and official seal.

_____
(Notary Public)

(NOTARIAL SEAL)   My commission expires: _____

FORM D – UNIFORM CONSENT TO SERVICE OF PROCESS

_____, (a corporation organized under the laws of the State of _____) (a partnership) (an individual) _____
_____, irrevocably appoints the _____
_____ (name of regulatory authority) and the successors in office, its attorney in the State of for service of notice, process or pleading in an action or proceeding against it arising out of or in connection with the sale of franchises, or a violation of the franchise laws of _____, and consents that an action or proceeding against it may be commenced in a court of competent jurisdiction and proper venue within _____ by service of process upon this officer with the same effect as if the undersigned was organized or created under the laws of _____
_____and had lawfully been served with process in _____. It is requested that a copy of any notice, process or pleading served this consent be mailed to:

_____

_____

(Name and address)

Dated: _____, 20_____

By _____

Title _____

(SEAL)

By _____

Title _____

FORM E – SALES AGENT DISCLOSURE FORM

1. List the persons who will offer or sell franchises in this state. For each person state:

   A. Name;

   B. Business address and telephone number;

   C. Home address and telephone number;

   D. Present employer;

   E. Present title;

   F. Social Security Number;

   G. Birth date; and

   H. Employment during the past five years. For each employment, state the name of the employer, position held, and beginning and ending dates.

2. State whether any person identified in 1. above:

   A. Has any administrative, civil or criminal action pending alleging a violation of franchise or securities law, fraud, embezzlement, fraudulent conversion, restraint of.trade, unfair or deceptive practices, misappropriation of property or any comparable allegations?
   YES _____ NO _____

   B. Had during the ten-year period immediately before the offering circular date:

      (1) Been convicted of a felony or pleaded nolo contendere to a felony charge or been held liable in a civil action by final judgment if the felony or civil action involved a violation of franchise or securities law, fraud, embezzlement, fraudulent conversion, restraint of trade, unfair or deceptive practices, misappropriation of property or comparable violations of law?   YES _____ NO _____

      (2) Entered into or been named in A consent judgment, decree, order or assurance under federal or state franchise, securities, anti-trust, monopoly, trade practice or trade regulation law?   YES _____ NO _____

      (3) Been subject to an order or national securities association or national securities exchange as defined in the Securities and Exchange Act of 1934 suspending or expelling the person from membership in the association or exchange?
      YES _____ NO _____

   C. For each above question answered "YES" state:

      (1) The name of the person or entity involved;

      (2) The court, agency, association or exchange involved;

      (3) A summary of the allegations;

      (4) If applicable, the date of the conviction, judgment, decree, order or assurance; and

      (5) The penalty imposed, damages assessed, terms and conditions of the judgment, decree, or order or assurance.

FORM F – GUARANTEE OF PERFORMANCE

For value received _____ located at _____,

(Address)

absolutely and unconditionally guarantees the performance by _____,

located at _____ of all of the obligations of

(Address)

of _____ under its franchise registration in the State

of _____ dated _____

(Name of state or province)   (Effective date of renewal)

and of its Franchise Agreement. This guarantee continues until all obligations of

_____ under the franchise registration and franchise agreement

are satisfied. _____ is not discharged from liability if a claim

by the franchisee against _____ remains outstanding. Notice of

acceptance is waived. Notice of default on the part of _____ is not

waived. This guarantee is binding on _____ and on its

successors and assignees. _____ executes this guarantee at

(Parent)

_____ on the _____ day of _____, 20____.

_____

(Parent)

By: _____

Title: _____

JRH:ufoc

Notes

Index

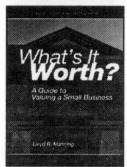

The Oasis Press®
Home to The Successful Business Library.

1-800-228-2275
International Calls +1.541.479.9464
http://www.psi-research.com/oasis

Mail: Send this completed order form and a check, money order or credit card information to:
PSI Research/The Oasis Press®, P.O. Box 3727, Central Point, Oregon 97502-0032

Fax: Available 24 hours a day, 7 days a week at **1-541-476-1479**

Email: info@psi-research.com (Please include a phone number, should we need to contact you.)

Web: Purchase any of our products online at our Website at **http://www.psi-research.com/oasis/**

Inquiries and International Orders: Please call **1-541-479-9464**

Indicate the quantity and price of the titles you would like:

TITLE	BINDER ISBN	PAPER ISBN	BINDER	PAPERBACK	QTY.	TOTAL
Advertising Without An Agency		1-55571-429-3		☐ 19.95		
Before You Go Into Business Read This		1-55571-481-1		☐ 17.95		
Bottom Line Basics	1-55571-329-7 (B)	1-55571-330-0 (P)	☐ 39.95	☐ 19.95		
BusinessBasics		1-55571-430-7		☐ 16.95		
The Business Environmental Handbook	1-55571-304-1 (B)	1-55571-163-4 (P)	☐ 39.95	☐ 19.95		
Business Owner's Guide to Accounting and Bookkeeping		1-55571-381-5		☐ 19.95		
businessplan.com		1-55571-455-2		☐ 19.95		
Buyer's Guide to Business Insurance	1-55571-310-6 (B)	1-55571-162-6 (P)	☐ 39.95	☐ 19.95		
California Corporation Formation Package		1-55571-464-1 (P)		☐ 29.95		
Collection Techniques for a Small Business	1-55571-312-2 (B)	1-55571-171-5 (P)	☐ 39.95	☐ 19.95		
College Entrepreneur Handbook		1-55571-503-6		☐ 16.95		
A Company Policy & Personnel Workbook	1-55571-364-5 (B)	1-55571-486-2 (P)	☐ 49.95	☐ 29.95		
Company Relocation Handbook	1-55571-091-3 (B)	1-55571-092-1 (P)	☐ 39.95	☐ 19.95		
CompControl	1-55571-356-4 (B)	1-55571-355-6 (P)	☐ 39.95	☐ 19.95		
Complete Book of Business Forms		1-55571-107-3		☐ 19.95		
Connecting Online		1-55571-403-X		☐ 21.95		
Customer Engineering	1-55571-360-2 (B)	1-55571-359-9 (P)	☐ 39.95	☐ 19.95		
Delivering Legendary Customer Service		1-55571-520-6 (P)		☐ 16.95		
Develop and Market Your Creative Ideas		1-55571-383-1		☐ 15.95		
Developing International Markets		1-55571-433-1		☐ 19.95		
Doing Business in Russia		1-55571-375-0		☐ 19.95		
Draw the Line		1-55571-370-X		☐ 17.95		
The Essential Corporation Handbook		1-55571-342-4		☐ 21.95		
Essential Limited Liability Company Handbook	1-55571-362-9 (B)	1-55571-361-0 (P)	☐ 39.95	☐ 21.95		
Export Now	1-55571-192-8 (B)	1-55571-167-7 (P)	☐ 39.95	☐ 24.95		
Financial Decisionmaking		1-55571-435-8		☐ 19.95		
Financial Management Techniques	1-55571-116-2 (B)	1-55571-124-3 (P)	☐ 39.95	☐ 19.95		
Financing Your Small Business		1-55571-160-X		☐ 19.95		
Franchise Bible	1-55571-366-1 (B)	1-55571-526-5 (P)	☐ 39.95	☐ 27.95		
The Franchise Redbook		1-55571-484-6		☐ 34.95		
Friendship Marketing		1-55571-399-8		☐ 18.95		
Funding High-Tech Ventures		1-55571-405-6		☐ 21.95		
Home Business Made Easy		1-55571-428-5		☐ 19.95		
Improving Staff Productivity		1-55571-456-0		☐ 16.95		
Information Breakthrough		1-55571-413-7		☐ 22.95		
Insider's Guide to Small Business Loans		1-55571-488-9		☐ 19.95		
Keeping Score: An Inside Look at Sports Marketing		1-55571-377-7		☐ 18.95		
Kick Ass Success		1-55571-518-4		☐ 18.95		
Know Your Market	1-55571-341-6 (B)	1-55571-333-5 (P)	☐ 39.95	☐ 19.95		
Leader's Guide: 15 Essential Skills		1-55571-434-X		☐ 19.95		
Legal Expense Defense	1-55571-349-1 (B)	1-55571-348-3 (P)	☐ 39.95	☐ 19.95		
A Legal Road Map for Consultants		1-55571-460-9		☐ 18.95		
Location, Location, Location		1-55571-376-9		☐ 19.95		
Mail Order Legal Guide	1-55571-193-6 (B)	1-55571-190-1 (P)	☐ 45.00	☐ 29.95		
Managing People: A Practical Guide		1-55571-380-7		☐ 21.95		
Marketing for the New Millennium		1-55571-432-3		☐ 19.95		
Marketing Mastery	1-55571-358-0 (B)	1-55571-357-2 (P)	☐ 39.95	☐ 19.95		
Money Connection	1-55571-352-1 (B)	1-55571-351-3 (P)	☐ 39.95	☐ 24.95		
Moonlighting: Earning a Second Income at Home		1-55571-406-4		☐ 15.95		
Navigating the Marketplace: Growth Strategies for Small Business		1-55571-458-7		☐ 21.95		
No Money Down Financing for Franchising		1-55571-462-5		☐ 19.95		
Not Another Meeting!		1-55571-480-3		☐ 17.95		
People-Centered Profit Strategies		1-55571-517-6		☐ 18.95		

Sub-total for this side:

TITLE		ISBN	BINDER	PAPERBACK	QTY.	TOTAL
People Investment	1-55571-187-1 (B)	1-55571-161-8 (P)	☐ 39.95	☐ 19.95		
Power Marketing for Small Business		1-55571-524-9 (P)		☐ 19.95		
Proposal Development	1-55571-067-0 (B)	1-55571-431-5 (P)	☐ 39.95	☐ 21.95		
Prospecting for Gold		1-55571-483-8		☐ 14.95		
Public Relations Marketing		1-55571-459-5		☐ 19.95		
Raising Capital	1-55571-306-8 (B)	1-55571-305-X (P)	☐ 39.95	☐ 19.95		
Renaissance 2000		1-55571-412-9		☐ 22.95		
Retail in Detail		1-55571-371-8		☐ 15.95		
The Rule Book of Business Plans for Startups		1-55571-519-2		☐ 18.95		
Secrets of High Ticket Selling		1-55571-436-6		☐ 19.95		
Secrets to Buying and Selling a Business		1-55571-489-7		☐ 24.95		
Secure Your Future		1-55571-335-1		☐ 19.95		
Selling Services		1-55571-461-7		☐ 14.95		
SmartStart Your (State) Business		varies per state		☐ 19.95		
Indicate which state you prefer:						
Small Business Insider's Guide to Bankers		1-55571-400-5		☐ 18.95		
Start Your Business		1-55571-485-4		☐ 10.95		
Strategic Insights		1-55571-505-2		☐ 19.95		
Strategic Management for Small and Growing Firms		1-55571-465-X		☐ 24.95		
Successful Network Marketing		1-55571-350-5		☐ 15.95		
Surviving Success		1-55571-446-3		☐ 19.95		
TargetSmart!		1-55571-384-X		☐ 19.95		
Top Tax Saving Ideas for Today's Small Business		1-55571-463-3		☐ 16.95		
Truth About Teams		1-55571-482-X		☐ 18.95		
Twenty-One Sales in a Sale		1-55571-448-X		☐ 19.95		
WebWise	1-55571-501-X (B)	1-55571-479-X (P)	☐ 29.95	☐ 19.95		
What's It Worth?		1-55571-504-4		☐ 22.95		
Which Business?		1-55571-390-4		☐ 18.95		
Write Your Own Business Contracts	1-55571-196-0 (B)	1-55571-487-0 (P)	☐ 39.95	☐ 24.95		

Success Series	ISBN		PAPERBACK	QTY.	TOTAL
50 Ways to Get Promoted	1-55571-506-0		☐ 10.95		
You Can't Go Wrong By Doing It Right	1-55571-490-0		☐ 14.95		

Oasis Software	FORMAT	BINDER		QTY.	TOTAL
Company Policy Text Files CD-ROM	CD-ROM ☐		☐ 49.95		
Company Policy Text Files Book & CD-ROM Package	CD-ROM ☐	☐ 89.95 (B)	☐ 69.95 (P)		
Winning Business Plans in Color CD-ROM	CD-ROM ☐		☐ 59.95		

Subtotal from other side	
Subtotal from this side	
Shipping	
TOTAL	

Ordered by: *Please give street address*

NAME _____ TITLE _____

COMPANY _____

STREET ADDRESS _____

CITY _____ STATE _____ ZIP _____

DAYTIME PHONE _____ EMAIL _____

Ship to: *If different than above*

NAME _____ TITLE _____

COMPANY _____

STREET ADDRESS _____

CITY _____ STATE _____ ZIP _____

DAYTIME PHONE _____

Shipping:

YOUR ORDER IS:	ADD:
0-25	5.00
25.01-50	6.00
50.01-100	7.00
100.01-175	9.00
175.01-250	13.00
250.01-500	18.00
500.01+	4% of total

91012960

PLEASE CALL FOR RUSH SERVICE OPTIONS.
INTERNATIONAL ORDERS, PLEASE CALL FOR A QUOTE
ON CURRENT SHIPPING RATES.

Payment Method:

☐ CHECK ☐ MONEY ORDER
☐ AMERICAN EXPRESS ☐ DISCOVER
☐ MASTERCARD ☐ VISA

CREDIT CARD NUMBER

EXPIRATION (MM/YY)   NAME ON CARD (PLEASE PRINT)

SIGNATURE OF CARDHOLDER (REQUIRED)

OASIS PRESS BOOKS & SOFTWARE